GOSPEL TRADITIONS
IN THE
SECOND CENTURY

Christianity and Judaism in Antiquity

CHARLES KANNENGIESSER, SERIES EDITOR

Volume 3

GOSPEL TRADITIONS IN THE SECOND CENTURY

Origins, Recensions, Text, and Transmission

studies by

BARBARA ALAND

TJITZE BAARDA

J. NEVILLE BIRDSALL

SEBASTIAN P. BROCK

JOEL DELOBEL

ELDON JAY EPP

HELMUT KOESTER

FREDERIK WISSE

WILLIAM L. PETERSEN
editor

University of Notre Dame Press

Notre Dame　　　　　　London

Cover illustration: recto of $\mathfrak{P}^{52}$ (Rylands Greek Papyrus 457), containing John 18:31-33. Used by permission of the John Rylands University Library of Manchester, England.

Library of Congress Cataloging-in-Publication Data

Gospel traditions in the second century : origins, recensions, text,
    and transmission / studies by Barbara Aland . . . [et al.] ; William
L. Petersen, editor.
        p.   cm. -- (Christianity and Judaism in antiquity ; v. 3)
    ISBN 0-268-01022-6
    1. Bible. N.T. Gospels—Criticism, Textual. 2. Bible. N.T.
Gospels—Criticism, Redaction. 3. Bible. N.T. Gospels—Criticism,
interpretation, etc. 4. Bible. N.T. Gospels—Harmonies—History
and criticism. I. Aland, Barbara. II. Petersen, William Lawrence,
1950-   III. Series.
BS2555.G622   1990
226'.04'09015—dc20   89-27807

Manufactured in the United States of America

Contents

Preface

This volume would not exist if a conference of the same name had not been held; that conference would not have been held except for the interest, generosity and vision of those who provided funding. Monies from the College of Arts and Letters' Institute for Scholarship in the Liberal Arts, from the Department of Theology, and from the William K. Warren Chair of Theology provided the requisite subvention. The support of Deans Michael J. Loux and Nathan O. Hatch, of Fr. Richard P. McBrien, and of Fr. Thomas F. O'Meara, O.P., the respective administrators of these funds, is acknowledged with thanks. It is hoped that this volume offers the world of scholarship a return commensurate with their investment.

Thanks are also due the eight scholars who presented papers—five of whom crossed the Atlantic to do so. Their papers were uniformly well-received; their easy participation in both formal and informal discussion brought real light to vexed problems. It was hoped that they would stimulate us with their learning, which they did; we hope that they too gained from the conference.

I must also acknowledge the assistance of my Graduate Assistant, Jon Nelson Bailey, now of Abilene Christian University. It was his care in standardizing the layout which makes this book a delight to the eye. He checked abbreviations and references, compiled the indices, oversaw the formatting, and made final corrections. The volume's defects are mine.

At numerous points in the project, various University colleagues and staff gave essential assistance, which I wish to acknowledge: Harriet Baldwin of the Center for Continuing Education handled conference arrangements; Robert Burke of the Institute for Scholarship in the Liberal Arts assisted in securing funding; Prof. William Davisson scanned one paper into electronic form, and translated various disk formats for us. Papers which could not be transferred electronically were retyped by Cheryl Reed of the Faculty Steno Pool. Finally, I wish to thank my colleagues in the Christianity and Judaism in Antiquity Seminar for their assistance in the planning and execution of the conference.

Notre Dame, Indiana   W.L.P.
May 5, 1989

vii

Contributors

BARBARA ALAND is Professor of New Testament and Ecclesistical History, and Director of the Institut für neutestamentliche Textforschung at the Westfälische Wilhelms-Universität (Münster, West Germany). In addition to co-editing the Nestle-Aland *Novum Testamentum Graece* and the UBS *Greek New Testament*, she is co-author of *Das Neue Testament in syrischer Überlieferung* (1986) and *The Text of the New Testament* (1987).

TJITZE BAARDA is Professor of New Testament and Judaica at the Rijksuniversiteit te Utrecht (the Netherlands). He is the author of numerous works, including *The Gospel Quotations of Aphrahat the Persian Sage* (1975), and a collection of essays entitled *Early Transmission of Words of Jesus: Thomas, Tatian and the Text of the New Testament* (1983). He is also the editor of *Text and Testimony: Essays on New Testament and Apocryphal Literature in Honor of A. F. J. Klijn* (1988).

J. NEVILLE BIRDSALL is University Professor emeritus of New Testament Textual Criticism at the University of Birmingham (England). He is the author of *The Bodmer Papyri of the Gospel of John* (1960), "The New Testament Text" in *The Cambridge History of the Bible* (1970), and the co-editor of *Biblical and Patristic Studies in Memory of Robert Pierce Casey* (1963). He was a member of the British Committee of the International Greek New Testament Project for many years, serving as the executive editor from 1970 to 1977.

SEBASTIAN P. BROCK is University Lecturer in Aramaic and Syriac at the Oriental Institute, University of Oxford (England). He is the editor of the *Journal of Jewish Studies;* has edited numerous Syriac texts, including *Isaiah* for the Peshitta Institute in Leiden (1987); co-edited the *Classified Bibliography of the Septuagint* (1973); and written extensively on Eastern Christianity. A collection of his essays has been published in a volume titled *Syriac Perspectives on Late Antiquity* (1984).

JOËL DELOBEL is Professor of New Testament at the Katholiek Universiteit van Leuven (Belgium). He is the author of several articles, essays, and books, including *L'onction de Jesus par la pecheresse* (1966). He has co-edited *Jean et les synoptiques* (1979) and *Logia: Les paroles de Jésus: The Sayings of Jesus: mémorial Joseph Coppens* (1982); and has edited *Études de critique textuelle du Nouveau Testament,* by Jean Duplacy (1987).

ELDON JAY EPP is Harkness Professor of Biblical Literature and Dean of Humanities and Social Sciences at Case Western Reserve University (Cleveland, Ohio, USA). He is author of *The Theological Tendency of Codex Bezae Cantabrigiensis in Acts* (1966); co-editor of *New Testament Textual Criticism: Its Significance for Exegesis: Essays in Honor of Bruce M. Metzger* (1981); and associate editor of the *Journal of Biblical Literature.* He also serves on the Editorial Board of *Hermeneia,* and on the American Executive Committee of the International Greek New Testament Project.

HELMUT KOESTER is John H. Morison Professor of New Testament Studies and Winn Professor of Ecclesiastical History in the Divinity School at Harvard University (Cambridge, Massachusetts, USA). He is the author of *Synoptische Überlieferungen bei den apostolischen Vätern* (1957), and a two-volume *Introduction to the New Testament* (1982); co-author of *Trajectories through Early Christianity* (1971); and co-editor of *Nag Hammadi Codex III, 5: The Dialogue of the Savior* (1984). He is also chairman of the New Testament Editorial Board of *Hermeneia.*

FREDERIK WISSE is Professor of New Testament at McGill University (Montréal, Québec, Canada). He has written several articles, essays, and books, including *The Profile Method for Classifying and Evaluating Manuscript Evidence* (1982); and has co-edited *Nag Hammadi Codices III,2 and IV,2: The Gospel of the Egyptians* (1975). He is also co-editor of the series *Nag Hammadi Studies.*

Abbreviations

AAST.M	Atti della Academia della Scienze di Torino, Classi di Scienze morali, storche e Filologiche
AnBib	Analecta Biblica
ANTT	Arbeiten zur neutestamentliche Textforschung
AUU	Acta Universitatis Upsaliensis; SLatU, Studia latina upsaliensia
BASP	British Academy Supplementary Papers
BEThL	Bibliotheca ephremeridum theologicarum Louvaniensium
BHTh	Beiträge zur historischen Theologie
Bib	*Biblica*
BWANT	Beiträge zur Wissenschaft vom Alten und Neuen Testament
BZNW	Beiheft zur Zeitschrift für die neutestamentliche Wissenschaft
CBM	Chester Beatty Monograph Series
CChr.SL	Corpus Christianorum, Series Latina
CSCO	Corpus Scriptorum Christianorum Orientalium
EL	Ephemerides Liturgicae
ET	*Expository Times*
EThL	*Ephemerides theologicae Louvanienses*
FKDG	Forschungen zur Kirchen- und Dogmengeschichte
FRLANT	Forschungen zur Religion und Literatur des Alten und Neuen Testamentes
GCS	Die griechischen christlichen Schriftsteller der ersten drei Jahrhunderte
HeyJ	*Heythrop Journal*
HThR	*Harvard Theological Review*
HThS	Harvard Theological Studies
JBL	*Journal of Biblical Literature*
JJS	*Journal of Jewish Studies*
JSAI	*Jerusalem Studies in Arabic and Islam*
JSOT	*Journal for the Study of the Old Testament*
JThS	*Journal of Theological Studies*
KlT	Kleine Texte für Vorlesungen und Übungen
KNT	Kommentar zum Neuen Testament, geg. T. Zahn
LeDiv	Lectio Divina
Muséon	*Le Muséon*
N-A[26]	*Novum Testamentum Graece,* ed. E. Nestle and K. Aland, 26th ed.
NT	*Novum Testamentum*
NTA	Neutestamentliche Abhandlungen
NT.S	Novum Testamentum, Supplements

NTS	*New Testament Studies*
NTTS	New Testament Tools and Studies
OECT	Oxford Early Christian Texts
OLoP	Orientalia Lovaniensia Periodica
OrChr	*Oriens Christianus*
OrChrA	Orientalia Christiana Analecta
OrSyr	*L'Orient syrien*
ÖTKNT	Ökumenischer Taschenbuchkommentar zum Neuen Testament
ParOr	*Parole de l'Orient*
PG	Patrologia cursus completus. Series Graeca, ed. Migne
PL	Patrologia cursus completus. Series Latina, ed. Migne
PO	Patrologia Orientalis, ed. Graffin
PS	Patrologia Syriaca, ed. Graffin
RB	*Revue Biblique*
RHT	*Revue d'historie des textes*
RSLR	*Rivista di Storia e letteratura religiosa*
RThL.C	Cahiers de Revue théologique de Louvain
SC	Sources Chrétiennes
SJ	Studia Judaica
SNTS.MS	Studiorum Novi Testamenti Societas Monograph Series
SPAW	Sitzungsberichte der (königliche) prussische Akademie der Wissenschaften
SS	*Studia Sinaitica*
StD	Studies and Documents
TaS	Texts and Studies
TBAW	Tübinger Beiträge zur Altertumswissenschaft
TDNT	*Theological Dictionary of the New Testament*
ThHK	Theologischer Handkommentar zum Neuen Testament
TRE	*Theologische Realenzyklopädie*
TU	Texte und Untersuchungen zur Geschichte der altchristlichen Literatur
UBS	United Bible Societies
UBS³	United Bible Societies' *Greek New Testament*, 3rd ed.
VigChr	*Vigiliae Christianae*

Prologue

Between April 15th and 17th, 1988, eight leading scholars from six nations met at the University of Notre Dame to discuss "Gospel Traditions in the Second Century: Origins, Recensions, Text and Transmission." Deployed around this central theme, each panelist was charged with presenting insights from his or her area of research: the Western Text, the papyri, the Eastern Versions, the text of the Fathers, the impact of findings from the second century upon the latest Nestle-Aland edition, the status of the synoptics, Gospel harmonies, and redactorial activity.

The last fifty years have seen an enormous growth in new material relating to the Gospels in the second century. The discoveries at Nag Hammadi, especially the *Gospel of Thomas*, come to mind. But there have been other significant finds. The Persian *Diatessaron* was first available in 1951, and the Syriac recension of Ephrem's *Commentary* on the *Diatessaron* turned up in the mid-1960s. New, more scholarly editions of Patristic texts (such as *Die griechischen christlichen Schriftsteller der ersten drei Jahrhunderte, Sources chrétiennes,* and *Patristische Texte und Studien*) have replaced those in Migne. Our understanding of first-century Judaism has been redrawn by the findings at Qumran. Collectively, these events have forced a reappraisal of the origin and early transmission of the Gospels. But it is not from these discoveries alone that we have come to new understandings of the second-century Gospel text; scholarly methods have evolved as well. The work of redaction and form critics has revolutionized our view of how the Gospels were put together and, indeed, has redefined the concept of a what a "Gospel" is. Theology itself has changed, as well. Today Protestants are comfortable with the idea that the Gospels were not immune to the exigencies of transmission which affect any document created in antiquity. Similarly, Catholics are no longer bound to a preconceived scheme of Gospel origins.

The conference was devoted to studying questions which confront the scholar as he or she moves back from the fourth-century uncials, Codex Sinaiticus and Codex Vaticanus, into the third, and finally the second century. Work on the second-century Gospels is specialized of necessity. Patristic scholars examine Patristic citations. Linguists examine the versions in their particular language. Textual critics occupy themselves with cataloging, collating, and editing. The higher critics seek the most primitive recoverable form of a given pericope—regardless of where it occurs. Although each works in his or her own bailiwick, a

1

synthesis is necessary: Patristic quotations can illuminate the work of the form critic; the most beautiful conjecture of the textual critic may flounder on the reading of another version. The conference sought to do two things. First, it sought to provide a forum where the speakers and forty registered guests might discuss the problems associated with research on the Gospels in the second century. Second, it sought to create a common frame of reference for future research and discussion. By defining problems more clearly, by isolating the precise points of disagreement and the logic for each position, it was hoped that scholarship would be enriched and stimulated.

It will be for you, the reader, to decide whether these goals have been achieved. The volume in hand contains the papers presented at the conference, revised by the contributors in light of the discussion. Occasionally their sequence has been altered to aid the reader, who will progress from the more general and familiar to the more intricate and esoteric. The terrain of Gospel traditions in the second century is largely uncharted; the existing maps are outdated. This volume is an invitation to accompany some of the most competent guides available today as they explore new territory.

The Western Text in the Second Century

J. Neville Birdsall

University of Birmingham (England)

The title which was proposed to me for this introductory lecture is awe-inspiring, even if we limit it to the field of the Gospel text, as—in the light of the general theme of the conference—I intend to do. In accepting the title, I feel, with Shakespeare's Malvolio, that "some men have greatness thrust upon them." I do not propose to give some new or final solution to the many problems which the term "Western Text" conceals. Rather, I will attempt, necessarily in a brief compass, a conspectus of data and opinion at present, and will draw attention to various data from sources of the earliest date, which should enable us to take preliminary bearings. I also hope that my paper will provide a framework for the various topics to which our colleagues will address themselves.

In taking up, along with the title, the term "Western Text," I am not defending any particular view of the term or of the data which it was long ago created to codify. There *is* a body of data for which the term was devised, and it continues to demand both examination and the erection of hypotheses to explain it, and no student of the earliest Christian centuries can avoid these. If an apologia is demanded for my title, it is found in that situation. The term appears to originate with Semler and was taken up by his pupil Griesbach, as a designation of a text known from the time of Tertullian on, mainly in the Western parts of the Empire. That the term is already a misnomer is shown by the fact that Griesbach, in recognizing the sporadic appearance of the Sahidic and the "Jerusalem Syriac" amongst the witnesses whose concurrence gave rise to the term, apologizes for the term with the phrase *haud inepte*, "not at all unsuitably."[1] Most of us met the term in the context of the theory of Westcott and Hort, which has dominated debate for the last century and which, in some circles, seems to

---

[1] Johann Jakob Griesbach, *Novum Testamentum Graece...*, *editio nova* (London, 1809), 1:lxxvi.

arouse a rationally inexplicable fury. Amongst their many contributions to textual debate was the introduction of two crucial new factors, namely the importance of the quotations of the Fathers for dating and placing the phenomenon, and the heavy stress which they laid upon the text of Codex Bezae (D) as a witness to "the Western Text." Otherwise, they were utilizing a basically Griesbachian scheme. Yet they made their task more complex than that set by their predecessors when they sought not only to establish on intrinsic grounds the text of the New Testament, but also to reconstruct the history of the text as a justification and explanation of the text established by them. (The stress on history, and the historical analysis in terms of a dialectic of two ancient texts resolving itself in the emergence of a third, might suggest an Hegelian influence upon their thinking: but their biographies give no grounds for asserting that this was so.)

The simplicity of their scheme was already belied by the data before them. Two points in their own analysis demonstrate this: (1) a fourth text, which they named "Alexandrian," breaks out of the overall pattern, and (2) within their main theory, those readings which they called the "Western non-interpolations" show that the attempted historical outline could not explain all features of the scene. The tortuous term itself showed at least an embryonic awareness of this on their part. The work of Rendel Harris and others on the Codex Bezae seems to me to have sprung from the problems which the scholars of the succeeding generation found in trying to use the text of Bezae as evidence for the text of the second century, as Hort was prepared to do. In the field of Acts, the work of Ropes continued this line of examination, with the conclusion that Codex Bezae is not as good a representative of the "Western Text" as some of its allies. About the same time, Streeter and the Harvard team of Lake and Blake (soon joined by New, the later Mrs. Lake), with some degree of collaboration, attempted a more basic revision of the inherited scheme in the notion of a spectrum of local texts spanning the bounds of ancient Christendom: F. C. Burkitt was critical of the notion of local texts which one might reconstruct, but nevertheless gave his support then and earlier to the proposal that the original text might be found in readings attested elsewhere than in the Alexandrian witnesses to which Westcott and Hort had given their contentious name of "Neutral."

Parallel to these theoretical developments ran a considerable increase in material discoveries. Foremost among these up to our own day are the increasing numbers of newly discovered manuscripts, many of them papyri, which have come mainly from Egypt. They show, however, a variety of textual types and affiliations, changing from time to time the evidence in the debate and making it more complex. Then, due in large part to the advances in the photographic art, manuscripts known in the last century are both better known in this century, and are more accessible in facsimiles and microfilms to all investigators. Furthermore, we can usually travel nowadays with greater ease to look at our sources for ourselves, while retaining in our photographed resources an accurate record of the new insights we have gained. What we have said of Greek manuscripts applies equally to the ancient versions: we now have more knowledge of every one than our predecessors had, although in some cases (such as that of Syriac) it is not proportionately much greater. We have certainly advanced in the editions of some versions, although the field as a whole is very unevenly provided: Coptic and Georgian are now very well provided for, although their presentation has not yet reached perfection; while versions such as the Armenian and the Ethiopic still lag far behind. In the editions of the Fathers, there is a similar inequality of attainment: we have great riches readily at our disposal for Tertullian or Irenaeus, for example; but for other authors of comparable importance, such as Hippolytus, we must rely still on very imperfect presentation. Furthermore, in the case of Hippolytus and others, our task is rendered more difficult by the unresolved debate amongst *Patristiker*, about the identity of the author or authors of works transmitted under a name.

It was necessary for earlier scholars—not only Westcott and Hort, but their successors as well—to extrapolate from evidence of a later date to the earlier centuries with which they were concerned in their reconstruction of the primitive text and its development. Recently, they have been quite unreasonably criticized for this, for what else could they have done? The proper response should be to alert ourselves to their practice, lest it escape our notice by its very familiarity, and to remain aware of the pitfalls and sources of error implicit in such a procedure. But, as we shall see, we deceive ourselves if we believe that we can escape the need for some such extrapolation. The papyrus discoveries of the present century, from the Oxyrhynchus to the Bodmer publications, have repeatedly raised great hopes that a royal road to a better understanding of the original text and its development had been opened by the new information which they provide. However, from the very start these hopes have been dashed upon the close investigation of the content of the newly discovered documents. This was so as soon as the Chester Beatty papyrus of the Gospels and Acts began to be studied, although it was not perhaps always very clearly perceived, since many scholars were still operating with "Hortian" categories or with the construct of local texts. The problems only intensified when the Bodmer papyri of John appeared: each new publication seemed to create a new confusion. As I perceive recent debate, I doubt if the situation is much different, even though we now have a few second-century papyri. A recent study by Kurt Aland of three papyri which share some common extent in chapters 18 and 19 of the Gospel of John ($\mathfrak{P}^{52}$, $\mathfrak{P}^{90}$ and $\mathfrak{P}^{66}$) is an instructive exercise, but is limited by the extent of the materials under review.[2] He himself acknowledges that it does not extend very far, and that the scope for conclusions is limited further by the lack of parallel quotations in the second-century Fathers writing in Greek, namely Clement and Irenaeus.

If we keep to second-century Greek evidence alone, we have no way of telling whether we have here a purely Egyptian text of the second century, or a text more representative of the New Testament throughout Christendom at that time. In the course of collation, however, it springs to the eye that there are a number of first-hand readings in $\mathfrak{P}^{66}$, not infrequently corrected away later, which find support in readings of later witnesses such as the Codex Sinaiticus ($\aleph$), the Freer Codex (W), or in such minuscules of interesting text as 565, Family 1 (f^1) or the Ferrar group (f^{13}). It might seem from this that there were in Egypt, at the time of the writing of $\mathfrak{P}^{66}$, two texts, one of which was used as a model, the other as a standard of correction. To gain any further bearings, we must extrapolate both geographically and in terms of time, to take into account readings of the Old Latin Codex Palatinus (e), which has been shown to coincide with the form of text known to Cyprian. Within the brief compass of the papyri in question there are not many coincidences of reading. But, the omission of part of John 19:5 ("And he says to them, Behold the man") by the first hand of $\mathfrak{P}^{66}$ is striking. We might proceed from such a beginning to investigate if—parallel to the texts known as variants in Egypt—there were different texts elsewhere in Christianity of the second century.

Another early manuscript witness, examined recently by Aland, is the uncial fragment **0171**, dated about 300 CE.[3] A collation of the recently identified Matthean portion (Matt 10:17-23, 25-32) reveals a fluctuating concurrence with the Codex Bezae (D). Within the short extent of the

---

[2]Kurt Aland, "Der Text des Johannes-Evangelium in 2. Jahrhundert," in *Studien zum Text und zur Ethik des Neuen Testaments. Festschrift zum 80. Geburtstag von Heinrich Greeven*, ed. W. Schrage, BZNW, no. 47 (Berlin: Walter de Gruyter, 1986), 1-10.

[3]Kurt Aland, "Alter und Entstehung des D-Textes im Neuen Testament. Betrachtungen zu $\mathfrak{P}^{69}$ u. 0171," in *Miscel.lànea papirològica Ramon Roca-Puig en el seu vuitantè aniversari* (Barcelona, 1987), 37-61.

extant text I count nine agreements and eleven disagreements, and some other interesting readings. In verse 25, it provides our earliest knowledge of the variant ἐκάλεσαν against ἐπεκάλεσαν. This has previously been recognized as the reading of the *Textus Receptus*, and attested in the Koridethi Codex (Θ), Family 1 (*f¹*), 700, 1424 and others. In the field of the versions, we can collate this section in the Codex Bobbiensis (*k*), which, as is agreed, represents a form of the African Latin which lacks the signs of revision which we find in both the Palatinus and the quotations in Cyprian, and therefore attests a form of text close to that from which the Latin was first translated in Africa. We have excellent materials for such a collation: there is a good edition in *Old Latin Biblical Texts no. II*, which we can compare with the data in Jülicher's *Itala*, and in any case of doubt, we have recourse to the photographic facsimile of Cipolla.[4] Plooij's former pupil Adolphine Bakker also produced work on the analysis of this Latin manuscript in a *Proefschrift* (of which only the first part was published), and in a full collation, produced in lithographed form.[5] Comparison with **0171** shows a number of striking coincidences of reading. In verse 19, we find the omission of any equivalent for πῶς ἤ, not omitted in Codex Bezae. In the same verse, on the other hand, we find that it is Codex Bezae that shares a variant, namely the omission of the words between the first and the second occurrence of λαλήσητε, by *homoioteleuton*, with Codex Bobbiensis. In verse 23, a long addition is attested in **0171**, known both in Codex Bezae and in Codex Bobbiensis. Within this, **0171** attests the rare future ἐκδιώξουσιν, apparently read only by L and 247 among Greek witnesses, to which *persecuti vos fueri(n)t* of Codex Bobbiensis might correspond. Lastly, we may mention the variant ἀποκτεῖναι for ἀπολέσαι in verse 28, which is unknown in the Greek tradition, but is read by Codex Bobbiensis, by Cyprian and by the Pseudo-Augustinian *Speculum* (*m* in earlier notation). Here again, then, a Greek text, of Egyptian provenance, shows a text known in a Western source at a very early date, but without consistent support in other Greek sources.

Any *apparatus criticus* will reveal a row of readings in common between the Old Latin materials and those available in Syriac. It was a mis-

---

[4] *Il codice evangelico k della Biblioteca Universitaria nazionale di Torino.* Raccolta di codici riprodotti in fac-simile a cura della Regia Accademia delle Scienze di Torino (Torino, 1913).

[5] Adolphine Bakker, *A Study of Codex Evang. Bobbiensis (k)* (Amsterdam, 1933); and idem, *A Full Collation of Codex Ev. Bobbiensis (k)* (No publisher or date is given, but presumably 1933, as a specimen page is found in the preceding).

take of the successors of Westcott and Hort to treat the Old Syriac Gospels
as second-century texts; but it cannot be ruled out that they may contain a
basis for determining the situation in Eastern Christendom at that date, an
exercise parallel to that done with the African Latin. Ephraem was acquainted with separated Gospels, which he termed "the Greek;" and
probably these were those which are known to us through the *Evangelion
da-Mepharreshe* (= the "Separated Gospel" = MSS Syr^{sin.cur}). New analysis
of the text of these Gospels is long overdue. Vööbus attempted to show
the widespread use of this Separated Gospel, but his demonstration of this
usage has largely taken the form of isolated verses taken from various
writers, sometimes from printed editions, often from manuscript sources
not previously collated. From the editions of the two manuscripts of the
Gospels themselves, we can see that their text owes something to the
Diatessaron and something to manuscripts which must have had affinity
with the Ferrar Group (*f^{13}*) and kindred minuscules. The hope was often
entertained that the Armenian and Georgian versions, as they became
better known, would serve as auxiliaries in this investigation, providing a
replica of lost Old Syriac manuscripts. The Old Armenian is unfortunately
still very difficult to ascertain. It must be painfully reconstructed—and
only partially at that—from citational materials, since no one manuscript
corresponding to the citations has come to light. The Georgian, of which
there are two early versions, one slenderly, one numerously attested in
manuscripts both complete and fragmentary, seems to have a far more
complex ancestry than the former hope presupposed.

The *Diatessaron* in its original form was no doubt a second-century
text; but while we have made considerable advances in recent years, due
in part to fortuitous discoveries and in part to the hard toil of investigators
in that field, we have a long way to go before we can be confident that we
know its text as it left the hand of Tatian. As Professor Baarda is dealing
with the *Diatessaron* in his paper, I shall not rehearse the questions raised
in that area of research, apart from one observation. On the basis of the
Diatessaronic materials published by Ortiz de Urbina,[6] Joseph Molitor es-
sayed a commented translation of the reconstructed *Diatessaron* text, with
a collation against the Old Syriac and Old Georgian material, which was

---

[6]*Biblia polyglotta Matritensia. Series VI. Vetus evangelium syrorum et exinde
excerptum Diatessaron Tatiani*, ed. I. Ortiz de Urbina, O. S. B. (Matriti, 1967).

published *seriatim* in *Oriens Christianus*.[7] Molitor's work has a number of faults and is not easy to use, but in working through it at the time of its publication, I was struck by the high incidence of short readings which may be ascribed to the work of Tatian. This impression coincides with that gained by Boismard, who in his work on the text of the Gospel of John suggested the existence in early times of a very short and ancient text of that Gospel, to which a number of ancient versions and the quotations of Syriac Fathers bear witness together with the various sources which quote the *Diatessaron*. Boismard believed, of course, that these ultra-short readings revealed the original text of John. Might it be the case, however, that abbreviation was a mark of Tatian's work, and that such readings when supported by that tradition, are to be treated with caution?

We must touch upon the Coptic evidence. There is considerable divergence of opinion about the dating of the origin of the version in general and of the dialect-differentiated varieties of text which we possess. A number of Coptologists are willing to place the Sahidic in the third century, and a few even in the second. The "minor" dialects have usually been placed a century or two later, while the Bohairic is generally dated late, as indeed its extant manuscripts are. The textual data appear to be similar to those of the Greek papyri which we have surveyed. Readings are found which intimate affiliation with the traditions of the Old Latin or of Codex Bezae, but many others counterbalance these. In the Gospels, certainly, we do not find the close support for peculiarities of the Bezan text, which in Acts is said to be provided by the Glazier Coptic manuscript, or by Greek witnesses such as $\mathfrak{P}^{38}$ and $\mathfrak{P}^{48}$.

The second-century Fathers may also be a source of information about text-forms in this period and have often previously been adduced as witnesses to the Western text. In the case of many, we have had no new critical advance, in the sense of editions or collections of Biblical materials. If we had a precise knowledge of Marcion's text, it would cast much light on a dark period; but we still rely upon the deductions of Zahn and von Harnack, working mainly from Epiphanius, Tertullian, and the strictly anonymous Adamantius *De recta in Deum fide*. My experience has been that, great though those two scholars were, it is often worthwhile in "Marcionite" textual studies to work over their materials again, going back to the editions and manuscripts of their three main sources, and the sparse

---

[7]Joseph Molitor, "Tatians Diatessaron und sein Verhältnis zur altsyrischen und altgeorgischen Überlieferung," *OrChr* 53 (1969): 1-88; ibid., 54 (1970): 1-75; ibid., 55 (1971): 1-61.

additional matter which one can find in Ephraem the Syrian, Eznik, and occasional others (Professor Delobel will deal with Marcion in his paper). Sometimes we arrive at different conclusions. The one Father in fact from whom we might expect a fruitful harvest for our sphere of interest is Irenaeus. In the hundred years since Westcott and Hort, several Greek fragments have come to light, some in fragmentary manuscripts, some in excerpts preserved in catenae and florilegia; and the Armenian of Books 4 and 5 of the *Adversus Haereses* has been discovered and studied, as well as a few fragments in other languages of Christian antiquity. The hoped-for edition in the Berlin Corpus has never appeared: but we do have a new edition in *Sources Chrétiennes*. This is a boon, as it brings together the new materials and the old, carefully studied, and presented with introductions and justificatory notes, book by book. But here too, we must exercise a certain caution: there was disagreement amongst the editors after the appearance of Book 4 (the first part to be published and the one of greatest interest to the Biblical textual critics). Recently the veteran Late-Latinist Sven Lundström[8] has joined in the debate, supporting various arguments of Hemmerdinger, the dissentient editor. In Lundström's judgement, the remaining editors have "over-estimated the Armenian version, have not studied the translation procedures of the Latin translator, and consequently, have removed genuine elements of vulgar Latin, and altered the Latin text arbitrarily." This is a densely documented and closely argued book of over 150 pages, and I have by no means worked through it. It may be that little will bear upon the scriptural text as quoted, but we should consult him on each point where he has commented.

In the discoveries of portions of the Greek text, there stand out two early papyri. The Oxyrhynchus papyrus 405, which contains part of book 3 (*haer*. 3.9.3: *SC* 211.106-109), is of striking importance since it is dated in the late-second or early-third century: it is thus nearly contemporary with the work of Irenaeus, written between 174 and 189 CE. It consists of seven fragments, and thus its text is uncertain, supplied by editors on the basis of line length in a number of places. Now however, we can have at a number of points some greater certainty, since the relatively recently discovered florilegium of Ochrida contains an excerpt of much the same extent. The verses in question are Matt 3:16-17. In addition to the form ἀνεῴχθησαν without superfluous temporal augment (which both witnesses share, but is a majority reading in the New Testament textual tradition) the most

---

[8]Sven Lundström, *Die Überlieferung der lateinischen Irenaeus-übersetzung*, AUU, SLatU, no. 18 (Uppsala, 1985).

striking reading is the second person singular σὺ (εἶ ὁ υἱός) which the text of Irenaeus was not previously known to attest, the Latin reading *hic est* in verse 17. The second person is the reading of the Codex Bezae, of the Old Latin *a* in addition to *d*, and of the two Old Syriac manuscripts. A further coincidence in a Bezan reading by the papyrus, but not supported by the florilegium, is ὡς for ὡσεί before περιστεράν, known also in D and Eusebius *on the Psalms*, and, according to von Soden, in MS 983 (attestation which cannot at present be checked). The papyrus in disagreement with the florilegium omits αὐτῷ after ἀνεῴχθησαν; reads τὸ πνεῦμα, and probably, on grounds of space, τοῦ θεοῦ following; and, with the florilegium, reads καί before ἐρχόμενον. Most of these variants, are insignificant, since they are readings of the majority of Gospel witnesses; but the omission of αὐτῷ in verse 16 is attested only by ℵ, B, some Vulgate manuscripts, the Old Syriac manuscripts, the Sahidic version, and Cyril of Jerusalem. Thus, in a copy of Irenaeus which is later than his activity by only a few decades, we find two readings subsingular to the Codex Bezae, and another, on the contrary, coincident with ℵ and B only, amongst Greek manuscripts. This fluctuation of the attestation of variants, in terms of later groupings, shows much the same pattern as we have seen in early papyri of the Gospels.

Also extremely early in the history of the transmission of the text of Irenaeus is the Jena papyrus, originating in the late-third or early-fourth century. Although very fragmentary, it is still significant for the original Greek form of three Gospel passages in book 5. (1) Luke 9:60 is found in column 5 of the papyrus (*haer.* 5.9.1: *SC* 153.108f). Variants attested are the plural ἄφετε for the singular ἄφες, and the present infinitive θάπτειν for the aorist θάψαι. This is a generalizing form of which the only other extant attestation for both variants together is from other Greek patristic sources. (2) Luke 6:46 is found in column 5 (*haer.* 5.8.3: *SC* 153.102-105). Here the reading agrees with the vast majority of attestation, which gives the plural ἃ λέγω; the singular ὃ λέγω is known from 𝔓⁷⁵, B, it (*e*), gothic, probably the Old Syriac and the Peshitta, and also the Latin sermon PS-AU s Cai I 15,3. (3) Lastly, in column 10 of the papyrus we have a small fragment of a passage by Irenaeus (*haer.* 5.13.1: *SC* 153.164f) concerning the raisings of the dead effected by Jesus: Jairus's daughter (Mark 5), the widow's son of Nain (Luke 7), and Lazarus (John 11). Details of the raising of Jairus's daughter are transferred to that of the widow's son, who is raised by the hand and whose feeding is commanded. Only the singular masculine pronoun in the dative αὐτῷ survives in the papyrus, but this alone is sufficient to confirm the ambiguous Latin and Armenian at this point. The two passages are not infrequently found exchanging details when quoted from memory, and it is interesting that another story of the restoration of a dependent, namely the centurion's boy, has intruded here into the Armenian tradition where Jarius's daughter (*op. cit.*, 162, line 2) has become the daughter of a centurion!

Although these instances have their own interest and open up a number of topics pertinent to the wider issues of our enquiry, this early patristic papyrus does not offer other variants which bear directly upon the question of second-century attestation for readings which are also known in the witnesses formerly deemed to attest the "Western Text," and thus to speak for its existence. For data of this kind we must go to a secondary source of our knowledge of the Greek text of Irenaeus, utilized from the time of the first critical editors, namely the excerpts known from *catenae* and *florilegia*. In the cases to be discussed here, both quotations are found in excerpts in the *Sacra Parallela* of John of Damascus. These enable us to look at examples from books 2 and 4 of the *Adversus Haereses*. In *haer.* 2.33.5 (*SC* 294.352-355), we have an instance where the florilegium of Ochrid duplicates the evidence for the Greek. Here, in an allusion in indirect speech, we find a variant of Luke 20:34, namely the addition of the items "beget and are begotten" to the phrase "marry and are given in marriage." In the Irenaeus passage here attested in Greek, already known from the Latin version, this phrase precedes the one relating to marriage. This is also attested in Origen, in Clement of Alexandria, in both manuscripts of the Old Syriac version, and in the margin of the Harklean (Syr[hmg]). In Codex Bezae, in the same position, the order is transposed to "are begotten and beget." This phrase alone, in one order or the other, is found in the Old Latin *e ff*[2] *l q*, while the phrase concerning marriage is added in other manuscripts of that version. It seems to me that it may also be significant that two manuscripts of the *Sacra Parallela* give the form γαμεῖσθαι in the phrase common to all texts, since γαμοῦνται is found in Codex Bezae alone. (In the opinion, however, of Dom Adelin Rousseau, in a report of his views by Marcel Richard, appended to the publication of the Ochrid fragment, the reading γαμίζεσθαι in a third manuscript of the *Sacra Parallela* and in the Ochrid florilegium is to be preferred as the original reading of Irenaeus.) An echo of knowledge of the "Bezan" reading in John of Damascus's work elsewhere may be heard in *Expositio Fidei* 100 (line 100)[9] where, speaking of the human state in the Resurrection, he declares (admittedly with a reference to the Matthaean

---

[9] *Die Schriften des Johannes von Damaskos....besorgt von P. Bonifatius Kotter O.S.B.*, vol. 2, *Expositio fidei* (Berlin: Walter de Gruyter, 1973), 237.

parallel to the passage of Luke here in point) that there will be "no longer marriage, nor begetting of children" (οὐ γάμος ἔτι, οὐ τεκνογονία).

The other passage in which we find a Greek quotation of scripture by Irenaeus which contains features attested by the "Western" witnesses is Matt 25:41. This is quoted or alluded to nine times in the *Adversus Haereses*, in seven of which there is clear reference—either verbatim or by paraphrase—to the reading known from the Codex Bezae, Family 1, Hippolytus and Origen: τὸ πῦρ τὸ αἰώνιον ὁ ἡτοίμασεν ὁ πατήρ (μου). One of the paraphrastic references (*haer.* 4.40.1: *SC* 100**.974f.) is found in Greek in a passage known from one manuscript of the *Sacra Parallela*: "It is the one and the same Father who has prepared good things by his side ... and who has prepared eternal fire ... who, for those who flee from His light, has prepared eternal fire and outer darkness." The reading so clearly known to Irenaeus is placed within second-century attestation yet more certainly by its presence in Justin and the Clementine *Homilies*.

These examples are few, but nevertheless they justify the view—on the basis of both the papyri of the Gospels and the best access that we can gain to the original Greek of the major work of Irenaeus—that distinctive Greek textual variants were known in the second century, and that these variants are not infrequently those which survived in the witnesses of the so-called "Western Text." (The paucity of Gospel references would be somewhat ameliorated if we were including the Paulines in our study, for Paul is quoted much more frequently than the Gospels in the papyri and *catenae* of Irenaeus which we examined.) The problem is, however, whether we should view these variations as indicating the existence of a "text." Our answer probably depends on how we define "text." We have still not freed ourselves from the Hortian schema, with its implicit model of three (or any number of) texts, viewed as quite specific and distinct each from other. (Such notions still survive in full strength, as the work of Boismard and Lamouille, and of Amphoux reveals.) We shall do better to be guided by the charts and tables of the various scholars, for instance Griffith or Duplacy,[10] who have attempted a taxonomy of the states of text in particular manuscripts. In such charts we find a picture of the text as a whole emerging, rather like a spectrum, in which, on the one hand, particular colours may be discerned quite distinctly, but, on the other, not

---

[10]J. Duplacy, "Classification des états d'un texte, mathématiques et informatique: repères historiques et recherches methodologiques," *RHT* 5 (1975): 249-309; reprinted in J. Duplacy, *Études de critique textuelle du Nouveau Testament*, BEThL, no. 78 (Leuven: University Press/Peeters, 1987), 193-257.

demarcated from one another by a ruled line. Moving through the spectrum, we find each colour shading into the next. Some recent work suggests a more complex model, requiring three dimensions rather than two, in order to reflect the interrelation of the various states of text. To exploit this new model, we would need to draw upon terminology more properly appropriate to a discipline such as solid geometry.

The scholars who have attempted taxonomic presentation of the interrelation of the states of text reflected within the manuscript tradition have considered the Greek tradition as a whole, using a significant number of instances from that tradition. From the second century we have not used all that is available, but we can, I believe, see that the picture, when complete, would resemble the taxonomists' presentation. One type would fade into another, the *differentia* being such signal variants as we have discerned in the papyri, in the Old Latin version, and in the Greek text of Irenaeus. Each color, or sector, or point (whichever model we are using) would correspond to forms which we know better from sources of later date. Rational criticism will help us to determine which variants, not known in the earliest strata, may nevertheless have existed at that earlier time. Historical reconstruction will then have to take over and play its part in explaining which variation at any given point is the original, and how the corruption of the text came about.

In this reconstruction we shall have to take into account some recent work. The papyrologist C.H. Roberts, in his important survey of early Christianity in Egypt,[11] presents a picture of a church whose transmission of its scriptures shows great care from an early date, even though professional scribes are not at first employed. This is shown early in the second century by the provision of reading signs, punctuation and chapter divisions. Later, critical signs begin to appear. We are reminded by the writer of the view of Günther Zuntz, based on the textual evidence of the Pauline Epistles, that by 100 CE there already existed a text in Alexandria upon which a careful criticism had been exercised. For the Paulines the argument is cogent. In that place, at any rate, the church was not only concerned that its sacred texts should be carefully and intelligibly read, but that those texts should be reliable in the textual sense. In the case of the Gospels, I wish to draw attention to an essay buried in the pages of the

---

[11]Colin H. Roberts, *Manuscript, Society and Belief in early Christian Egypt,* The Schweich Lectures, 1977 (London: Oxford University Press, 1979), 20-25.

Kilpatrick *Festschrift* published in 1976,[12] in which I attempted an assessment of the significance of the variations between the two earliest extensive witnesses to the text of Luke, namely the then recently published Bodmer papyrus, $\mathfrak{P}^{75}$, and the Chester Beatty papyrus $\mathfrak{P}^{45}$. Assessment was made in the light of Hellenistic morphology, grammar and syntax, and led to the conclusion—surprising to me at that time—that, in most areas of comparison, it was $\mathfrak{P}^{75}$ which was nearest to the linguistic norms of the period, whereas $\mathfrak{P}^{45}$ showed signs of the influence of the Atticizing tendency and of other kinds of correction of a stylistic kind. This appears to bear out, for this Gospel, the notion of a careful tradition which maintained an original text in linguistic respects in the face of cultural pressures for change.

In the case of the Pauline Epistles, Zuntz made a convincing case, however, that although a protective and careful transmission of the text was to be found at such an early time, there were cases where corruption had taken place. We need to be alert to the possibility that this was true in the case of the text of the Gospels as well. Indeed, as we have pointed out, Westcott and Hort were convinced that this was so, even in that text which they so confidently called "Neutral." Working with different models, we may find in some cases that most of the tradition has lost the original reading: take for instance the form of the saying of Jesus about marriage and divorce in Mark 10:11-12, found in W, Family 1, the Sinaitic Syriac and the Adish manuscript of the Old Georgian. In this form, the first part of the sentence treats of the woman who divorces and remarries, the second treats of the case of the man who so behaves. In all other forms of the verse, man precedes woman. Paul appears to have in mind a dominical saying in which the same order was found, since he gives the woman precedence in the moral teaching of 1 Cor 7:10-11. The evangelist Matthew leaves out the woman altogether in his version, while the parallels in Matt 5:32 and Luke 16:18, although mentioning the woman, do not see her as initiating the divorce. Burkitt argued that the form of the saying in these few witnesses was probably original, since it fitted the situation faced first by John the Baptist and then by Jesus in the scandal of the behavior of Herodias and her *paramour*. Once the historical background had been forgotten, the saying in the Gospel of Mark lent itself to

---

[12]J. Neville Birdsall, "Rational Eclecticism and the Oldest Manuscripts: A Comparative Study of the Bodmer and Chester Beatty Papyri of the Gospel of Luke," *Studies in New Testament Language and Text. Essays in Honour of George D. Kilpatrick on the Occasion of his Sixty-fifth Birthday*, NT.S, no. 44 (Leiden: Brill, 1976), 39-51.

the various corrections of the complex tradition here, in all of which the man's action comes first. In this instance, only a few witnesses preserve the original; but in the same textual vicinity, the readings of this group do not command respect upon examination. We could multiply many instances of this sort of problem. Certain witnesses may preserve a higher number of readings which we may find to be original, but not even the most careful tradition will be without erroneous readings—nor perhaps the worst without traces of the original.

Corruption will not usually take the form of the obliteration of details coherent with the historical background of the Gospel materials. In rational criticism we shall have to bear in mind more often other factors. Firstly, oral tradition continued as a living force well into the second century: as a written record became more and more established, material which had previously circulated orally could be added to the written Gospels. Secondly, as the specific definition of the faith became clearer by inner debate and outward defence and propagation, and the separate Gospels came to be treated more as a unity, readings could be made more precise in their reflection of church belief or of the beliefs of groups within the church, and harmonious with emerging doctrine. Harmonization of the Gospels is another aspect of this. Thirdly, scholarship played its part, sometimes preserving (as in the example of the text of $\mathfrak{P}^{75}$, to which I have alluded), but sometimes corrupting the text—as the later intrusion of the conjectural Βηθαβαρά of Origen at John 1:28 into Gospel texts reveals.

As emphasized at the beginning of this paper, I share common ground with the recent critics of Westcott and Hort, that the text of the Codex Bezae cannot be identified with any entity of the second century *tout simple*: if "Western Text" means "the text of the Codex Bezae," then it is not to be found in the second century. The text of that fascinating manuscript has developed under the influence of all the factors which have been outlined, intermingling with the surviving original readings. If the hypothesis be correct that the manuscript is the product of the provision of lections in parallel languages in an Eastern church (such as Jerusalem in the beginning of the pilgrim period), then we shall find the explanation of the features of the mutual interaction of the Greek and Latin columns in its evolution, and, perhaps, of the data of an apparent Syriac interaction (on which Chase based himself), which sometimes seem to explain the otherwise inexplicable. An Eastern origin would also explain the presence of features which might reflect Aramaisms or other possible links with "original" features. The text of the Codex Bezae is the product of more centuries than the one on which we are concentrating.

But in the second century textual forms already existed which were not characteristic of the Alexandrian tradition; the data I have brought before you present a *prima facie* case. The form of this second-century proto-Western text or texts has not yet been determined. Many lines of research might be open to us: no one, for instance, has investigated the view of Henry Sanders that the first five chapters of Mark in the Freer Codex (W) are a Greek equivalent of the African Latin (*e*);[13] nor has anyone pursued an explanation of the indubitable links of that manuscript with readings of the Old Syriac tradition or the Ferrar group. There is much to investigate and that is the only way forward: dogmatisms will render us no service.

"The Western Text in the Second Century," to revert to the title proposed to me and the topic undertaken by me, is an object which we do not yet perceive with absolute clarity, but of whose existence (in the sense of a body of textual data of major influence upon the evolution of the Gospel text in the earliest centuries) there can be no doubt, as even our brief survey of the data demonstrates. We are still rather like *Alice Through the Looking Glass*, on her first encounter with the poem Jabberwocky which she has discovered and deciphered. She exclaimed, having read it, "It's rather hard to understand" (you see, she didn't like to confess, even to herself, that she couldn't make it out at all). "Somehow it seems to fill my head with ideas—only I don't exactly know what they are! However, *somebody* killed *something*, that's clear, at any rate—." As we pursue the study of the "Western Text," especially in the second century, do my colleagues admit with me, that we often feel as Alice did?

---

[13]*The New Testament Manuscripts in the Freer Collection. Part I. The Washington Manuscript of the Four Gospels*, ed. Henry A. Sanders, University of Michigan Studies, Humanistic Series, no. 9 (New York: Macmillan, 1912), 67.

The Text of the Synoptic Gospels in the Second Century

Helmut Koester

Harvard University (USA)

Since there is no second-century manuscript evidence,[1] the quest for the text of the Synoptic Gospels in the second century is identical with the question of the earliest usage of their text in other writings. The evidence consists not only of such writers as the Apostolic Fathers and early Apologists but also of later Gospel writers, like Matthew and Luke, as external attestations for the text of an older Gospel.

There are fundamental differences between a second-century user of a Gospel and a fourth- or fifth-century quotation in a Church Father: (1) For a later user, the Gospels of the New Testament were available as part of the four-Gospel canon; in the period before the year 200 CE, the Gospels were usually transmitted separately. (2) In the later period, the Gospels were considered holy scripture; no such respect was accorded them in the earliest period. (3) Beginning only with the third century can we assign quotations to certain text types, attested in extant manuscripts, and often confirmed by translations into Syriac, Coptic, and Latin; for the earlier period, we have no manuscript evidence at all, and text types can be identified only by the evidence that comes from those who used Gospels.

The problems for the reconstruction of the textual history of the canonical Gospels in the first century of transmission are immense. The assumption that the reconstruction of the best archetype for the manuscript tradition is more or less identical with the assumed autograph is precarious. The oldest known manuscript archetypes are separated from the autographs by more than a century. Textual critics of classical texts know that the first century of their transmission is the period in which the most serious corruptions occur. Textual critics of the New Testament writings have been surprisingly naïve in this respect.

---

[1] The fragment of John in $\mathfrak{P}^{52}$ is so small that is immaterial as a textual witness.

Moreover, there can be no question that the Gospels, from the very beginning, were not archive materials but used texts. This is the worst thing that could happen to any textual tradition. A text, not protected by canonical status, but used in liturgy, apologetics, polemics, homiletics, and instruction of catechumens is most likely to be copied frequently and is thus subject to frequent modifications and alterations. What then can be learned from these users of Gospels about the alterations they introduced and about the texts which they used?[2]

Evidence for Matthew's and Luke's Use of Mark

The Synoptic two-source hypothesis asserts that Matthew and Luke used the Gospel of Mark as their primary source. The alterations which they made in their employment of this source have often been discussed and need not be repeated here. They include not only numerous instances of improving Mark's style and language, but also the rearrangement of larger blocks of materials and the addition of similar materials from other sources. Notable is the assembling of the Markan miracle stories into a single collection by Matthew (chaps. 8-9). Matthew also expanded existing Markan collections: in reproducing Mark's parable collection (chap. 4), Matthew (chap. 13) added a number of parables from his special source. Luke, on the other hand, left the order of Markan pericopes mostly intact. However, he constantly interwove materials from the Synoptic Sayings Source and from his special source with Markan materials. Among the few departures from the Markan order, the most striking is the placement of Mark 6:1-6 (Jesus' Rejection at Nazareth) at the beginning of Jesus' ministry (Luke 4:16-24; following upon Luke 4:14-15 = Mark 1:14-15).[3]

---

[2]Francois Bovon ("The Synoptic Gospels and the Noncanonical Acts of the Apostles," *HThR* 81 [1988]: 19-36) gives examples from the transmission of the apocryphal acts as possible analogies for the way in which the gospels might have been transmitted and copied before their canonization.

[3]Furthermore, two Markan pericopes have been placed into the Lukan "Travel Narrative" (Luke 9:51-18:14): Luke 10:25-28 = Mark 12:28-31 (The Great Commandment); Luke 11:15-22 = Mark 3:22-27 (Beelzebul Controversy).

Matthew and Luke not only provide examples for changes in the text of an older gospel, they are also important witnesses for the oldest text of their source. It is possible, to be sure, that there are instances in which Matthew and Luke, independently of each other, made the same stylistic improvements of Mark's text. But there should be no question that the oldest accessible text of the Gospel of Mark is preserved in most instances in which Matthew and Luke agree in their reproduction of their source— even if the extant Markan manuscript tradition presents a different text.

These instances of agreement are numerous. They include cases in which Matthew and Luke agree in the wording of a phrase or sentence that is different from Mark's text; and cases in which Markan words, sentences, or entire pericopes are absent from both Matthew and Luke. I cannot repeat the entire material here. It has been presented and discussed in detail recently by Frans Neirynck in defense of the two-source hypothesis,[4] and by Hans-Herbert Stoldt in his criticism of this hypothesis.[5] In the following I shall discuss only some striking examples.

According to the overwhelming majority of textual witnesses, the text of Mark 4:11 reads: "To you is given the mystery of the rule of God" (Ὑμῖν τὸ μυστήριον δέδοται τῆς βασιλείας τοῦ θεοῦ). However, the parallel passages in Matthew (13:11) and Luke (8:10) agree in reading "to know" (γνῶναι) after "is given" (δέδοται) and the plural "mysteries" (μυστήρια) instead of the singular "mystery" (μυστήριον) of Mark 4:11.[6] Thus Matthew and Luke agree in their formulations: "To you is given to know the mysteries of the rule of God (Matthew: of the heavens)" = Ὑμῖν δέδοται γνῶναι τὰ μυστήρια τῆς βασιλείας τοῦ θεοῦ (τῶν οὐρανῶν).

---

[4]Frans Neirynck, *The Minor Agreements of Matthew and Luke against Mark*, BEThL, no. 37 (Louvain: Leuven University Press, 1974); see also C. M. Tuckett, *The Revival of the Griesbach Hypothesis*, SNTS.MS, no. 44 (Cambridge: Cambridge University Press, 1983).

[5]Hans-Herbert Stoldt, *History and Criticism of the Marcan Hypothesis* (Macon, GA: Mercer University Press, 1980).

[6]There is considerable variation in the manuscript tradition. Both singular and plural occur in manuscripts of all three gospels. However, the occurrence of the singular in manuscripts of Matthew and Luke and the occurrence of the plural in manuscripts of Mark is due to later corruption and is not the survival of a more original reading. The archetype for all Markan manuscripts read the singular.

As far as the context is concerned, both Matthew and Luke drew everything surrounding this discourse of Jesus with the disciples (the Parable of the Sower and its allegorical interpretation) from the Gospel of Mark, not from any different common source. Thus, they must have preserved the original Markan text also in the statement of Jesus to the disciples in Mark 4:11. Moreover, the plural "mysteries" is appropriate here: each parable is "a mystery," that is, a mysterious saying or a riddle that must be explained.[7] This use is more original,[8] while the singular "mystery" as a designation of the entire preaching of Jesus or of the entire Gospel occurs only in later Christian literature.[9]

In numerous instances, Matthew and Luke agree against Mark in the choice of a particular term. One of the most striking cases is the use of ἐγερθῆναι in Matthew and Luke instead of Mark's ἀναστῆναι in two of the Predictions of the Passion. In the first Prediction of the Passion, Matt 16:21 and Luke 9:22 are in agreement in their reading "and on the third day he will be raised" (καὶ τῇ τρίτῃ ἡμέρᾳ ἐγερθῆναι), while the extant text of their common source, Mark 8:31, says: "and after three days he will rise" (καὶ μετὰ τρεῖς ἡμέρας ἀναστῆναι).[10] In the reproduction of the second and

---

[7]Joachim Jeremias (The Parables of Jesus, 2d ed. [New York: Scribner's, 1972], 13-18) has shown that Mark 4:11-12 is an older and originally independent saying. He points to the antithetical parallelism of the phrases, "to you the mystery is given" and "to those outside it comes in parables." However, Jeremias fails to explain why Mark 4:11 reads the singular "mystery" as antithesis to the plural "parables" (cf. also the plural in Mark 4:34: "to his disciples he explained all these things"). The problem is resolved if the plural form in the first half of the antithesis in Matt 13:11 and Luke 8:10 ("to you it is given to know the mysteries") was also the original reading of Mark 4:11.

[8]The Gospel of Thomas uses the plural in a saying that introduces several parables: "It is to those who are worthy of my mysteries that I give my mysteries" (62). Paul confirms the analogous usage; when referring to an individual saying, he uses the singular (Rom 11:25; 1 Cor 15:51), otherwise he uses the plural; cf. 1 Cor 13:2: "and if I knew all the mysteries" (see also 1 Cor 4:1; 14:2). See Günther Bornkamm, "μυστήριον," TDNT 4:802-828.

[9]Typical for later usage is the identification of "mystery" and "gospel," or the close association of the two terms; cf. Eph 6:19: "to make known the mystery of the gospel" (see also Eph 3:1-7).

[10]Mark's phrase "after three days" instead of "on the third day" is peculiar. It contradicts Mark's own dating of the resurrection: the empty tomb is found on the morning of the third day. M. Smith (Clement of Alexandria and a Secret Gospel of Mark [Cambridge, MA: Harvard University Press, 1973], 163-164) points out that "after three days" actually means "on the fourth day" and that there is an interesting parallel in John 11:17 and 39, the Johannine parallel to the story of the raising of the young man reported in the Secret Gospel of Mark: Lazarus was raised on the fourth day after his death.

third Predictions of the Passion (Mark 9:31; 10:34), Matthew (17:23; 20:19) also uses the term "he will be raised" (ἐγερθήσεται) instead of Mark's "he will rise" (ἀναστήσεται). In these last two instances, the evidence is less conclusive with respect to the original reading of Mark, because a Lukan parallel to Mark 9:31 is missing and in the parallel to Mark 10:34, Luke (18:33) agrees with Mark's extant text "he will rise" (ἀναστήσεται). But "to be raised" (ἐγερθῆναι) is more common in the oldest Christian usage (see also 1 Cor 15:4) and is, therefore, most likely the term that appeared in Mark's original text.[11]

The two words "to teach" (διδάσκειν) and "teaching" (διδαχή) were certainly used in the oldest text of the Gospel of Mark. Matthew or Luke or both reproduce them in their usage of the following Markan passages: 1:21, 22; 6:2, 6; (7:7); 11:18; 12:14; 14:49. However, there are a number of Markan passages in which the term occurs without equivalent terms occurring in the corresponding parallels in Matthew and Luke. In Mark 1:27, the witnesses to Jesus' exorcism (1:23-26) respond by saying "a new teaching with authority" (διδαχὴ καινὴ κατ' ἐξουσίαν). The phrase "new teaching" appears only in one other New Testament passage, Acts 17:19: "What is this new teaching that is proclaimed by you?" (τίς ἡ καινὴ αὕτη ἡ ὑπὸ σοῦ λαλουμένη διδαχή;). As Acts 17:32 reveals, this new teaching is "the resurrection from the dead." Another important parallel occurs in the Gospel fragment from P. Oxy. 1224, 2 v. col. I: "Which new teaching do they say you teach, and which new baptism do you proclaim?" (π[ο]ίαν σέ [φασιν διδα]χὴν καιν[ὴν διδάσκειν ἢ τί β]ά[πτισμ]α καινὸν [κηρύσσειν;] . . .).[12]

In Mark 6:7 the Twelve are sent out "with power over the unclean spirits"; when they return (Mark 6:30) they announce to him "all they had done and what they had taught" (πάντα ὅσα ἐποίησαν καὶ ὅσα ἐδίδαξαν). The parallel passages (Matt 14:12 and Luke 9:10) do not present the latter phrase καὶ ὅσα ἐδίδαξαν. In the subsequent introduction to the story of the Feeding of the Five Thousand, Mark 6:34 says, "and Jesus began to teach (διδάσκειν) them many things." Matt 14:14 only reports that Jesus healed the sick; Luke 9:11 contains a similar remark and notes that Jesus was "speaking" (ἐλάλει) about the rule of God. Mark 8:31 and 9:31 introduce the first and second Predictions of the Passion with the words "he began to teach" and "he taught"; no such statement appears in the parallels in

---

[11]See the use of ἐγείρειν in other formulaic passages such as Rom 4:24; 1 Thess 1:10.

[12]Erich Klostermann, *Apocrypha II: Evangelien*, KlT, no. 8, 3d ed. (Berlin: Walter de Gruyter, 1929), 26.

Matthew and Luke.   In addition to these passages, Mark 2:13; 4:1-2; 10:1;
11:17; 12:35, 37, 38 also use the word "to teach" for the activity of Jesus,
while Matthew and Luke use different verbs in their parallel passages.

The story of the Healing of the Epileptic Child, Mark 9:14-29, is the
most complex miracle narrative in Mark and presents the most difficult
problems for the explanation of its origin and its relationship to the
parallels in Matthew (17:14-21) and Luke (9:38-43a).[13]   Mark's version of
the story is more than twice as long as the parallel versions in Matthew
and Luke.   Besides, Mark 9:14b-16, 21, 22b-24, parts of 25-27, and 28 have no
parallels in either Matthew or Luke.   It seems that both read a version of
this story in their copy of Mark which did not contain these verses.
Especially the phrases and sentences of Mark 9:25-27 which are missing in
the other two Synoptic Gospels have the appearance of secondary alterations or additions.   Matt 17:18 and Luke 9:42b must have read a common
source which reported briefly that Jesus exorcised the unclean spirit
(ἐπετίμησεν κτλ.), that the child was healed (Matt: ἐθεραπεύθη, Luke:
ἰάσατο), and perhaps a reaction of the crowd (preserved only in Luke 9:43).
The extant text of Mark, however, quotes in full the wording of an
exorcistic formula, indeed the longest such formula in the Synoptic
Gospels.[14]   "You mute and deaf spirit, I command you, go out of him and
never enter into him again" (Τὸ ἄλαλον καὶ κωφὸν πνεῦμα, ἐγὼ ἐπιτάσσω
σοι, ἔξελθε ἐξ αὐτοῦ καὶ μηκέτι εἰσέλθῃς εἰς αὐτόν).   Surprisingly, this is an
exorcism for a deaf-mute person, not for an epileptic child.[15]   Apparently,
the redactor shows little interest in the healing of the disease.   Rather, he
wants to describe the effect of a powerful exorcism and thus introduces the
following action of Jesus which has no parallel whatever in Matthew and
Luke: the demon departs with appropriate demonstration, the boy is left
"as if dead" (ὡσεὶ νεκρός) and the bystanders say "he died" (ἀπέθανεν).   This
prepares for an action of Jesus which is described as the raising of a dead

---

[13]Commentaries try to explain the complexity of the Marcan story as the result of
an inept redaction by the author of the Gospel who may have tried to conflate two older
stories. However, they do not use the much simpler forms of the story in Matthew and Luke
as a guide for the reconstruction of the original story in Mark. For discussion and literature,
see Walther Schmithals, *Das Evangelium nach Markus*, ÖTKNT, no. 2/1 (Gütersloh:
Gütersloher Verlagshaus, 1979), 407-424.

[14]The other exorcistic formulae cited in the Synoptic Gospels are very brief; cf.
Mark 1:41; 2:11; 3:5; 10:52; Luke 8:54; 13:12; 17:14.

[15]Mark, or a later redactor, has changed 9:17 accordingly (ἔχοντα πνεῦμα ἄλαλον),
although the original description of the disease is still visible in Mark 9:18, 20, 22.

person: Jesus takes him by the hand (κρατήσας τῆς χειρὸς αὐτοῦ), raises him, and he rises (ἤγειρεν αὐτόν, καὶ ἀνέστη).

There are several "major omissions" of Markan pericopes or parts of pericopes which Matthew and Luke share. At least in two instances, they apparently did not appear in the original Markan text that was used by Matthew and Luke.

The Parable of the Seed Growing Secretly (Mark 4:26-29) is not reproduced by either Matthew or Luke. If Matthew found the parable in his copy of Mark, one must resort to the explanation that he replaced it with the Parable of the Tares (Matt 13:24-30). However, the additions to the Markan parable chapter in Matt 13 show that he was eager to expand this chapter.[16] Since also Luke does not reproduce this parable in his version of the parable chapter (Luke 8:4-18) nor anywhere else in his Gospel, it is more likely that the original text of Mark did not include it.[17]

In Mark 12:28-31 (= Matt 22:34-40 and Luke 10:25-28) the pericope about the Great Commandment is provided with an appendix about "the scribe who is not far from the rule of God" (Mark 12:32-34). Günther Bornkamm has demonstrated that this appendix is a later addition to the text of Mark, written from the perspective of Hellenistic propaganda.[18] The scribe acknowledges that Jesus "in truth" (ἐπ' ἀληθείας) puts forward first of all the confession of Hellenistic Jewish and Christian propaganda that "God is one" (εἷς ἐστιν, Mark 12:32)—thus the quote of Deut 6:3 which appears only in Mark (12:29) is also an expansion; adds the phrase "out of your whole understanding" (ἐξ ὅλης τῆς συνέσεως, Mark 12:33) in the repetition of the commandment to love God (Deut 6:5); and contrasts love of one's neighbor with "burnt offerings and sacrifices," another typical commonplace of Jewish and Christian propaganda. Jesus finally answers that the scribe has spoken "with understanding" (νουνεχῶς, Mark 12:34).[19]

---

[16]Cf. Matt 13:33, 44-46, 47-50, 51-52.

[17]Philipp Vielhauer (*Geschichte der frühchristlichen Literatur* [Berlin: Walter de Gruyter, 1975], 273-275) considers this the only certain evidence for the thesis that the original text of Mark differed from the canonical text.

[18]Günther Bornkamm, "Das Doppelgebot der Liebe," in *Neutestamentliche Studien für Rudolf Bultmann*, ed. Walther Eltester, BZNW, no. 21 (Berlin: Töpelmann, 1954), 85-93.

[19]I leave aside here the problem of Mark 6:45 - 8:26, the "Bethsaida section," which is completely missing in Luke. It is at least possible that Luke had a text of Mark in which this section was missing, whether or not this was a defective or a more original copy

The Evidence from the Apostolic Fathers

At an earlier time in New Testament scholarship, the Apostolic Fathers played a major role in attempts to establish an early *terminus ante quem* for the composition of the canonical Gospels.[20] Though one may still find occasional claims that Matthew and Luke were used in the *First Epistle of Clement*, in the *Epistle of Barnabas*, and in the *Didache*, or that the Gospel of John was used by Ignatius of Antioch, it is now more generally acknowledged that there is no basis for such assumptions. The careful investigation by a British committee of scholars at the beginning of this century[21] has made scholars more cautious in this respect.[22]

The earliest use of the Gospel of Matthew appears in the letter of Polycarp of Smyrna. In *Phil.* 2.3, he quotes sayings of Jesus from *1 Clem.* 13.2.[23] However, Polycarp does not reproduce these sayings as they appear in *1 Clement*. Rather he revises the text in order to achieve a more exact agreement with the Matthean parallels.[24] It is not certain that this use of

---

of Mark. As is well known, this Markan section contains a number of doublets to the preceding chapters. This would support the view that this section is a secondary addition.

[20]The classical work was written by Constantin Tischendorf, *Wann wurden unsere Evangelien verfaßt?* 4th ed. (Leipzig, 1866); the most comprehensive material was brought together by Theodor Zahn, *Geschichte des neutestamentlichen Kanons*, 2 vols. (Erlangen and Leipzig, 1888-92). These works were primarily directed against the arguments for second-century dates of the Gospels of the New Testament which were based on the lack of certain quotations from these Gospels in the Apostolic Fathers; cf. I. H. Scholten, *Die ältesten Zeugnisse betreffs der Schriften des Neuen Testaments* (Bremen, 1867).

[21]*The New Testament in the Apostolic Fathers*, By A Committee of the Oxford Society of Historical Theology (Oxford, 1905). For a more comprehensive study see Helmut Köster, *Synoptische Überlieferung bei den Apostolischen Vätern*, TU, no. 65 (Berlin: Akademie-Verlag, 1957).

[22]The more recent work of Eduard Massaux, *Influence de Saint Matthieu sur la littérature chrétienne avant Saint Irénée* (Louvain, 1950), now also available in English translation, is too uncritical in this respect and assumes the use of Matthew in numerous instances in which reliance on oral or an apocryphal tradition is the more appropriate explanation.

[23]That Polycarp is dependent upon 1 Clement is evident in the quotation formula: μνημονεύοντες δὲ ὧν εἶπεν ὁ κύριος, διδάσκων, cf. *1 Clem.* 13.1: μεμνημένοι τῶν λόγων τοῦ κυρίου Ἰησοῦ, οὓς ἐλάλησεν διδάσκων, οὕτως γὰρ εἶπεν. See Köster, *Synoptische Überlieferung*, 115-118.

[24]Knowledge of the text of Matthew is also evident in Polycarp, *Phil.* 7.2, where he combines an allusion to the Lord's Prayer ("Lead us not into temptation") with a sentence

Matthew can be dated early in the second century CE. More likely, the part of the letter of Polycarp in which these quotations appear was not written until the middle of the second century, as Harrison has argued quite convincingly.[25]

The information of Papias about Mark and Matthew[26] may indeed refer to the two canonical Gospels transmitted under these names.[27] But Eusebius has not preserved anything that Papias may have quoted from these Gospels. Thus, nothing can be learned from Papias about the text of these Gospels.

The *Second Epistle of Clement*, written around the middle of the second century, is the only writing from the corpus of the Apostolic Fathers in which a number of quotations of sayings of Jesus appear which could be claimed as evidence for the use of canonical Gospels. These quotations are very instructive.[28] (1) Nowhere does one find allusions to narrative materials from any written Gospel known to us. (2) The sayings quoted here are certainly not taken directly from any canonical Gospel by the author of this writing; rather, they derive from a collection of sayings into which apocryphal sayings have also been incorporated.[29] (3) Almost all the sayings are harmonizations of parallel texts of Matthew and Luke, reflecting redactional changes introduced by these two Gospel writers.

The third point is evident in 2 *Clem.* 4.2, 5, quoting parts of Matt 7:21-23 = Luke 6:46 and 13:22-28. A fuller harmonized text of these sayings occurs in two quotations in Justin Martyr, 1 *Apol.* 16.9-12 and *Dial.* 76.5.

---

spoken by Jesus in the Gethsemane narrative: "As the Lord said, 'the flesh is willing, but the spirit is weak'" (Mark 14:38 = Matt).

[25] P. N. Harrison, *Polycarp's Two Epistles to the Philippians* (Cambridge: Cambridge University Press, 1936).

[26] Cf. Eusebius, *h.e.* 3.39.15, 16.

[27] The reference to Matthew has been taken by some scholars as a witness to the Synoptic Sayings Source, though more recently arguments have been presented which reaffirm the traditional view that the canonical Gospel of Matthew was known to Papias. For a more complete discussion, cf. Ron Cameron, *Apocryphon of James*, HThS, no. 34 (Philadelphia: Fortress, 1984), 93-116.

[28] For these sayings, see Köster, *Synoptische Überlieferung*, 70-105.

[29] 2 *Clem.* 4.5 contains a sentence ("If you were assembled on my breast...") that is commonly assigned to the *Gospel of the Nazoreans*. 2 *Clem.* 12.2, 6 quotes a saying ("When the two are one...") that Clement of Alexandria (*Strom.* 3.13, 92.2) found in the *Gospel of the Egyptians* and which is now also attested in the *Gospel of Thomas* (22).

2 *Clem.* / [Justin]	Matthew	Luke
οὐ πᾶς ὁ λέγων μοι	οὐ πᾶς ὁ λέγων μοι	τί δέ με καλεῖτε
[εἰσελεύσεται...]	εἰσελεύσεται...	
ἀλλ' ὁ ποιῶν...	ἀλλ' ὁ ποιῶν	
[πολλοὶ ἐροῦσίν μοι	πολλοὶ ἐροῦσίν μοι	τότε ἄρξεσθε λέγειν
ἐφάγομεν		ἐφάγομεν ἐνώπιόν
καὶ ἐπίομεν		σου καὶ ἐπίομεν
καὶ προεφητεύσαμεν	καὶ ἐπροφητεύσαμεν	
καὶ	καὶ τῷ σῷ ὀνόματι	
δαιμόνια ἐξεβάλομεν]	δαιμόνια ἐξεβάλομεν	
καὶ	καὶ τότε	καὶ
ἐρῶ ὑμῖν [αὐτοῖς]	ὁμολογήσω αὐτοῖς	ἐρεῖ λέγων ὑμῖν
[ἀποχωρεῖτε ἀπ' ἐμοῦ]	ἀποχωρεῖτε ἀπ' ἐμοῦ	ἀπόστητε ἀπ' ἐμοῦ
ἐργάται	οἱ ἐργαζόμενοι	πάντες ἐργάται
ἀνομίας	τὴν ἀνομίαν	ἀδικίας

The last phrase of this saying is drawn from the Synopotic Sayings Source which in turn uses Ps 6:9: ἀπόστητε ἀπ' ἐμοῦ, πάντες οἱ ἐργαζόμενοι τὴν ἀνομίαν.[30]   It is likely that this wording appeared in the Synoptic Sayings Source. Matt 7:23 changed the beginning of the sentence to ἀποχωρεῖτε ἀπ' ἐμοῦ..., whereas Luke 13:27 changed only the second half of the sentence to πάντες ἐργάται ἀδικίας. That 2 *Clement* and Justin present a mixture of these redactional changes is evident. It is unlikely that this is just an accidental mixture of the parallel versions. Other parallels in Justin's quotations confirm that these harmonized sayings derive from a systematic harmonization of Matthew and Luke; special features of Mark's text never occur.

Justin Martyr as a Witness to the Text of the Gospels

The mixture of Synoptic parallels in the quotations of sayings of Jesus in Justin Martyr has, of course, been observed for a long time. Many solutions have been proposed, ranging from use of a pre-synoptic source,[31]

---

[30]For a presentation of all parallels, see Köster, *Synpotische Überlieferung*, 88.

[31]Wilhelm Bousset, *Die Evangeliencitate Justins des Märtyrers in ihrem Wert für die Evangelienkritik* (Göttingen: Vandenhoeck & Ruprecht, 1891).

exclusive use of the canonical Gospels,[32] use of an apocryphal Gospel,[33] careless quotation from memory,[34] to the employment of a systematic harmony of the canonical Gospels.[35] In an investigation of all sayings quoted in Justin's writings, Arthur Bellinzoni has demonstrated that Justin's quotations rest on a systematic harmonization of written Gospels and that only the Gospels of Matthew and Luke have been used in order to produce these harmonized texts.[36] However, Bellinzoni does not believe that Justin possessed a full harmony of these two Gospels. Rather, for the sayings he presupposes a written catechism for which harmonized forms of the sayings were produced. The occasional appearance of non-canonical sayings in Justin's writings is explained as deriving from the use of "traditional sources, such as liturgical texts or early Christian handbooks known in similar form to other fathers in the early church."[37]

The reference to one or several catechisms with a harmonized text may seem a satisfactory explanation of the sayings in Justin. The question, however, remains, whether the "catechisms" from which Justin quotes are composed as harmonies on the basis of the two separate Gospels of Matthew and Luke or whether they are excerpts from a previously composed harmony of Matthew and Luke. It seems to me that the way in which Justin's catechisms move from one saying to another suggests that he is not composing a catechism and, at the same time, harmonizing the readings of the two Gospels for that particular purpose. Rather, the sayings he included in his catechism were already harmonized in his *Vorlage*. Whoever produced this *Vorlage*—and I am inclined to think

---

[32]Eduard Massaux, "Le texte du Sermon sur la Montagne de Matthieu utilisé par Saint Justin," *EThL* 28 (1952): 411-448; idem, *Influence de l'Évangile de St. Matthieu*.

[33]Adolf Hilgenfeld, *Kritische Untersuchungen über die Evangelien Justins, der Clementinischen Homilien und Marcions* (Halle, 1850).

[34]Theodor Zahn, *Geschichte des neutestamentlichen Kanons* (Erlangen, 1888), 1.2, passim.

[35]Ernest Lippelt, *Quae fuerint Justini Martyris ΑΠΟΜΝΕΜΟΝΕΥΜΑΤΑ* (Halle, 1901).

[36]Arthur J. Bellinzoni, *The Sayings of Jesus in the Writings of Justin Martyr*, NT.S, no. 17 (Leiden: Brill, 1967). See *ibidem* for full bibliography on the various hypotheses summarized above.

[37]Bellinzoni, *The Sayings of Jesus*, 138; cf. *idem*, "The Source of the Agraphon in Justin Martyr's Dialogue with Trypho 47:5," *VigChr* 17 (1963): 65-70.

that it was Justin himself or his "school"—did not intend to construct a
catechism, but was composing the *one* inclusive new Gospel which would
make its predecessors, Matthew and Luke (and possibly Mark), obsolete.

To illustrate the method used by the composer of this harmony, I
shall consider one example which also includes the passage already cited
above in the discussion of *2 Clement*: Justin *1 Apol.* 16.9-13.[38]

1 Apol. 16.9   = Matt 7:21 = Luke 6:46.

1 Apol. 16.10 = Luke 10:16 which is a variant of Luke 6:47 with a
                   phrase from Luke 6:46 not quoted in *1 Apol.* 16:9.

1 Apol. 16.11 = harmonization of Matt 7:22-23 and Luke 13:26-27.

1 Apol. 16.12 = harmonization of Matt 13:42-43 and Luke 13:28.

1 Apol. 16.13 = combination of Matt 24:5 with Matt 7:15-16, 19.

The writer of this new Gospel used Matthew 7 as the basis, moved
from Matthew 7 to the proper Lukan parallel (6:46), replaced the following
verse in Luke (6:47) with a variant found in Luke 10:21, returned to the
Matthean context (7:22-23), harmonized it with the Lukan parallel (13:26-
27), quoted the following Lukan verse (13:28) and harmonized it with the
appropriate Matthean parallel (13:42-43), then returned to another saying
from Matthew 7 (verse 15-16) and combined it with a variant from
Matthew 24 (verse 5).[39] This is a complex procedure which the composition of catechetical materials would hardly require, but could well be the
result of a systematic composition of a new Gospel on the basis of several
older sources. The procedure resembles that of Matthew who frequently
combines and amalgamates parallels from his two sources Mark and Q,
whereas Luke more often reproduces such variants twice in separate
sections of his Gospel.

The harmonized quotations of Gospel narrative materials in Justin
also call for an explanation. More detailed analysis would demonstrate
that, also in this respect, Justin follows the "School of St. Matthew." Justin
(or his source) wants to bring the narrative texts into closer agreement
with scriptural prophecy. In almost all instances, Justin quotes such

---

[38]This passage is also discussed in Bellinzoni, *The Sayings of Jesus*, 98-100.

[39]It is, of course, possible that the quote stood before Matt 7:21 in Justin's *Vorlage*.

narrative materials from the Gospels in order to demonstrate the fulfillment of Biblical prophecies, and his choice of sentences and phrases from
either Matthew or Luke is dictated by the requirements of such scriptural
proof. One example must suffice here, a section from the passion narrative quoted as a proof for the fulfillment of Psalm 21:8-9.

Psalm 21:8-9	Justin, *Dial.* 101.3[40]	Synoptic Gospels
		Luke 23:35:
πάντες οἱ	οἱ	εἱστήκει ὁ λαὸς
θεωροῦντές με	θεωροῦντες αὐτὸν	θεωρῶν
		Matt 27:29:
ἐκίνουν κεφαλὴν	τὰς κεφαλὰς ἕκαστος	κινοῦντες τὰς
	ἐκίνουν	κεφαλὰς
ἐλάλησαν ἐν	καὶ τὰ χείλη	
χείλησιν	διέστρεφον	
		Luke 23:35:
ἐξεμυκτήρισάν με	καὶ τὰς μυξωτῆρσιν	ἐξεμυκτήριζον
	ἐν ἀλλήλοις	καὶ οἱ ἄρχοντες
	διαρρινοῦντες ἔλεγον	λέγοντες
	εἰρωνευόμενοι	
		Matt 27:40:
ἤλπισεν ἐπὶ κύριον	υἱὸν θεοῦ αὐτὸν	εἰ υἱὸς εἶ τοῦ θεοῦ
	ἔλεγε	
ῥυσάσθω αὐτόν	καταβὰς περιπατεῖτο	καὶ κατάβαθι ἀπὸ
		τοῦ σταυροῦ
σωσάτω αὐτόν.	σωσάτω αὐτὸν ὁ θεός.	σῶσον σεαυτόν.

It is well known that Matthew's changes of Mark's text in the
Passion Narrative are often based on the desire to establish a closer agreement with the text of the prophetic Biblical passages.[41] Justin's further
improvement of the Gospel texts—in his case the texts of Matthew and

---

[40]A similar, but less complete, harmonization of parallel passages from Matthew
and Luke appears in *1 Apol.* 38.8. This parallel demonstrates that Justin did not compose
such harmonizations *ad hoc*, but relied on previously redacted written materials.

[41]The most striking example is Matt 27:34, where Matthew substitutes οἶνον μετὰ
χολῆς μεμιγμένον for Mark's ἐσμυρνισμένον οἶνον (Mark 15:23) in order to establish closer
agreement with Ps 68:22.

Luke—continues this process. But while Matthew does not always quote the Biblical reference for his development of the text of Mark, Justin lays his cards on the table, quoting his Biblical texts in full. The process, however, is exactly the same as the procedure that must be assumed for Matthew. Like Matthew, Justin is creating a new text of the "Gospel," harmonizing what he has inherited, adding phrases which are missing in the texts of Matthew and Luke. That Justin is not just doing this *ad hoc*, but is relying on a previously composed new Gospel text is evident in the passage quoted above: in his quotation of Ps 21:9 in *Dial.* 101.3, the phrase σωσάτω αὐτόν is actually missing in his quote from the Psalm, while the corresponding phrase appears in his quotation of the Gospel text. On the other hand, Justin does not list only those phrases which prove the fulfillment of scripture; he also includes such phrases from the text of the Gospels which do not have a scriptural base.

The hypothesis I am proposing here is that Justin (or someone in his "school") continues the literary activity that is most clearly evident in Matthew. Justin wants to create again the *one* Gospel, now combining Matthew and Luke, strengthening at the same time the close bond between prophecy and fulfillment, and thus expanding the text of this Gospel to achieve an even closer agreement than is evident in Matthew.

Another instance of bringing the text of the Gospels into closer conformity to the scripture is a "Western Text" reading in Justin's quotation of the account of Jesus' baptism in *Dial.* 88.8 and 103.6: instead of "You are (Matt: this is) my beloved son in whom I am well pleased" (Matt 3:17; Mark 1:11; most manuscripts of Luke 3:22) which mirrors Isa 42:1, Justin reports the heavenly voice in an exact quote from Ps 2:7: "You are my son, today I have begotten you." This latter reading appears in Luke 3:22 in Codex D, manuscripts of the Vetus Latina, and several fathers.[42] Justin's reading is usually quoted as evidence for the original text of Luke. There is indeed one Lukan feature in *Dial.* 88.8: ἐν εἴδει περιστεράς (Matt: ὡς περιστεράν). But ἅμα τῷ ἀναβῆναι in *Dial.* 103.6 (cf. Matt: ἀνέβη) reveals that Justin was using a harmonized text also in this instance. This makes it difficult to consider Justin as a witness for an early Lukan text. The quotation from Ps 2:7 was probably contributed by the author of Justin's harmony in an attempt to bring its text closer to a scriptural prophecy. The possibility that Ps 2:7 was inserted *ad hoc* by Justin himself is unlikely; he

---

[42]Numerous editions adopt this reading as the original text of Luke: Huck, Huck-Greeven, Boismard. Yet, Aland and Nestle-Aland have the reading of the majority of manuscripts (= Mark 1:11).

never refers to Ps 2 in the context of his quotations from the story of Jesus' baptism.[43]

There are more "Western Text" readings in Justin's quotations which cannot be discussed in detail here. Is Justin a witness for the early existence of the Western Text, especially for the Gospel of Luke? Or is the Western Text a testimony for the influence of Justin's Gospel harmony? And is Justin's new Gospel also responsible for the large number of harmonized readings found in subsequent Gospel quotations from Clement of Alexandria and Irenaeus to the *Apostolic Constitutions* and other Church Fathers?

What was the motivation and purpose of the composition of a new Gospel on the basis of Matthew and Luke? And why was the composer of this Gospel interested in strengthening the ties to the prophecy of the Scriptures? Justin knew Marcion, opposed him, and even composed a *Syntagma* against Marcion which is, unfortunately, lost.[44] Marcion was the first Christian theologian who called a writing containing the words and deeds of Jesus a "Gospel,"[45] and Justin must have learned this designation from Marcion. There is no evidence for the use of this designation before Marcion and Justin.[46] It is not unlikely, then, that the harmony of Matthew and Luke which Justin composed and/or used was also produced in the context of the reaction to Marcion's work. While Marcion severed the ties between Gospel and scripture, Justin's harmony wants to reestablish the close relationship between prophecy and fulfillment and thus continued the work that is already evident in Matthew's harmony of Mark and Q.

---

[43]Psalm 2:7-8 is quoted in full in Justin, *Dial.* 122:6; but there is no reference to the story of Jesus' baptism.

[44]For Justin against Marcion, see *1 Apol.* 26.8 (*Syntagma* against all heresies); Irenaeus, *haer.* 4.6.9; Eusebius, *h.e.* 4.11.8 (*Syntagma* against Marcion).

[45]Hans von Campenhausen, *The Formation of the Christian Bible* (Philadelphia: Fortress, 1972), 147-65. For a fuller account of this argument, see my forthcoming essay in *NTS* 35 (1989).

[46]In a few instances, Justin explicitly states that what he otherwise calls "Memoirs of the Apostles" are called "Gospels." In *1 Apol.* 66.3 he relates: "In the memoirs which the apostles have composed which are called Gospels (ἃ εὐαγγέλια καλεῖται) they transmitted that they had received the following instructions..." In *Dial.* 10.2, Justin introduces Trypho the Jew, his partner in the dialogue, as saying: "I know that your commandments which are written in the so-called gospel (ἃ γέγραπται ἐν τῷ λεγομένῳ εὐαγγελίῳ) are so wonderful and so great that no human being can possibly fulfill them."

Canonical and Secret Mark

The quote of a portion of a *Secret Gospel of Mark* in a letter of Clement of Alexandria[47] has been the subject of controversy ever since its publication.[48] I shall base the following discussion on the assumption that the quotations from the *Secret Gospel* are genuine.[49] There are several peculiar features in the extant canonical text of the Gospel of Mark which seem to be related to the quote from the *Secret Gospel* in the letter of Clement of Alexandria. I have discussed these in a previous article.[50] Let me point to the four most striking peculiarities.

(1) In the *Secret Gospel*, the young man (νεανίσκος) who has been raised by Jesus "looks at Jesus and loves him" (ἐμβλέψας αὐτῷ ἠγάπησεν αὐτόν). In Mark's version of the story of the "Rich Man" (Mark 10:17-22) Jesus "looks (at the rich man) and loves him" (ἐμβλέψας αὐτῷ ἠγάπησεν αὐτόν, 10:21). There is no parallel to this sentence in either Matthew or Luke. However, in the Johannine version of the story of the raising of Lazarus, Jesus weeps as he comes to the tomb and the Jews say: "Behold, how he loved him" (ἴδε πῶς ἐφίλει αὐτόν, John 11:36). This feature does not belong into the story of the Rich Man, but may have been a genuine part of the story of the raising of the youth/Lazarus. The latter story has been introduced into the text of Mark by the *Secret Gospel* after Mark 10:32. It could be argued that the same redactor inserted Mark 10:21 in order to establish an identity of the rich man who had encountered Jesus with the youth who was raised by Jesus. This is confirmed by the remark included in the *Secret Gospel* that the youth was rich (ἦν γὰρ πλούσιος)—a feature

---

[47]Morton Smith, *Clement of Alexandria and a Secret Gospel of Mark* (Cambridge, MA: Harvard University Press, 1973); the text, plates, and translation are found on pages 445-454. The Greek text has been republished in Otto Stählin and Ursula Treu, *Clemens Alexandrinus, vol. 4.1: Register*, GCS, 2d ed. (Berlin: Akademie-Verlag, 1980), xvii-xviii.

[48]For discussion on this controversy, see Morton Smith, "Clement of Alexandria and Secret Mark: The Score at the End of the First Decade," *HThR* 75 (1982): 449-61.

[49]Even if the letter of Clement of Alexandria should not be genuine, it must be an ancient forgery written in order to defend the *Secret Gospel of Mark* as apostolic. The gospel text quoted here is certainly genuine and possibly written early in the second century. The story of the raising of the youth told in the quote from the *Secret Gospel* is a version of a story which is, form-critically, earlier than the story of the raising of Lazarus of John 11.

[50]"History and Development of Mark's Gospel: From Mark to Secret Mark and 'Canonical' Mark," in *Colloquy on New Testament Studies: A Time for Reappraisal and Fresh Approaches*, ed. Bruce C. Corley (Macon, GA: Mercer University Press, 1983), 35-58.

that is missing in the Johannine version, i.e., it is due to the redactor who inserted the story into the Gospel of Mark.[51]

(2) The *Secret Gospel* reports that the young man (νεανίσκος) comes to Jesus to be initiated into the mystery of the kingdom of God "dressed in a linen cloth over his naked body" (περιβεβλημένος σινδόνα ἐπὶ γυμνοῦ). Mark 14:50-51 reports that, when Jesus was arrested in the Garden of Gethsemane, a young man "dressed in a linen cloth over his naked body" (νεανίσκος περιβεβλημένος σινδόνα ἐπὶ γυμνοῦ) lets go of his linen cloth and flees naked. There are no parallels to this brief Markan pericope in either Matthew or Luke. No satisfactory explanation for this episode in Mark's Gospel has ever been proposed,[52] nor has anyone been able to explain why both Matthew and Luke should have deleted it completely without any trace. If this account was missing in the copy of Mark that Matthew and Luke used, it is reasonable to suggest that it was added by the redactor of the *Secret Gospel*.

(3) The original edition of the text of the *Secret Gospel* had already proposed that the six-day instruction by Jesus which the youth receives after he is raised must be understood as the preparation for baptism which is here understood as a secret initiation rite.[53] In Mark 10:38b/39b Jesus refers to the disciples receiving "the same baptism with which I am baptized." This statement, which is usually taken as a reference to martyrdom, is problematic. It is not included in the Matthean parallel (Matt 20:23-24 = Mark 10:38a/39a) which only refers to "drinking the same cup which I am drinking."[54] This latter expression is attested early as a metaphor for martyrdom; but "baptism" is never used as a martyrological metaphor in the early period of the Christian church.[55] In the earliest text

---

[51]It can be argued that also Mark 10:24 is due to this same redactor. After Jesus' saying about the difficulty of the rich people to enter the kingdom of God (Mark 10:23 = Matt 19:23 and Luke 18:24), Mark states the amazement of the disciples (ἐθαμβοῦντο) and repeats Jesus' saying, but without reference to wealth: "Children, how difficult it is to enter the kingdom of God." There are no parallels in either Matthew or Luke.

[52]Rudolf Bultmann (*A History of the Synoptic Tradition* [New York: Harper, 1963], 16-17) suggested that this was a remnant of an ancient historical report. Few exegetes after him have seriously entertained this explanation.

[53]Morton Smith, *Clement of Alexandria and a Secret Gospel of Mark*, 174-188.

[54]A Lukan parallel is missing, because Luke skips the entire pericope.

[55]Hans von Campenhausen, *Die Idee des Martyriums in der alten Kirche*, 2d ed. (Göttingen: Vandenhoeck & Ruprecht, 1953), 60-61.

of Mark, there was probably no reference to "baptism," but to the "cup" as symbol of martyrdom.[56] Once the parallel sentence referring to "baptism" had been added, Mark 10:38-39 no longer referred to martyrdom, but to the Christian "sacraments" of baptism and eucharist (= the cup). Was the redactor of the *Secret Gospel* responsible for this addition?

(4) According to the letter of Clement of Alexandria, the *Secret Gospel* did not only report the story of the raising of the youth after Mark 10:34, but also told of an encounter after Mark 10:46a ("And they came into Jericho"): "And the sister of the youth whom Jesus loved and his mother and Salome were there and Jesus did not receive them." In the extant text of Mark 10:46 the two clauses "And they came into Jericho," and "when he came out of Jericho," seem to be remnants of this episode, thus creating the strange statement that Jesus and his disciples went into Jericho for no reason whatsoever. Matthew only speaks of Jesus coming out of Jericho, introducing the situation of the healing of the (two) blind men (Matt 20:29).[57] This may be exactly what stood originally in the Markan text.

If the *Secret Gospel* redaction of the original text of the Gospel of Mark has left traces in the extant manuscript text of Mark, the conclusion is unavoidable that the canonical text is the result of a further redaction of the *Secret Gospel of Mark*, an edition in which some of the questionable passages were omitted. One may debate whether any of the other peculiarities in the canonical text of Mark, discussed in the first part of this paper, are also the product of the redaction of the *Secret Gospel*. This is most likely the case with respect to the singular μυστήριον (Mark 4:11), the only instance of the singular in the canonical Gospels. There is a parallel in the statement of the *Secret Gospel*:: ἐδίδασκε αὐτὸν . . . τὸ μυστήριον τῆς βασιλείας τοῦ θεοῦ. Also the present form of the healing narrative of Mark 9:14-29 was probably created by the same redactor who thus presented a story of the raising of a child which shared many features with the story of the raising of the youth inserted into the following chapter of Mark. As a result, the *Secret Gospel of Mark* presents a story reporting the raising of a person by Jesus between the first and second prediction of the passion and resurrection as well as between the second and third of these predictions.

---

[56]Cf. also the use of "cup" in the Gethsemane pericope (Mark 14:26 and parallels).

[57]Luke locates the encounter with Zacchaeus at Jericho (Luke 18:35-19:9).

Conclusion

This paper has not surveyed all of the available evidence for the second-century text of the Synpotic Gospels. Further corroboration would have to come from the investigation of those apocryphal Gospels which are dependent upon the canonical Gospels.[58] An investigation of the apocryphal acts of the apostles, the Pseudo-Clementines, and a number of writings from the Nag Hammadi corpus would also be required. Finally, the further history of Gospel harmonies and harmonized readings in the Church Fathers would probably confirm that Justin Martyr's harmony of Matthew and Luke was an influential document.

All of the evidence presented here points to the fact that the text of the Synoptic Gospels was very unstable during the first and second centuries. With respect to Mark, one can be fairly certain that only its revised text has achieved canonical status, while the original text (attested only by Matthew and Luke) has not survived. With respect to Matthew and Luke, there is no guarantee that the archetypes of the manuscript tradition are identical with the original text of each Gospel. The harmonizations of these two Gospels demonstrate that their text was not sacrosanct and that alterations could be expected, even if they were not always as radical as in the case of Marcion's revision of Luke, the *Secret Gospel's* revision of Mark, and Justin's construction of a harmony.

New Testament textual critics have been deluded by the hypothesis that the archetypes of the textual tradition which were fixed ca. 200 CE— and how many archetypes for each Gospel?—are (almost) identical with the autographs. This cannot be confirmed by any external evidence. On the contrary, whatever evidence there is indicates that not only minor, but also substantial revisions of the original texts have occurred during the first hundred years of the transmission. The story of the text of the Gospel of Mark and the revisions of its text—documented by Matthew, Luke, and the *Secret Gospel of Mark* —illustrates this, as well as the harmonizations of Matthew and Luke in Justin and in other witnesses.

---

[58]Especially the *Gospel of the Ebionites* which presents some harmonized readings similar to those found in 2 *Clement* and Justin Martyr. *The Gospel of Thomas, The Dialogue of the Savior, The Apocryphon of James, The Gospel of the Egyptians,* and *The Gospel of the Hebrews* are most likely independent of the Gospels of the NT canon.

The Nature and Purpose of
Redactional Changes in Early Christian Texts:
The Canonical Gospels

Frederik Wisse

McGill University (Canada)

It is widely taken for granted in Biblical scholarship that early Christian texts were extensively redacted during the first century of their transmission. These redactional changes are thought to have served mainly ideological purposes, i.e., to change or augment the theological outlook of a writing in order to make it conform to changes in the beliefs or practices of a particular community or those of a different community.

Since this view has for many the status of a virtual fact,[1] one would expect that it is based on clear textual evidence. However, this is not the case. The New Testament manuscript evidence attests to only two major redactional additions, though there are a considerable number of minor ones.[2] None of these interpolations change in an appreciable way the theology of the writing in question, though a few appear to have been theologically motivated.[3] Furthermore, their is no agreement in critical New Testament scholarship on any interpolation which lacks textual evidence, though many have been suggested in almost every book of the New Testament.[4] This raises the question how scholars can be virtually certain about the general phenomenon of extensive ideological redaction

---

[1]Of course, this does not include conservative scholarship, for whom the possibility of extensive redactional changes in the Holy Scriptures is theologically unacceptable.

[2]See *infra*, pp. 49-51.

[3]See *infra*, pp. 51-52.

[4]I have tended to agree that 2 Cor 6:14-7:1 and John 21 are later additions, but the arguments to the contrary cannot readily be dismissed; see W. G. Kümmel, *Introduction to the New Testament* , trans. H. C. Kee, 17th ed. (Nashville: Abingdon, 1975), 287-292; and Paul Minear, "The Original Function of John 21," *JBL* 102 (1983): 85-98.

in spite of the fact that there are no unambiguous instances. Does the frequent resort by scholars to interpolations in early Christian literature deserve the aura of scientific rigor which it has enjoyed?[5] Is this a useful and legitimate scholarly option to resolve instances of lack of unity in style or theology within early Christian writings?[6]

These questions seem urgent but are seldom asked. William O. Walker, Jr. deserves credit for raising the larger problem of interpolations in a recent article.[7] The question has special urgency for him since he wants to argue that 1 Cor 11:3-16 is an interpolation.[8] He admits that the burden of proof rests properly with the argument that a passage is an interpolation. However, this might mean in practice that it is virtually impossible to make a convincing case for any interpolation. The criteria for identifying interpolations must be high enough to protect the text against arbitrary treatment.[9] This means that even such sure cases as the *pericope adulterae* (John 7:53-8:11) and the so-called Longer Ending of Mark (Mark 16:9-20) could not be proven—and might even have escaped notice!—if it had not been for the textual evidence. Hence it would seem that as a rule the identification of passages as interpolations is beyond proof or disproof, and thus is of no scholarly value. That would mean

---

[5]The frequent argument that the early Christian author must have utilized or incorporated an otherwise unknown source has the same purpose, i.e., to specify that a part of the text does not represent the thought of the author and, therefore, does not need to be accounted for in terms of the author. This scholarly technique is, in principle, the same as the claim that part of the text is an interpolation, and both are open to the same critique.

[6]Increased attention in Biblical studies to the methods of literary criticism has tended to weaken the appeal and prestige of source and redaction theories.

[7]William O. Walker, "The Burden of Proof in Identifying Interpolations in the Pauline Letters," *NTS* 33 (1987): 610-618.

[8]William O. Walker, "1 Corinthians 11:2-16 and Paul's Views Regarding Women," *JBL* 94 (1975): 94-110. Walker's method and conclusions were rejected by Jerome Murphy-O'Conner, "The Non-Pauline Character of 1 Corinthians 11:2-16?" *JBL* 95 (1976): 615-621. It should be noted that Walker's proposal is subject to the same suspicion as the suggestions of interpolations in Rom 13:1-7; 1 Cor 14:33b-36, and 1 Thess 2:13-16. It would appear that such passages do not so much violate Paul's style and theology as offend the sensibilities of the modern reader. This was shown conclusively for 1 Thess 2:13-16 by Tjitze Baarda in his essay "Maar de toorn is over hen gekomen...! 1 Thess. 2:16c," in *Paulus en de andere Joden: Exegetische bijdragenen discussie*, ed. T. Baarda, H. Jansen, S. J. Noorda, and J. S. Vos (Delft: Meinema, 1984), 15-74.

[9]That this is not an imaginary danger is evident from the curious claim by the advocates of "radical criticism" that none of the letters of Paul are authentic.

that we are dealing with nothing more than educated guesses which lead nowhere and needlessly clutter the scholarly literature.

It is clear to Walker that the only way out of this impasse is to lower the burden of proof. Therefore, if there are good reasons to assume that, for example, the Pauline corpus was extensively interpolated, then this "significantly reduces the weight of the burden of proof attaching to any argument that a particular passage is, in fact such an interpolation."[10] Although Walker leaves unresolved how this might change the criteria for identifying an interpolation, his basic argument has some weight.[11] Before we can argue for a specific interpolation we must first establish the probability that early Christian texts were extensively redacted.

Walker built his case on the basis of literary-critical and text-critical considerations. He appeals to the widely held belief that the Pauline letters underwent extensive editing in the process of being collected into a corpus. Of course, this may well have occurred, but that it did is itself an assumption and thus can hardly function as proof that the corpus was extensively interpolated. Both assumptions are in need of similar external evidence to make them plausible; the one cannot serve as proof for the other. Walker's literary-critical argument is circular and thus of no help.[12]

More promising, at least in the case of the canonical Gospels, is the text-critical evidence and the historical considerations associated with it. For the Pauline corpus Walker had to play down the textual evidence, for there is no manuscript attestation for any significant interpolations.[13] He tries to explain this by arguing that all the interpolations were introduced before the beginning of the third century and that all of the manuscripts

---

[10]Walker, "The Burden of Proof," 615.

[11]It is widely admitted that the current criteria to distinguish possible sources or redactions in a text are ineffective. It is in the nature of the matter that only very clumsily incorporated sources and interpolations have a possibility of being spotted. As a general rule, ancient authors and redactors were not that clumsy. Thus, the hope that further study will lead to more effective criteria is mere wishful thinking.

[12]Walker failed to deal with Harry Gamble's important contribution to the subject ("The Redaction of Paul's Letters and the Formation of the Pauline Corpus," *JBL* 94 [1975]: 403-418). Gamble shows that hypotheses are untenable which attribute major redactional intervention to the collector(s) of the Pauline corpus.

[13]Rom 16:25-27 is the only significant interpolation for which there is any strong textual evidence. There is some manuscript evidence for the dislocation of 1 Cor 14:34-35 after 14:40, but this does not really help the case of those who want to argue that 1 Cor 14:33b-36 is an interpolation.

which lacked these redactional additions were eliminated by the Catholic leadership.[14] Such a "conspiracy" theory to account for the lack of direct evidence is crucial to Walker's argument, and we must return to it later.

The issue of redactional changes in the canonical Gospels is quite different from the question of the role of the evangelists as redactors of the oral and written traditions about Jesus. To the ancient reader the Gospels of Matthew and Luke did not look like interpolated versions of the Gospel of Mark. The obviously different beginnings and endings of these Gospels were sufficient indication that they were distinct texts. Until the modern age the remarkable overlap in content and wording between the Synoptic Gospels was explained simply as multiple witness to the same events.

However, modern insights into the redactional activities of the authors of the Gospels of Matthew and Luke are instructive for the issue at hand. They give us vivid examples of the freedom taken with a text used as a source when the author is not *accountable* to that text. In spite of the liberties taken with Mark, it is clear that this Gospel was not handled with disrespect. The two new Gospels do not appear to stand in a polemical relationship to their sources. No doubt some wording and details in Mark were changed or omitted because they were considered obscure or problematic, but there is no evidence or reason to suspect that the Gospels of Matthew and Luke were written because the Gospel of Mark had become unacceptable in certain parts of the church. The main theological emphases of Mark are not dropped or corrected; they are still there in Matthew and Luke, although they tend to be overshadowed by other concerns and interests.

The situation is very different where redactional changes occur in a document which keeps its identity. In this case the redactor is in the first place the transmitter of a text and he can be held *accountable* in terms of other copies which are in existence.[15] Redactional changes—omissions, additions, changes, and transpositions—would therefore run the risk of showing up as corruptions unless they could be justified as restorations of

---

14Walker, "The Burden of Proof," 614. In support of this theory, he appeals to Walter Bauer, *Orthodoxy and Heresy in Earliest Christianity*, trans. and ed. Robert A. Kraft and Gerhard Krodel (Philadelphia: Fortress, 1971), 160-167.

15The weight of accountability was felt considerably less by a translator than by a copyist. Therefore, readings in the versions which are not attested in the Greek text are best attributed to the translator, and not to the lost Greek *Vorlage*. One could say that a translation gives a text a new identity. Its readers are seldom in a position to compare the translated text with a copy in the original language.

what was believed to have been the original wording or intent of the author. The normal excuse for redactional changes was the belief that the text had suffered at the hand of previous copyists.[16] The conscious changing of the meaning of the original author would have been difficult to justify. To assume that during the early years of the transmission of the text Christian scribes saw a need for and were involved in such high-handed redactional activities is to set this *undocumented* period apart from the *documented* history of the transmission of early Christian texts. There would have to be compelling reasons to make such an assumption.

Claims and arguments for ideological redaction in the canonical Gospels are largely limited to the Gospel of John. Speculations in the past about an *"Urmarkus"*[17] or an *"Urlukas"* did assume a process of redaction, but such speculations do not play a significant role in recent discussions. More plausible is the idea of an ecclesiastical (Gentile) redactor in Matthew to account for the tension between passages which are thought to have a Jewish-Christian outlook and those which have an obvious Gentile bias.[18] However, the Gentile viewpoint is so pervasive in Matthew that it is thought to be simpler to attribute apparent Jewish-Christian elements to the traditions the evangelist incorporated.[19]

In contrast, the presence of the hand of an "ecclesiastical" redactor in the Gospel of John enjoys considerable scholarly support. It was posed to account especially for those passages in the Fourth Gospel which reflect futuristic eschatology or an interest in the sacraments.[20] They are seen as an attempt to correct the theology of the author which lacked these ele-

---

[16]This belief was fostered by the accusation that the heretics had introduced false readings into the scriptures. As far as we know, there is little substance to this accusation. Heretical redaction of the New Testament texts applies only to Marcion, and he did not willfully interpolate the text of Luke and Paul, but "purged" it from what he believed to be false readings and passages.

[17]According to Clement, there existed in Alexandria a "Secret Gospel of Mark" which was an interpolated version of the canonical Gospel of Mark and which was composed by Mark himself; see M. Smith, *Clement of Alexandria and a Secret Gospel of Mark* (Cambridge, MA: Harvard University Press, 1973). However, it is clear from Clement's description that this Secret Gospel of Mark had its own identity distinct from the canonical Mark in that it was intended for a very restricted audience.

[18]See E. L. Abel, "Who Wrote Matthew?" *NTS* 17 (1970-1971): 138-152.

[19]See especially G. Strecker, *Der Weg der Gerechtigkeit*, FRLANT, no. 82, 2nd ed. (Göttingen: Vandenhoek and Ruprecht, 1966), 15-35.

[20]The suggested interpolations are: John 5:28-29; 6:39b, 40b, 44b, 52b-59; 12:48b.

ments. Behind this lies the assumption that gnostic and apocalyptic theology differed in that the former rejected futuristic eschatology while the latter had no room for a gnostic type of a "now" or "vertical" eschatology. However, this view of Gnosticism and Apocalypticism reflects the state of knowledge at the early part of the twentieth century. From recent studies it is becoming increasingly clear that a stress on futuristic and vertical eschatology can be found side by side in apocalyptic writings, and that a considerable number of the gnostic tractates from Nag Hammadi are preoccupied with the last judgement and the end of the present age.[21]

Although serious questions could be raised about the criteria used to distinguish between author and redactor in John, our purpose here is to address the more basic question of whether or not there are reasons to believe that any early Christian texts were redacted for ideological purposes. We shall first consider whether there are historical reasons to distinguish the early history of the transmission of the text from the later one with respect to redactional activity.[22] Secondly, we need to consider the nature and purpose of the redactional activity for which there is manuscript attestation. Finally, these considerations will be brought to bear on the issue of interpolations for which there is no textual evidence.

History of Transmission

The strongest argument in favour of setting the early history of transmission of the text apart from the later periods is the fact that it took a considerable amount of time for the New Testament writings to gain full canonical status. This has led to the assumption that Christian scribes would have been very reluctant to tamper with the text of a canonical writing, but would have felt free to introduce changes before a text was recognized as apostolic and authoritative. There are, however, good reasons to challenge this assumption. If true, this would mean that those New Testament writings for which the canonical status was long in doubt would have suffered more extensive and more serious textual corruption,

---

[21]These recent developments and their significance for the Gospel of John are the subject of a McGill dissertation by Robert A. Hill.

[22]Walker ("The Burden of Proof," 614), claims that interpolations in the Pauline corpus came to an end by the beginning of the third century.

but this is not at all the case.[23] It is only when a text is considered authoritative that its teachings become problematic if they do no longer conform to current beliefs and practices. It is indeed possible that in the pre-canonical period scribes were less hesitant to take liberties with the text,[24] but at the same time there would have been less urgency to change or adapt the theology of these writings.

Furthermore, if we judge by the interpolations for which there is textual evidence then it appears that the numbers increase rather than decrease after the second century. Many of them, including the *pericope adulterae*, are not attested before the fourth century.[25] It would appear that the frequency of copying was a much more important factor in the creation of interpolations than was the canonical status of a writing.

These facts speak against the common assumption that by the early third century emerging orthodoxy brought about an end to the period of considerable redactional freedom by deciding on a "standard" text and by suppressing all manuscripts which deviated. Long after the third century the church was in no position to establish and control the biblical text, let alone eliminate rival forms of the text. Though there may have been an attempt at establishing a standard text as early as the fourth century, only beginning with the twelfth century do we have evidence for a large scale effort. This is von Soden's group K^r which shows evidence of careful control. Even at that late date there was no way to prevent the creation of many divergent copies. Only a small number of manuscripts were consistently corrected to conform to the text of K^r or to that of other groups or text-types. There is no evidence for the Byzantine period or for an earlier date of efforts to eliminate divergent copies of New Testament manuscripts.[26]

---

[23]These New Testament writings suffered far fewer redactional changes than those which enjoyed unquestioned canonical status at an early date. The many interpolations which were claimed for the Apocalypse of John in the early part of this century are today generally considered unwarranted. Furthermore, ideological redaction is seldom considered applicable to Patristic and later Christian texts.

[24]This is generally assumed by textual critics (*e.g.*, Kurt Aland and Barbara Aland, *The Text of the New Testament*, trans. Erroll F. Rhoades [Grand Rapids, MI: Eerdmans, 1987], 64), but the evidence for this is scant.

[25]See the discussion of interpolations *infra*, pp. 48-49.

[26]The high cost of producing Biblical manuscripts and their resulting value makes it improbable that there was any interest in eliminating deviant copies. We do know of concerted efforts in the late-fourth and in the fifth centuries to destroy copies of heretical

The appeal to a "conspiracy" theory to overcome the obvious lack of textual evidence for extensive ideological editing of New Testament texts must face still another serious objection. It runs counter to the obvious tenacity of the shorter form of a text in spite of the overwhelming acceptance of many of the interpolations.[27] Kurt and Barbara Aland have stressed and illustrated this fact in their treatment of the praxis of New Testament textual criticism.[28]

Invariably Marcion is mentioned as a second-century example of high-handed tampering with the New Testament writings.[29] However, as far as we know, Marcion did not interpolate the text,[30] but rather excised the many parts which he believed the Judaizers had succeeded in adding to the true Gospel defended by Paul in Galatians. Apparently he believed that the original Gospel had been preserved; it only needed to be purged from contamination. The criteria he used to distinguish between the original Gospel and the later interpolations can still be perceived. Thus Marcion is not an example of the allegedly common second-century tendency to interpolate but of the fact that theological editing was done mainly by excision and by replacement of individual words and phrases.[31]

It is not even possible to make Marcion typical for his time in excising parts of the text. Other second-century heretics are accused of taking

---

writings—such as those of Origen. In spite of the fact that the number of copies of these writings must have been very limited, the attempt to eliminate them was only partially successful. It appears that as late as the fourth century, the Nag Hammadi codices—with clearly heretical content—were produced in an "orthodox" Pachomian monastery.

[27]The acceptance of these interpolations was not due to hierarchical decision and enforcement, but to the fact that they commended themselves to almost all copyists and readers. Until the modern period, *lectio facilior* was *potior*, and not *lectio difficilior* or *lectio brevior*!

[28]See especially K. Aland's important essay, "Glosse, Interpolation, Redaktion und Komposition in der Sicht der neutestamentlichen Textkritik," in *Studien zur Überlieferung des Neuen Testaments und seines Textes*, ANTT, no. 2 (Berlin: Walter de Gruyter, 1967), 35-57. In their more recent publication, K. Aland and B. Aland (*The Text of the New Testament*) stress that "major disturbances in the transmission of the New Testament text can always be identified with confidence, even if they occurred during the second century or at its beginning" (290), and "every reading ever occurring in the New Testament textual tradition is stubbornly preserved, even if the result is nonsense" (291).

[29]*E.g.* Walker, "The Burden of Proof," 614.

[30]A. von Harnack, *Marcion: Das Evangelium vom fremden Gott*, TU, no. 45, 2nd ed. (Leipzig: Akademie-Verlag, 1924), 61.

[31]See *infra*, p. 52.

liberties with the scriptures, but normally this consisted of their methods of interpretation and not redactional changes. Gnostics were able to manipulate the meaning of the text in such a way that it always supported their views.[32] However, their "orthodox" opponents were no less adept. This greatly reduced the need to excise or interpolate the sacred text. Conse-quently there was little reason for ideological redaction on either side of the controversy.

Since there is no basis to assume that the early, poorly attested history of the transmission of the text was governed by factors different from those operative in the canonical period, the existing textual evidence may be taken to be indicative of the nature and purpose of redactional activity from the beginning. We shall proceed to review this textual evidence for the canonical Gospels. Since the argument for ideological redaction involves mainly additions to the text, the focus will be on evidence for larger and smaller interpolations.[33]

Major Interpolations

There is evidence for only two long interpolations in the New Testament, Mark 16:9-20 and John 7:53 - 8:11. The so-called Longer Ending of Mark is attested for the second century.[34] In spite of the fact that it provided a far more satisfactory ending to the Gospel, it still was not widely accepted by the fourth century. It was not even able to replace a competing shorter ending. The longer ending is clearly based on the accounts in the

---

[32]Gnostic exegesis of the early chapters of Genesis illustrates how a "hostile" text could be infused with gnostic meaning. Elaine H. Pagels concludes: "While Marcion sought to exclude elements of the texts he considered inauthentic, Valentinus tended instead to accept the full texts available to him, interpreting them esoterically. Valentinus' followers accepted, apparently, the full texts of Paul's own letters; and while they virtually ignored the Pastorals, they willingly included (and, indeed, highly revered) Ephesians, Colossians, and Hebrews as sources of Pauline tradition" (*The Gnostic Paul: Gnostic Exegesis of the Pauline Letters* [Philadelphia: Fortress, 1975], 163).

[33]The manuscript evidence shows only a few significant omissions compared to a considerable number of interpolations. Clearly, scribes were very hesitant to omit text.

[34]For a discussion of the textual evidence see B. M. Metzger (on behalf of the UBS Editorial Committee), *A Textual Commentary of the Greek New Testament* (London: United Bible Society, 1975), 122-128, and K. Aland and B. Aland, *The Text of the New Testament*, 287-288. W. R. Farmer's argument for the originality of the longer ending has found little acceptance (W. R. Farmer, *The Last Twelve Verses of Mark* [Cambridge: Cambridge University Press, 1974]).

other three canonical Gospels and is thus is an example of harmonization. No theological motivation is evident for its creation. Rather, it is obvious that the abrupt ending in Mark 16:8 was thought to be in need of a supplement. The shorter ending was an independent answer to the same need.

The *pericope adulterae* (John 7:53-8:11) was introduced into the manuscript tradition of John perhaps as early as the second, but more likely during the third century.[35] The reason for placing it after John 7:52 was likely the reference to inappropriate judging in 7:51.[36] In any case, the purpose of this interpolation clearly was not to change or adapt the theology of the Fourth Gospel, but simply to accommodate a noble anecdote about Jesus known in the "free" tradition. That this major interpolation could establish itself in spite of wide awareness of the antiquity of the shorter text serves as further proof that before printing there was little or no opportunity for ecclesiastical control on the transmission of the text. It also illustrates well the tenacity of the shorter text which is still well attested in the late Byzantine period in spite of the wide acceptance of the interpolated text.

Minor Interpolations

There is attestation for many small interpolations into the text of the canonical Gospels, ranging from a phrase to a full sentence. The bulk of these, some 75%, are obvious harmonizations to a parallel passage in one of the other Gospels or, in some cases, within the same Gospel:[37]

> Matt 5:44; 6:13[38]; 17:21; 18:11; 19:9; 20:16, 22-23; 21:44;
> 23:14; 25:13; 26:39; 27:35, 49.

---

[35]For an overview of the manuscript attestation for this passage, see K. Aland, "Studien zur Überlieferung" in *Studien zur Überlieferung des Neuen Testaments und seines Textes*, 38-46. He presents it as a major example of the "ripple effect" in the manuscript tradition caused by an interpolation into the text.

[36]The Ferrar family of manuscripts (f^{13}) places it after Luke 21:38.

[37]The textual evidence for these passages is readily available in UBS. They are discussed by B. M. Metzger, *A Textual Commentary*. Some of the more important ones are also included in K. Aland and B. Aland, *The Text of the New Testament*, 292-305.

[38]This is a harmonization to the liturgical form of the Lord's Prayer.

Mark 1:34; 2:16; 3:14; 7:7-8, 16; 9:44, 46; 10:21, 40; 11:26; 14:65; 15:28.

Luke 1:28; 4:4; 8:43, 45; 10:22; 11:2-4, 11, 33; 12:21, 39; 15:21; 17:24, 36; 18:24; 22:19b-20[39]; 23:17, 38, 53; 24:1-2, 12, 36, 40.

John 1:51; 3:20, 31b-32; 8:59; 13:26.

It is likely that all these harmonizations originated after the four Gospels began to be copied together late in the second century.[40] This process of harmonization continued well into the Byzantine period. However, this kind of interpolation was not theologically motivated. Scribes had a ready excuse to supplement the text of one Gospel on the basis of the parallel pericope. The fact that this was not done far more often, and that the shorter readings remained preserved in the tradition indicates the conservative nature of the transmission process. It is no surprise that there are far fewer interpolations in the Gospel of John than in the Synoptic Gospels.[41]

A second and far smaller group of interpolations was made up of material from the free-floating tradition. The addition to Matt 20:28 in Codex Bezae (D) and a few other witnesses may be from the free tradition or it could have been created on the basis of Luke 14:8-10. Luke 22:43-44 is also not a certain case since it could be simply an omission witnessed by the Alexandrian text.[42] Similarly, Luke 9:54-56 may well involve a theologically motivated omission rather than an interpolation from the free tradition.[43] The addition in Luke 6:5 in Codex Bezae fits its well known anti-Judaistic bias. More likely from the free tradition is Luke 23:34. The addition of "and from a honeycomb" in Luke 24:42 is thought to reflect later liturgical usage. John 5:4 appears to be an explanatory gloss to give

---

[39]This is probably a harmonization to 1 Cor 11:24b-25.

[40]It hard to understand how the *Diatessaron* can be cited in UBS as a witness for Matt 17:21, which is a harmonization on the basis of Mark 9:29.

[41]Matt 16:2-3; Mark 14:68; 15:12; and John 13:32 were not included since it is very difficult to decide whether they involve interpolations or omissions.

[42]It appears that Heb 5:7 is based on Luke 22:43-44; in any case, the author of Hebrews saw no difficulty in attributing fear of death to Jesus.

[43]So K. Aland and B. Aland, *The Text of the New Testament*, 304; against B. M. Metzger, *A Textual Commentary*, 148-149.

background for 5:7; it was likely created for this purpose. In so far as a purpose is visible in such interpolations, it was the desire to enhance the text. The few cases which may have been theologically motivated will be mentioned again below.

A third category of interpolations are interpretive glosses. They are found in the textual tradition of Matt 10:23; Mark 8:26; 9:49; 10:24; Luke 10:38; 22:62; John 2:3; 3:13; 7:46. They are relatively minor in importance and do not change the theological sense of the text.

Theologically Motivated Redaction

In an article published in 1953, Kenneth W. Clark took issue with the earlier opinion of textual critics that the variant readings in New Testament manuscripts do not affect matters of Christian doctrine.[44] Of course, what such critics as F. J. A. Hort, K. Lake, L. Vaganay, F. Kenyon, F. C. Grant and J. Knox had in mind was that decisions on variants do not change the basic, traditional Christian doctrines; but Clark thought they meant that variants do not touch on theological issues. He set out to disprove this on the basis of nine variants found in $\mathfrak{P}^{46}$. Actually what he showed was that some variants affect the basic meaning of the sentence. No textual critic of past or present would want to deny this. It is also beyond doubt that such changes in meaning sometimes have theological implications, though the previous generation of textual critics may still be correct that no significant doctrine stands or falls by such changes. Of the many variants which involve a change in meaning only relatively few are clearly theologically motivated in that the original meaning was found to be objectionable and thus replaced by another.[45] Only one of the variants discussed by Clark falls in that category.[46]

---

[44]Kenneth W. Clark, "Textual Criticism and Doctrine," in *Studia Paulina in honorem Johannis de Zwaan septuagenarii*, ed. J. N. Sevenster and W. C. van Unnik (Haarlem: Bohn, 1953), 52-65.

[45]Far more often the change is from the obscure to the clear meaning, or the meaning is enhanced or augmented.

[46]1 Cor 15:51, where some witnesses corrected the factual incorrectness of the first clause by shifting the negative to the second clause.

Normally the scribes "corrected" objectionable meaning by change (replacement) or omission[47] and not by interpolation. This should not be surprising, for interpolations are effective mainly in enhancing[48] and adding meaning[49] and not so much as a corrective device. Some of the more obvious examples of corrective changes and omissions in the textual tradition of the canonical Gospels are:

Matt 27:9

Mark 1:2; 3:21; 8:31; 10:13; 13:32

Luke 2:33, 41, 43, 48; 5:39; 22:43-44; 23:32; 24:51-52

John 7:8; 8:53.

These "corrections" involve matters of historical fact—usually a perceived contradiction with a statement elsewhere in the text—or items that might conflict with a major aspect of orthodox Christology such as the virgin birth or the *homoousian* doctrine. There is no concern for more subtle matters of doctrine visible in these variants.

Conclusions

There is very little direct textual evidence from the second century relevant to the canonical Gospels. The few New Testament papyri from this period are too small to be relevant. The later New Testament writings and the Apostolic Fathers only provide allusions to the Gospels; more precise citations begin with the writings of Irenaeus who is also the first author who witnesses the four Gospels as a group. Though the evidence before Irenaeus is very difficult to evaluate,[50] there is no indication that

---

[47]This is the technique Marcion is reputed to have used.

[48]Eldon J. Epp has demonstrated that the longer text of Acts enhances the anti-Judaic element of the book (*The Theological Tendency of Codex Bezae Cantabrigiensis in Acts*, SNTS.MS, no. 3 [Cambridge: Cambridge University Press, 1966]).

[49]One of the best known examples of this is Mark 9:29, where most witnesses add "fasting" to "prayer."

[50]See the important studies by H. Koester, *Synoptische Überlieferung bei den apostolischen Vätern*, TU, no. 65 (Berlin: Akademie-Verlag, 1957), and A. J. Bellinzoni,

the Gospels circulated in a form different from that attested in the later textual tradition.[51]

The textual tradition of the canonical Gospels attests to two major and a considerable.number of minor interpolations. In the Gospels these serve mainly harmonizing purposes, but there are also some interpretive glosses and a few cases in which bits of free tradition are interpolated. There is evidence for this kind of redactional activity from the second century, but it clearly continues unabated throughout the manuscript tradition.[52] There is also a limited amount of evidence for ideological redaction, i.e., attempts to correct what appear to be factual "errors" or questionable theological statements. However, this is not done through interpolations but by changing words and by minor omissions.

Thus the claims of extensive ideological redaction of the Gospels and other early Christian literature runs counter to all of the textual evidence. This lack of evidence cannot be explained away by speculations about an extensively interpolated "standard" text which was imposed by the orthodox leadership late in the second century, and the successful suppression of all non-interpolated copies. The Church certainly lacked the means and apparently also the will to do this. The remarkable tenacity of the shorter text, in spite of the obvious attractiveness of the interpolated readings, shows that the transmission process could not be effectively controlled even during the Byzantine period.[53] If indeed the text of the Gospels had been subjected to extensive redactional change and adaptation during the second century, the unanimous attestation of a relatively stable

---

The Sayings of Jesus in the Writings of Justin Martyr, NT.S, no. 17 (Leiden: Brill, 1967). It is clear that even in later Patristic writings Biblical citations are frequently quoted from memory and are thus imprecise and liable to conflation and *ad hoc* modification; see M. J. Suggs, "The Use of Patristic Evidence in the Search for a Primitive New Testament Text," *NTS* 4 (1957-1958): 139-147; and Gordon D. Fee, "The Text of John in Origen and Cyril of Alexandria: A Contribution to Methodology in the Recovery and Analysis of Patristic Citation," *Bib* 52 (1971): 357-394.

[51]One cannot take the minor agreements between Matthew and Luke against Mark in the triple tradition to be indicative of the state of the text of Mark at the time of composition of the first and third gospels. In most of these cases the text of Mark is clearly the *lectio difficilior*.

[52]E. W. Saunders gives examples of interpretive glosses which were introduced into a thirteenth-century manuscript (Gregory MS 2614 = Duke 7), from the eleventh-century commentary of Theophylact; see his "Studies in Doctrinal Influences on the Byzantine Text of the Gospels," *JBL* 71 (1952): 85-92.

[53]There are even a few cases in which a scribe appears to have been influenced by the oft-condemned text of the arch-heretic Marcion.

and uniform text during the following centuries in both Greek and the versions would have to be considered nothing short of a miracle.

One further argument can be mentioned against the claim that the pre-canonical period was characterized by extensive ideological redaction of Christian literature. This pre-canonical period was not characterized by rival "orthodoxies," as is often assumed, but by an inevitable heterodoxy.[54] The limits of "sound doctrine" were still ill-defined or even non-existent. There were no established ways or technical vocabulary to adjudicate between conflicting views. Such conflicts are only apparent from a later, fully developed, theological viewpoint. The original author and readers were most likely oblivious to them. To those familiar with later Christian thought, writings from the Church's first century appear uneven, eclectic, and idiosyncratic. However, it is anachronistic to expect full coherence in composition, style,[55] and theology from them. For this reason exegetes of early Christian literature should be extremely reluctant to assume the existence of incorporated sources or later interpolations for a text in order to resolve apparent inconsistencies in style or content. The burden of proof and the weight of the textual evidence are such that one can only suggest the possibility of an interpolation as a last resort, for it is tantamount to an admission of failure to resolve the alleged problems in the text.

---

[54]I have discussed this in "The Use of Early Christian Literature as Evidence for Inner Diversity and Conflict," in *Nag Hammadi, Gnosticism, & Early Christianity*, ed. C. W. Hedrick and R. Hodgson (Peabody, MA: Hendrickson, 1986), 177-190.

[55]This is recognized by E. Haenchen for the Gospel of John (*John 1: A Commentary on the Gospel of John Chapters 1-6*, trans. Robert W. Funk and Ulrich Busse [Philadelphia: Fortress, 1984], 71-90). However, he still expects this Gospel to reflect a coherent theology.

Die Münsteraner Arbeit am Text des Neuen Testaments und ihr Beitrag für die frühe Überlieferung des 2. Jahrhunderts: Eine methodologische Betrachtung

Barbara Aland
Westfälische Wilhelms-Universität (West Germany)

Freundlichkeit und Geschick unseres Gastgebers haben uns hier in einer, was unsere Sachgebiete betrifft, besonders günstigen Zusammensetzung versammelt. Woran wir, jeder auf seinem Feld, arbeiten, kann zusammengefaßt werden unter einem weit, aber sachgemäß verstandenen Begriff der *Textforschung*. Diese Disziplin leidet an der überall zu beobachtenden Spezialisierung und Atomisierung der einzelnen Arbeitsgebiete. Das ist unbefriedigend, und auf unserem gemeinsamen Feld, wie mir scheint, auch überwindbar. Ich erlaube mir daher, die Gunst der Stunde zu nutzen und die Aufgaben zu bedenken, die sich m.E. vom Aspekt der Textkritik im engeren Sinne her unserer Disziplin stellen. Die im folgenden vorgetragenen Reflexionen sind durchaus nur Anregungen und bedürfen in vielerlei Weise Ihrer Ergänzung und Korrektur. Sie ergeben sich aus der Institutsarbeit, es kann ihnen durch das Institut aber nicht allein nachgegangen werden. Hier ist das Zusammenwirken von uns allen notwendig.

Im Blick auf die Berichterstattung, die das mir gestellte Thema impliziert, kann ich mich aus zwei Gründen kurz fassen. Zum einen ist jüngst der neue Bericht der Stiftung zur Förderung der neutestamentlichen Textforschung erschienen, der Sie über die Arbeit der letzten drei Jahre informiert.[1] Zum anderen gilt, daß die Arbeit des Münsteraner Instituts zur Zeit aus guten Gründen nicht schwerpunktmäßig auf das Thema unserer Tagung—"Gospel Traditions in the Second Century: Origins, Recensions, Text and Transmission"—konzentriert ist. Dennoch ist der Blick auf unsere Arbeit, wie ich hoffe, hier von Nutzen.

---

[1]*Bericht der Hermann Kunst-Stiftung zur Förderung der Neutestamentlichen Textforschung für die Jahre 1985 bis 1987* (Münster/Westphalia, 1988).

Das Institut für neutestamentliche Textforschung in Münster
verfolgt ja seit seiner Gründung die Konzeption, mit einem eingespielten
Mitarbeiterteam die Aufgaben zu erfüllen, die einzelne Forscher nicht
leisten können und die auch sinnvollerweise an einem Ort konzentriert
werden. Auf diese Weise hoffen wir in Münster, der gelehrten Welt
dienen zu können. Entsprechend dieser Konzeption wurden in der ersten
Phase der Institutsarbeit, wie Sie wissen, die Handschriften des Neuen
Testaments so vollständig gesammelt wie möglich. Sie stehen jetzt auf
Mikrofilm jedem Interessierten im Institut zur Verfügung. Die zweite
Phase der Arbeit galt der ersten Gruppierung der Handschriften. Dabei
sollte vor allem die große Menge der Zeugen des byzantinischen Reichs-
textes und seiner Untergruppen identifiziert werden, damit die restlichen,
textkritisch vielfältig interessanten neutestamentlichen Handschriften
vollständig identifiziert und Verwandte unter ihnen schon soweit wie
möglich erkannt werden konnten. Diese Phase ist bis auf die Arbeit am
Johannesevangelium abgeschlossen, ihre Ergebnisse sind ebenfalls im
Institut einzusehen. Diese zweite Phase ist die unmittelbare Voraus-
setzung für das gegenwärtige dritte Stadium der Arbeit, das der Auswertung und Interpretation des gesamten Handschriftenbefundes der
einzelnen neutestamentlichen Corpora gewidmet ist. Dabei wird u.a. das
vollständige Material zu jeder neutestamentlichen Schrift, jetzt mit Hilfe
von Datenverarbeitung, so aufbereitet, daß jeder einzelne Forscher damit
die Handschriften, samt sämtlichen Verwandten näheren oder ferneren
Grades, für seine speziellen Interessen finden kann.

Suchen Sie z.B. eine bestimmte Textpassage aus einer Rezension
des 2. Jahrhunderts und wollen Sie prüfen, ob sich diese durch die
Jahrhunderte hin erhalten hat bzw. in ähnlichen Formen in späteren
Jahrhunderten vorkommt, so können Sie das anhand der von uns
erarbeiteten Hilfsmittel tun.[2] Allerdings ist dabei folgende Einschränkung
zu machen: Wenn Ihre Textpassage sich unter den Teststellen befindet,
aufgrund derer unsere publizierten Hilfsmittel erarbeitet sind, werden Sie
sofort die exakte Zahl und Bezeichnung der Handschriften ersehen
können, die Ihre Textpassage wörtlich oder mit kleinen Änderungen
enthält. Wenn sie sich nicht unter den Teststellen befindet, müssen Sie
keineswegs resignieren. Denn in diesem Fall können Sie bei sachgemäßer

---

[2]Bereits publizierte Bände: *Text und Textwert der griechischen Handschriften des
Neuen Testaments, I. Die Katholischen Briefe;* Bd. 1: *Das Material,* Bd. 2,1 und 2,2: *Die
Auswertung,* Bd. 3: *Die Einzelhandschriften, in Verbindung mit A. Benduhn-Mertz und G.
Mink hrsg. v. K. Aland,* ANTT, no. 9-11 (Berlin/New York: Walter de Gruyter, 1987).

Benutzung der Hilfsmittel *die* Handschriften vollständig aus der Gesamt-
menge herausfinden, bei denen am ehesten die Wahrscheinlichkeit
besteht, daß sie Ihre Textpassage enthalten. Es handelt sich meist nur um
wenige Handschriften, die Sie dann selbst überprüfen müssen. Das kann
auch der einzelne Forscher tun. Er kann *nicht* im gesamten Meer der
etwa rund 1800 Texthandschriften der Synoptiker ziellos selbst auf die
Suche gehen. Kurz: unsere publizierten Arbeitsmaterialien erschließen
Ihnen die unübersehbare Handschriftenfülle und liefern Ihnen eine Art
Kompaß dafür, und zwar aufgrund von objektiven und stets nachprüf-
baren Daten. Diesen Kompaß können Sie nach Ihren ganz speziellen
Interessen ausrichten und können und müssen dann mit den gefundenen
Handschriften selbständig aufgrund von Vollkollationen weiterarbeiten.[3]

Diese Arbeitsmaterialien sind für die Katholischen Briefe bereits
veröffentlicht und werden jetzt für die Paulinen vorbereitet. Es empfahl
sich mit diesen neutestamentlichen Corpora zu beginnen, weil hier
verglichen mit den Evangelien eine begrenztere Handschriftenfülle und
weniger komplizierte—wenn auch immer noch höchst schwierige—
Überlieferungsprobleme vorliegen. Wir hoffen, damit Erfahrungen zu
sammeln, um so für die anspruchsvollste Aufgabe, die Erforschung der
Textüberlieferung der Evangelien, angemessen gerüstet zu sein.

Dennoch kann auch über die Textform jeder Handschrift der
synoptischen Evangelien im Münsteraner Institut auf Wunsch schon
Auskunft erteilt werden. Das ist aufgrund der beschriebenen zweiten
Arbeitsphase möglich, dementsprechend zwar zunächst nur in einer
ersten, noch nicht differenzierten Form, die aber zur groben Charakteri-
sierung und Einordnung der Handschriften ausreichend ist.

Trotz des großen Reichtums an griechischen Handschriften und
Fragmenten aus frühester und früher Zeit muß man sich stets vor Augen
halten, daß nur ein Bruchteil, und zwar ein zufällig ausgewählter Bruchteil, erhalten ist. Das ist zwar eine Binsenwahrheit, die aber nicht oft
genug wiederholt werden kann. Es kann deswegen nicht darauf
verzichtet werden, jeden Hinweis auf die früheste Überlieferung zu
finden und angemessen zu würdigen. Das geschieht vor allem durch die
beschriebene Auswertung sämtlicher neutestamentlicher Minuskeln,
unter denen sich—insbesondere wenn sie in Provinzwinkeln des

---

[3]Ein Beispiel für eine Benutzung der Arbeitsinstrumentarien zu einem sehr
speziellen Zweck (viele andere sind entsprechend denkbar und auszuprobieren) ist
ausführlich dargestellt in *Das Neue Testament in syrischer Überlieferung, I. Die Großen
Katholischen Briefe, in Verbindung mit A. Juckel hrsg. und untersucht v. B. Aland*, ANTT,
no. 7 (Berlin/New York: Walter de Gruyter, 1986), vgl. insbesondere 41-90.

byzantinischen Reiches, abseits vom Strom des Üblichen, abgeschrieben wurden—Abschriften von alten Handschriften finden können.

Es geschieht aber auch durch eine systematische Nutzung der neutestamentlichen Zitate bei den kirchlichen Schriftstellern. Hier muß nach unserer Überzeugung noch viel geschehen. Denn befriedigend können die Väter nur genutzt werden, wenn ihre individuelle Zitierweise erkannt wird. Dafür müssen sie einer nach dem andern vollständig gelesen werden, und an jeder einzelnen Stelle muß aus dem Kontext erhoben werden, warum ein Zitat beispielsweise verkürzt oder verändert wurde. Das kann man nämlich sehr häufig genau erkennen, präzise Kenntnis des Autors und des Kontextes vorausgesetzt. Man wird dann nicht mehr in Versuchung kommen, ein von den uns bisher bekannten, überlieferten Variationen eines Textes verschiedenes Zitat als mögliche, nur bei dem bestimmten Vater erhaltene Textüberlieferung zu werten. Die Zitate werden also insgesamt weniger werden. Die aber, die bei dieser strengen und zugleich sensiblen Durchsicht übrig bleiben, können als— sekundäre—Textüberlieferung mit der Primärüberlieferung der Handschriften zuverlässig in Bezug gesetzt werden. Viel Mißbrauch der Zitate kann so vermieden werden. Andererseits wird viel an kostbarer Information gewonnen. Denn nur von dem "Text," wie er uns auf diese Weise durch die Zitate erschlossen wird, wissen wir ja genau, wann er in welcher Kirchenprovinz benutzt wurde.[4]

Daß diese Neubearbeitung der Väter auf ihre Zitate hin ihre Zeit braucht, liegt auf der Hand. Wir haben bei den frühen Vätern begonnen, Irenäus ist abgeschlossen, Clemens von Alexandrien steht kurz vor dem Abschluß. Für junge, sprachlich begabte Theologen und Philologen mit sehr guten Griechisch-Kenntnissen steht hier noch ein fruchtbares Arbeitsfeld, geeignet auch für Dissertationen, offen.[5]

Die Zitate spielen schließlich auch bei unserer Arbeit an der syrischen Überlieferung des Neuen Testaments eine entscheidende Rolle. Es zeigt sich, daß man mit ihrer Hilfe die Entwicklung des neutestamentlichen Textes in einer bestimmten Kirchenprovinz, hier im syrisch-

---

[4]Was hier über die Textüberlieferung gesagt wurde, gilt *mutatis mutandis* auch für das sog. apokryphe Material.

[5]Für Interessierte bin ich gern bereit, die Art unserer Bearbeitung der Väter näher zu erläutern. Ich kann versichern, daß es noch sehr viel mehr und Spannendes zu entdecken gibt als es die bekannten Zitatsammlungen zu einzelnen Vätern auch nur ahnen lassen. Vielmehr wird der Umgang des jeweiligen Vaters mit dem Text und damit, an einem bestimmten Ausschnitt, Text- und Interpretationsgeschichte selbst lebendig.

sprachigen Gebiet, rekonstruieren und verfolgen kann. Darüber, wie auch über die weiteren Unternehmungen des Institutes zu berichten, ist hier nicht der Ort. Hier sollte lediglich verdeutlicht werden, daß ein scheinbar zeitlich begrenztes Thema wie das unsrige —"Gospel Traditions in the Second Century: Origins, Recensions, Text and Transmission"— nur behandelt werden kann, wenn das Material dafür methodisch zuverlässig aus der gesamten Überlieferung gewonnen und bereitgestellt wird, was das Institut in Münster u.a. sich zu tun bemüht.

Damit erlaube ich mir zum zweiten Teil meines Referates überzugehen, der jedoch, wie angegeben, lediglich den Charakter von Erwägungen aufgrund erster Beobachtungen hat.

Eines der entscheidenden Probleme der Textforschung, insbesondere zur Überlieferung der frühen Zeit, scheint mir heute das Methodenproblem zu sein. Was wollen, was müssen wir heute tun? Wie können wir dem Reichtum der Überlieferung, der auf uns gekommen ist, gerecht werden? Meinem Eindruck nach herrscht darüber durchaus noch keine Klarheit, kaum ein Bewußtsein für die Notwendigkeit der Sache. Das gilt insbesondere hinsichtlich der frühen Papyri, die erst in diesem Jahrhundert die Überlieferung des Neuen Testaments auf völlig neue Grundlagen gestellt haben.

Obwohl die frühen Papyri, die ein oder mehrere neutestamentliche Bücher ganz oder nahezu vollständig enthalten, die schlechterdings einzigartige Besonderheit der neutestamentlichen Überlieferung gegenüber der aller anderen antiken Texte sind, läßt sich nicht sagen, daß sich schon eine befriedigende *Methode* für ihre Erschließung herausgebildet hätte. Eine Methode zu finden, ist also ein Hauptdesiderat. Eine der Schwierigkeiten besteht dabei darin, angemessene Vergleichsmaßstäbe für diese frühesten Handschriften und ihren Text zu finden. Außer dem Stil der jeweiligen Schrift,[6] der aber kein ausreichender Wegweiser sein kann, bietet sich dafür kaum etwas an.

Sicher jedoch muß die Methode zur Erforschung der frühen Papyri der Eigenart dieser Handschriften (sowie der Gesamtüberlieferung) entsprechen. Welches ist diese Eigenart? Zwei sich scheinbar wider-

---

[6]Darauf wies richtig erstmals J. N. Birdsall in einer frühen Studie zum 𝔓66: *The Bodmer Papyrus of the Gospel of John* (London, 1960), hin. Mit einer Auswahl wichtiger Majuskeln sowie dem textus receptus, vergleicht Gordon Fee in seiner wichtigen Arbeit zu 𝔓66 die frühe Handschrift: *Papyrus Bodmer II, P66: Its Textual Relationships and Scribal Characteristics*, StD, no. 34 (Salt Lake City: University of Utah Press, 1968). Das ist vernünftig, auch für eine erste große Untersuchung zu nur einem Papyrus ergiebig, läßt aber grundsätzliche methodische Wünsche offen.

sprechende Charakteristika zeichnen sich ab. Einerseits enthalten fast alle Papyri (und es sind immerhin bis zum 3./4. Jahrhundert über 40) einen erheblichen Anteil an sog. alexandrinischem Text. Das ist eine nicht zu leugnende Tatsache. Sie ist nicht damit schon erklärt und abgetan, daß man darauf verweist, es handle sich eben um einen "Lokaltext," da alle Papyri ja aus Ägypten stammten. Vielmehr können die Vorlagen der in Ägypten entstandenen frühen Handschriften aus dem gesamten römischen Reich stammen. Beispiele lassen sich nachweisen.[7] Andererseits sind diese Papyri in ihrem Text jedoch auch so verschieden voneinander, daß sie nicht direkt miteinander verglichen werden können. Statistische Vergleiche der Übereinstimmungen und Abweichungen einzelner früher Zeugen voneinander ergeben fast immer—auf welcher Basis sie auch immer gefertigt sein mögen—so wenig aussagekräftige Ergebnisse, daß sie unbrauchbar werden. Allenfalls lassen sich gewisse tendenzielle Vergleichswerte entnehmen (x stimmt mehr mit y überein als mit z). Meist ergeben jedoch die Gegenproben jeweils viel zu hohe Werte, um zu irgendwelchen klaren Ergebnissen zu führen. Die frühen Handschriften sind also trotz ihres gemeinsamen großen Anteils an sog. alexandrinischen Text "Sonderlinge," "Solitäre," voneinander unableitbar. Woran liegt das?

Es liegt gewiß daran, daß zu wenige Handschriften aus früher Zeit (einschließlich der frühen Majuskeln des 4. und 5. Jahrhunderts) und diese dazu noch in zufälliger Auswahl erhalten sind. Auch eine gewisse Kontamination wird eine Rolle spielen. Doch können beide Gründe, insbesondere der zweite, nicht ausschlaggebend gewesen sein. Denn die Zeitspanne zwischen der Entstehung der neutestamentlichen Schriften und den frühesten Handschriften ist so kurz, daß eine so starke Auseinanderentwicklung allein aus diesen Gründen kaum denkbar ist.

Was ist also die Ursache dafür, daß jene frühen Handschriften bis etwa zum 5. Jahrhundert diesen Solitärcharakter haben, d.h. sich der Ableitung voneinander so sehr widersetzen, obwohl sie einen so erheblichen gemeinsamen Anteil an sog. alexandrinischem Text als gemein-

---

[7]Der Oxyrhynchus-Papyrus 405 enthält beispielsweise ein Fragment aus Irenäus, *haer.* 3.9.3. Da er nach übereinstimmender Einschätzung der Paläographen und Editoren Grenfell/Hunt, Roberts und Wessely gegen Ende des 2. bzw. zu Anfang des 3. Jahrhunderts geschrieben ist und in Oxyrhynchus gefunden wurde, muß also der erst kurz vorher entstandene Text des Irenäus sehr schnell von Gallien nach Oberägypten gekommen sein (Hinweis von H. U. Rosenbaum). Ähnliches ist von neutestamentlichen Texthandschriften annehmbar. Zu P. Oxy. 405 vgl. Grenfell/Hunt, *The Oxyrhynchus Papyri* (London: Egypt Exploration Fund, 1903), Part III, 10-11; und Part IV, 264, Erstedition.

same Grundschicht aufweisen? Für klassisch-pagane Schriften besitzen
wir häufig insgesamt nur zahlenmäßig wenig mehr Handschriften (diese
allerdings stammen aus der Zeit vom 9. Jahrhundert ab) als beim Neuen
Testament allein für die Zeit bis zum 6. Jahrhundert und doch lassen sich
im klassischen Bereich meist eindeutige Stemmata erstellen. Der Vergleich macht die Besonderheit des neutestamentlichen Phänomens
deutlich. Es handelt sich um den Unterschied einer Überlieferung aus
früher Zeit (bis zum 6. Jahrhundert) zu der aus später Zeit (vom 9. Jahrhundert ab), die jeweils aufgrund sehr verschiedener Bedingungen zu-
stande gekommen sind.

Um die Gründe für die genannte Eigenart früher Handschriften des
Neuen Testaments zu finden, müssen die Variationen bzw. Fehler der
frühen Handschriften untersucht und ihre Intentionen und Tendenzen
so genau wie möglich beschrieben und erklärt werden.

Es handelt sich (nur grob charakterisiert, ich gehe aus von vorläufigen Beobachtungen am Johannesevangelium) etwa um drei Fehler-
gruppen, die nicht scharf voneinander zu trennen sind: Nachlässigkeit
beim Abschreiben, stilistische Glättung mit Minimaleingriffen aller Art
oder stilistische sowie—seltener—inhaltliche Eingriffe in den Text, die
den ohnehin gegebenen Sinn deutlicher hervorheben. Zur zweiten und
dritten Gruppe gehören Auslassungen und Zufügungen im Kleinstum-
fang, kleinere Umstellungen mit gelegentlicher Betonungsverstärkung,
Angleichungen an den Kontext und den Stil des Autors, um den Text
noch "authentischer" zu machen, oder Kürzungen, um ihn verständ-
licher und klarer erscheinen zu lassen, Partikeländerungen, Tempus-
änderungen in Richtung des gebräuchlicheren Griechisch, gelegentlich
auch der Gebrauch von Synonyma etc.

Die *Intention* dieser Textänderungen läßt sich, abgesehen von den
reinen Nachlässigkeits- und Flüchtigkeitsfehlern, aus einem Willen zur
Glättung im weitesten Sinne verstehen. Sie äußert sich überwiegend nur
stilistisch, seltener durch Eingriffe in den Sinn. Diese Glättungsvarianten
machen m.E. ein wichtiges Charakteristikum der frühen neutestamentlichen Papyri aus. Je nachdem wie häufig sie vorkommen, sprechen wir
in Münster von einem festen, einem normalen, einem freien Text oder
besser: einer festen, normalen oder freien Textüberlieferung.

Für alle diese sog. Glättungsvarianten gilt, daß das *Ausmaß des
Eingriffs in den Text* meist nur sehr begrenzt ist (Kürzungen und
Umstellungen umfassen nur wenige Worte, Zufügungen oft noch
weniger usw.). Wie begrenzt es ist, wie behutsam also die Schreiber als die
Verursacher der Glättungsvarianten verfahren, lehrt eindrücklich ein

Vergleich mit neutestamentlichen Zitaten, und zwar denen bei frühen Autoren (bis etwa 150) einerseits sowie späteren Kirchenschriftstellern andererseits. Während die frühen "Zitate" bekanntermaßen von größter Freiheit im Umgang mit dem zu zitierenden Wort zeugen, ist schon bei den Autoren der zweiten Hälfte des 2. Jahrhunderts durchaus der Wille zu sorgfältiger Wiedergabe der ihnen vorgegebenen neutestamentlichen Textform zu beobachten. Dennoch gehen sie mit dem Text immer noch ein gut Teil freier um, als es sich die Kopisten der Handschriften mit ihrer Vorlage erlauben. Die Art der Eingriffe in den Text ist bei zitierenden Autoren mit der der Handschriften zu vergleichen. Auch hier handelt es sich häufig um eine Art "Glättung," nur eben in größerem Ausmaß.

Nun kann man einwenden, daß sich diese *Glättungsvarianten mit begrenztem Umfang* in der gesamten Überlieferung aller Jahrhunderte finden und sie daher kein markantes Kennzeichen der frühen Überlieferung sein können. Das ist zwar richtig, aber in der späten Überlieferung vom 9. und auch schon in der vom 6. Jahrhundert ab sind *solche* Varianten *aus der Vorlage abgeschrieben.* Im 2. Jahrtausend pflegen Handschriften aus denselben Familien oft in den kleinsten Partikeln miteinander übereinzustimmen. In der frühen Zeit dagegen fügt offensichtlich jeder Schreiber einen recht erheblichen Anteil dieser Varianten *individuell in seine Kopie* ein. Nur so läßt sich meines Erachtens der Tatbestand erklären, von dem wir ausgingen: daß die frühen Handschriften trotz eines erheblichen gemeinsamen Anteils an sog. alexandrinischem Text doch viel-fältige Abweichungen voneinander aufweisen, die sie im Sinne eines Stemmas unableitbar voneinander machen.

Für die frühen Schreiber scheint also eine größere Freiheit in "Kleinigkeiten" eher kennzeichnend zu sein als für die späterer Jahrhunderte. Ihre Vorlagen sind daher, weil von frühen Kopisten geschrieben, schon durch jene Kleinigkeiten gegenüber dem ursprünglichen Text verändert. Sie selbst begeben sich in eben demselben Geist wie ihre Vorgänger an die Abschrift, d.h. bewahren den Text im Großen getreu, ändern aber wiederum individuell in jenen Kleinigkeiten. So entwickeln sich im Laufe des Kopierprozesses die entstehenden Kopien auseinander (im bezeichneten engen Rahmen, in diesem aber doch recht beträchtlich). So entstehen auch, wenn im Sinne ihrer Änderungsintention verwandte Schreiber einander folgen, gewisse Überlieferungsstränge mit besonderen Charakteristika.

Als Beispiel nenne ich $\mathfrak{P}^{45}$ und $\mathfrak{P}^{66}$. Beide sind das Ergebnis einer im Rahmen der frühen Überlieferungsgesetze relativ freien Kopierauffassung. Die Intention der Fehler beider Papyri möchte ich unter dem Stichwort der Glättung im weitesten Sinne zusammenfassen. Während jedoch $\mathfrak{P}^{66}$ überwiegend kleinere stilistische Änderungen in diesem Sinne und Anpassungen an das Normalgriechisch aufweist, die später charakteristischerweise häufig vom byzantinischen Text aufgenommen werden, zeigt $\mathfrak{P}^{45}$ eine andere Art der Glättung: Hier finden wir über die üblichen glättenden Kleinständerungen hinaus bestimmte Eingriffe in den Text (häufig Umstellungen, zum Teil Kürzungen), die den Wortlaut prägnanter und den Sinn klarer machen. Es handelt sich also um eine Glättung des vorgegebenen Textes in einem ganz anderen Sinn als bei $\mathfrak{P}^{66}$.[8] Auch diese Änderungen werden teilweise von späteren Handschriften aufgenommen, charakteristischerweise aber nur von wenigen und nicht immer denselben Zeugen (W; Θ; ℵ*; D), die nun ihrerseits wieder in ähnlichem Sinne in den Text modifizierend eingreifen. Auf diese Weise entstehen keine genealogisch voneinander ableitbaren Familien, aber möglicherweise "Überlieferungsstränge," die durch die gleiche Intention und Tendenz ihrer Fehler zusammengeschlossen sind.

Dafür, daß die frühe Überlieferung sich in dieser Weise durch getreue Übernahme im ganzen, aber jeweils individuelle glättende Gestaltung im einzelnen, vollzogen hat, gibt es einen merkwürdigen Beweis. Ihn stellen die wenigen Zeugen des sog. "westlichen" Textes mitsamt ihren Vorstufen dar. Der "westliche" Texttyp fällt natürlich aus dem bisher Besprochenen völlig heraus. Die Änderungen, die ein oder mehrere Redaktoren am neutestamentlichen Text vornahmen, sind so tiefgreifend, daß sie keineswegs nur unter dem Stichwort der Glättungsintention verstanden werden können. In einem Punkt sind jedoch die Handschriften, die die "westliche" Redaktion bezeugen, den übrigen frühen Papyri und Majuskeln durchaus vergleichbar: Auch sie übernehmen den ihnen vorliegenden "westlichen" Text im ganzen, ändern jedoch, jeder individuell, aber im Sinne der "westlichen" Redaktion, noch über ihre Vorlage hinaus. Es gibt keine zwei Zeugen des "westlichen" Textes, die nur pure Abschriften wären. Der Vorgang der Änderung läßt sich beim sog. "westlichen" Text mit seinen starken Umformungen

---

[8]Beide bezeichnen wir in Münster als Zeugen eines sog. "freien" Textes bzw. besser einer "freien" Textüberlieferung. Man sieht aus den angeführten Beispielen, daß diese Qualifizierung zwar als erstes Grundraster, das die numerische Abweichung einer Handschrift vom hypothetisch erarbeiteten ursprünglichen Text angibt, von Nutzen ist. Sie genügt aber nicht, wie wir wohl wissen. Vielmehr muß die Art der "Freiheit" genauer qualifiziert, d. h. die Fehler der "freien" Überlieferung müssen beschrieben werden.

besonders gut beobachten. Da ich ihn an anderem Ort beschrieben habe,[9] gehe ich hier nicht näher darauf ein. Im Prinzip ist die Individualänderung jedes einzelnen Kopisten aber mit dem der übrigen frühen neutestamentlichen Handschriften vergleichbar, wenn sie hier auch nicht entfernt so starke Ausmaße annimmt wie dort.

Wenn mit den im Sinne einer Arbeitshypothese beschriebenen Phänomenen von *Glättung im weitesten Sinne* und *begrenzter individueller Freiheit der Kopisten* wesentliche Merkmale der frühen Überlieferung ungefähr getroffen sein sollten, dann muß die Methode ihrer Erforschung diesen Merkmalen entsprechen. D.h. zunächst im Negativen: es entfällt weitgehend jede Genealogie und Stemmatologie (denn die potentiell überall vorhandene Individualänderung läßt sie nicht zu). Es entfallen statistische Erhebungen aufgrund von Teststellen oder aufgrund von Gesamtkollationen ausgewählter Textabschnitte. Das Ergebnis wird dabei immer nur sein, daß zwei frühe Handschriften nur "bis zu einem gewissen Grad" verwandt sind, meistens aber bis zu einem ebenso hohen Grad auch nicht. Selbst wenn man die Varianten der frühen Handschriften erst charakterisiert und gewichtet und dann dementsprechend statistische Erhebungen anstellt, wird man im günstigsten Fall Annäherungswerte, keine verläßlichen Ergebnisse bekommen, weil das Gewichten der Varianten der frühen Überlieferung von zu viel Subjektivität abhängig ist und damit die Statistik verfälscht.[10] Es entfällt auch ein Vergleich der frühen Handschriften mit späteren "Texttypen." Damit multiplizieren sich die Unsicherheitsfaktoren nur noch, weil die sog. Texttypen (außer der Koine und dem sog. "westlichen" Text in seinen großen Umformungen) keine fest umrissenen, sondern viel zu unscharfe Größen sind. Sie bieten zwar eine Reihe einzelner charakteristischer Lesarten, sind aber auf das Ganze des Textbestandes hin gesehen keine eindeutig definierten Vergleichsmaßstäbe. Daher ist auch die Zugehörigkeit der Handschriften zu ihnen durchaus umstritten.

Im Positiven müßte die gesuchte Methode m.E. folgende Merkmale aufweisen. Auszugehen wäre von den Textstellen, an denen der "Urtext"

---

[9]B. Aland, "Entstehung, Charakter und Herkunft des sog. westlichen Textes— untersucht an der Apostelgeschichte," *EThL* 62 (1986): 5-65.

[10]Es ist mir bewußt, daß auch mein hier skizziertes Vorgehen "Subjektivität" enthält, wie das selbstverständlich von aller textkritischen Arbeit gilt, die vom Urteil des Textkritikers ausgeht. Der Unterschied besteht darin, daß ich die hier vorgeschlagene Methode, die auf einer sensiblen Beschreibung der einzelnen Papyri beruht, nicht in eine Statistik, schon gar nicht eine recht einfacher Art, pressen zu können meine.

sicher oder mit größter Wahrscheinlichkeit zu rekonstruieren ist. Diese Stellen sind sehr zahlreich! Bedenken Sie, daß sich die Menge der bekannten Varianten des Neuen Testaments durch die Papyrusfunde nur in erstaunlich geringem Umfang vergrößert hat! Fast alle Varianten, die in den Papyri vorkommen, waren vorher schon aus späteren Handschriften bekannt. Von Singulärlesarten der Papyri kann man weitgehend absehen, weil sie im allgemeinen deutlich als Fehler erkennbar sind und in keiner Weise für den Urtext in Frage kommen. Die Ursache dafür liegt in Reichtum und Fülle der neutestamentlichen Überlieferung sowie in der Tenazität der Handschriften.

Bei der Überlieferung klassischer Texte ist das durchaus anders. Die wenigen erhaltenen Handschriften haben hier nur einen bestimmten, zufälligen Ausschnitt aus der einst vorhandenen Variantenfülle erhalten. Es werden daher Papyri gefunden, die neue, noch unbekannte Varianten enthalten und die bei der Textkonstitution beachtet werden müssen (sei es als Urtext selbst, sei es als Bindeglied zwischen bisher bekannten Varianten, wodurch die Entstehung der einen Variante aus der anderen deutlich wird).

Beim Neuen Testament kann man dagegen—zugespitzt gesagt— den "Urtext" in beträchtlichem Umfang schon aufgrund der Unzialen und Minuskeln rekonstruieren, so weit er überhaupt rekonstruierbar ist (s. dazu unten S. 68-69). Der hohe Wert der frühen Papyri liegt einerseits darin, daß durch sie die Textkonstitution sicherer gemacht, weil auf noch frühere Zeugen gestützt wird, andererseits darin, daß durch sie die Bedingungen und Gesetze der frühen Überlieferung erhellt werden können.

Ausgehend von den "sicher" zu rekonstruierenden Textstellen also sollten die Eigenheiten jedes einzelnen der großen Papyri und der Majuskeln so genau wie möglich beschrieben und klassifiziert werden, und zwar jeweils der ganzen Handschrift, nicht nur einzelner Stücke daraus. Bewertende Beobachtung und noch einmal Beobachtung ist das Gebot der Stunde! Als Beispiel seien die jeweils zu ihrer Zeit wegweisenden Arbeiten von Günther Zuntz[11] und Carlo Martini[12] genannt. In Ihrem Land hat vor allem Ernest Colwell[13] schon stark in diese Richtung

---

[11]G. Zuntz, *The Text of the Epistles. A Disquisition upon the Corpus Paulinum*, The Schweich Lectures, 1946 (London: Oxford University Press, 1953).

[12]C. M. Martini, *Il problema della recensionalità del codice B alla luce del Papiro Bodmer XIV*, AnBib, no. 26 (Roma: Istituto Biblica, 1966).

[13]E. C. Colwell, *Studies in Methodology in Textual Criticism of the New Testament*, NTTS, no. 9 (Leiden: Brill, 1969), vgl. bes. 106ff und 148ff.

plädiert. Aber nicht nur, wie er vorschlug, von den Singulärlesarten allein darf ausgegangen werden. Denn ihre Behandlung vermag zwar einen gesicherten Ersteindruck von der Individualität der Schreiber zu geben, aber eben auch nur von den Schreibern der aktuell vorliegenden Papyri, nicht von der Überlieferungstradition, die zu dem einzelnen Papyrus hinführte, von der "Ahnenreihe" des Papyrus also. Zudem vermitteln die Singulärlesarten nur einen sehr begrenzten Einblick. Daher muß die Ausgangsbasis breiter gewählt werden, das ist auch in sehr vielen Fällen mit ausreichender methodischer Sicherheit möglich.

Auf dieser Basis muß beobachtet werden, wo überhaupt Varianten vorliegen und nicht Variationen, die auf Dialektgewohnheiten und Orthographie der Schreiber zurückgehen. Aufgrund der neuen Grammatik zu den griechischen Papyri von Francis Gignac[14] mit ihren zahllosen neuen Belegen lassen sich weit genauere Feststellungen treffen als früher. Es müssen Nachlässigkeitsfehler aller Art registriert und jeweils nach Häufigkeit festgehalten werden. Vor allem aber müssen die echten Varianten jeder frühen Handschrift, die als Fehler zu erkennen sind, so genau wie möglich beschrieben und auf die Intention dieser Fehler hin untersucht werden. Entsprechend könnte der Charakter der einzelnen Handschriften bestimmt werden, wie es oben andeutungsweise mit $\mathfrak{P}^{45}$ und $\mathfrak{P}^{66}$ geschah. Es muß sich dabei auch zeigen, inwieweit von Glättungstendenzen in den frühen Papyri tatsächlich die Rede sein kann bzw. inwiefern hier genauer differenziert werden kann und muß.

Bestätigen sich dabei die bisherigen Beobachtungen zumindest insofern, als von einer allgemeinen Tendenz zur Glättung im weitesten Sinn gesprochen werden kann, so müßte diese als eine Art "Rostfraß" (oder "Oxydation") betrachtet werden, der nahezu alle frühen Handschriften befallen hat. Dieser "Rostfraß" wäre methodisch vergleichbar mit dem Einfluß der Koine, der sich vom 6. Jahrhundert ab in allen neutestamentlichen Handschriften, gleich welcher Textform, bemerkbar macht. Die Textform der Koine, der byzantinische Text also, dringt auf vielerlei Wegen in nahezu alle neutestamentlichen Handschriften im Laufe des Tradiervorganges ein. Das kann als ein Gesetz der späteren neutestamentlichen Überlieferung betrachtet werden. Entsprechend könnte jene Glättungstendenz, der in der einen oder anderen Form sehr viele frühe Handschriften unterliegen, ein Gesetz der frühen Über-

---

[14]F. Gignac, *A Grammar of the Greek Papyri of the Roman and Byzantine Periods* (Milano: Istituto editoriale cisalpino-La goliardica, 1976-1981), vol. 1: *Phonology*; vol. 2: *Morphology*.

lieferung sein. Der Koinetext selbst verdankt sich ihm. "Gute Handschriften" wären dann jene unter den frühen Zeugen, die sich diesem "Rostfraß" am meisten widersetzen ($\mathfrak{P}$75).[15]

Erst in einem zweiten Schritt kann dann der Vergleich mit anderen frühen Handschriften sowie auch den Unzialen des 4. bis 6. Jahrhunderts stattfinden, nachdem auch diese je für sich in der beschriebenen Weise charakterisiert worden sind. Bei solchem Vergleich darf aber nicht, wie bisher, nur die Suche nach genealogischer Verwandtschaft im Vordergrund stehen. Denn dann wählt man eine zu enge Optik. Man sucht nach etwas, was es im strengen Sinne nicht geben kann. Vielmehr muß, gemäß der beschriebenen Arbeitshypothese von der individuellen Freiheit der frühen Schreiber, auch nach Übereinstimmungen der Handschriften in den Fehler*tendenzen* gesehen werden. So könnte man der Eigenart der frühen Transmission Rechnung tragen und aus Handschriften mit gleicher Fehlerintention (nach Art des beschriebenen "westlichen" Textes) Überlieferungsstränge erkennen. Damit könnte eine der frühen Überlieferung sachlich angemessene, nicht stemmatische, Ordnung der Handschriften aus den ersten Jahrhunderten erreicht werden.

Schließlich müssen in diesen Vergleich auch jene Minuskeln einbezogen werden, die von alten Manuskripten abgeschrieben sind, also alte Textformen enthalten. Das anfangs erwähnte Teststellenprogramm in Münster wird bei der Auswahl dieser Minuskeln hilfreich sein.

Um die so beschriebene neutestamentliche Überlieferung auch von ihren historischen Bedingungen her zu verstehen, muß sie dann in den weiteren Rahmen gestellt werden, der unsere Arbeitsgebiete verbindet. Es muß gefragt werden: In welcher Beziehung stehen die Schreiber unserer neutestamentlichen Handschriften mit ihrer begrenzten Freiheit zu dem Prozeß der Umprägung des vorkanonischen Stoffes über die kanonischen Evangelien bis hin zu den außerkanonischen Apokryphen? Gibt es überhaupt eine Beziehung oder sind Kopistentradition und redaktionelle Arbeit voneinander grundsätzlich geschieden? Stellen die frühen Zitate und Übersetzungen mit ihrer größeren Freiheit gegenüber der Vorlage ein Bindeglied zwischen beiden dar? In welcher Beziehung steht der Umgang mit dem vorgegebenen Text in den sog. Texttypen der neutestamentlichen

---

[15]Damit ist eine genaue Definition dessen, was ich "gute" Handschriften nennen möchte, impliziert. In diesem sehr überlegten Sinne, basierend auf methodisch verantwortetem und nachprüfbarem Urteil über die Textkonstitution, scheint es mir durchaus vertretbar, wie klassische Philologen, von "besseren" und "schlechteren" Handschriften zu reden. Daß auch die "guten" unter ihnen niemals ohne Fehler sind, ist selbstverständlich und muß beachtet werden.

Überlieferung und in den Apokryphen wie etwa dem Papyrus Egerton 2, von dem vor kurzem wieder ein neues Fragment veröffentlicht worden ist? Wie arbeiten die Verfasser von Harmonien im Vergleich zu den Kopisten? Meine vorläufige Vermutung geht zwar dahin, daß die Aufgabe und das Selbstverständnis der Schreiber unabhängig von redaktioneller Arbeit zu sehen sind. Dafür sprechen wohl auch Gründe der antiken Buchherstellung, der Zweck der jeweiligen Arbeit hier wie da, sowie Person, Beruf und Herkunft der Schreiber wie der Redaktoren. Über die mit diesen Stichworten angeschnittenen Fragen beginnen freilich erst die Untersuchungen. Aber es muß dabei zur Kenntnis genommen werden, daß die frühen Kopisten in einem Klima arbeiteten, das der Um- und Neuformung des vorgegebenen Stoffes günstig war, ganz anders als in jeder späteren Epoche der Überlieferung.

Um so erstaunlicher ist der große Anteil an sog. alexandrinischem Text in allen frühen Papyri. Sollen wir wirklich fortfahren, ihn "alexandrinisch" zu nennen? Sollen wir damit weiter einen Terminus benutzen, den unsere Väter unter ganz anderen Voraussetzungen, ohne die Kenntnis der Papyri, prägten? Ist das noch sachlich angemessen? Muß nicht vielmehr ernsthaft die Möglichkeit ins Auge gefaßt werden, daß es sich bei diesem sog. alexandrinischen Text um eine sehr frühe "Ausgabe" des ursprünglichen Textes handelt?

Das führt schließlich zur letzten Frage: Welcher neutestamentliche Text kann überhaupt rekonstruiert werden? Die Frage ist möglicherweise nicht exakt zu beantworten, sie muß aber als Problem stets lebendig bleiben, und wir müssen uns einer Antwort mindestens annähern. Andernfalls könnte nicht gesagt werden, welchen Text wir eigentlich zu rekonstruieren und zu edieren beanspruchen. Die hier besprochenen, durchaus vorläufigen Beobachtungen und Überlegungen weisen m.E. deutlich darauf hin, daß unsere Handschriften auf eine sehr frühe Ausgabe oder autorisierte Abschrift o.ä. (der Terminus muß offen bleiben) zurückgehen. Der Grund dafür ist nicht nur die häufig besprochene Übereinstimmung zwischen $\mathfrak{P}^{75}$ und B, sondern vielmehr der starke Anteil an eben der Textform von $\mathfrak{P}^{75}$ und B in allen frühen Papyri, und das, obwohl diese Papyri die redaktionelle Hand eines Schreibers oder mehrerer Schreibergenerationen deutlich verraten! Die Grundschicht auch so verschiedener Textformen wie der von $\mathfrak{P}^{45}$ und $\mathfrak{P}^{66}$ bleibt nichts-destoweniger deutlich "alexandrinisch" bzw. mit $\mathfrak{P}^{75}$ und B überein-stimmend. In die gleiche Richtung weist außerdem, daß der Korrektor von $\mathfrak{P}^{66}$ die vielen offensichtlichen Irrtümer der 1. Hand ebenfalls nach dieser Textform verbessert. Wie sollte das anders zu erklären sein als damit, daß die Papyri auf *eine* Textform zurückgehen? Wenn diese aber keine Rezension des 2. Jahrhunderts war, wie C. Martini, G. Fee, und K. Aland in den verschiedensten Zusammenhängen überzeugend dargelegt haben,[16] bleibt dafür nur der "Urtext" bzw. besser und wahrscheinlicher: eine (oder mehrere) frühe editorische Abschrift(en) desselben übrig. Damit sind zwar keineswegs alle Fragen geklärt. Denn wir kennen z.B. nicht den Abstand zwischen dem Urtext und jener editorischen Abschrift, auf die unsere Handschriften zurückgehen. Wir wissen auch nichts über die technische Form der Manuskriptherstellung jener frühen Ausgabe. Sie barg wohl ebenso Fehlerquellen wie die noch davor liegenden Abschriften sie enthalten haben mögen. Daher können wir selbstverständlich nicht in jedem zu entscheidenden Falle bei der Textkonstitution eine Handschrift wie $\mathfrak{P}^{75}$ oder B orakelhaft befragen und ihr und ihr folgen. Wohl aber ist die Übereinstimmung mehrerer früher Zeugen, etwa die von $\mathfrak{P}^{45}$, $\mathfrak{P}^{66}$ und $\mathfrak{P}^{75}$ (z.B. in Joh 10) ein ganz starkes Indiz dafür, daß wir es hier mit der Lesart jener frühen editorischen Abschrift zu tun haben. Diese kann—der Fall ist denkbar—immer noch falsch sein, weil jene frühe "Edition" an dieser Stelle schon einen Fehler bot. Aber wir sollten uns von dieser theoretischen und zweifellos zu beachtenden Möglichkeit doch nun auch andererseits nicht den Blick dafür verstellen lassen, was es bedeutet, daß wir in so sehr vielen Fällen mit jener frühen "Ausgabe" so nahe an den ursprünglichen Text herankommen! Der Text des Neuen Testaments ist weitaus genauer zu konstituieren als der jeder anderen antiken Schrift. Ein Vergleich, der hier wie da vorhandenen Zeugen, zeigt das eindrücklich. Er wird leider zu selten von denen unternommen, die mit dem Neuen Testament umgehen. Ich plädiere daher für einen bewußten und selbstverständlich methodisch reflektierten Einsatz der äußeren Kritik neben der sog. inneren Argumentation. Dafür ist es auch notwendig, wie oben beschrieben, die Fehlerintention einer frühen Handschrift genau zu kennen bzw. allgemeiner: die Gesetze der frühen Kopierweise sorgfältig zu studieren. Sie sind von denen späterer Jahrhunderte und ganz gewiß des 2. Jahrtausends durchaus unterschieden.

---

[16]C. M. Martini a.a.O. (s. oben S. 65, Anm. 12); Gordon D. Fee, "P[75], P[66], and Origen: The Myth of Early Textual Recension in Alexandria," in *New Dimensions in New Testament Studies* (Grand Rapids: Zondervan, 1974), 19-45; u.ö.; Kurt Aland, "Neue neutestamentliche Papyri II," *NTS* 9 (1962-1963): 303-316; und: idem, "Die Bedeutung des $\mathfrak{P}^{75}$ für den Text des Neuen Testaments. Ein Beitrag zur Frage der 'Western non-interpolations'," in *Studien zur Überlieferung des Neuen Testaments und seines Textes*, ANTT, no. 2 (Berlin: Walter de Gruyter, 1967), 155-172.

Im Voranstehenden ist versucht worden, eine Methode für eine sachgemäße Behandlung der frühesten Handschriften des Neuen Testaments zu skizzieren. Im besten Falle kann damit jedoch nur *eine* methodische Annäherung an die Papyri angedeutet sein. Das genügt jedoch noch nicht. Wir brauchen eine Vielfalt der Methoden, die sich gegenseitig ergänzen und kontrollieren. Das Gespräch darüber, das wir hier so hoffnungsvoll pflegen können, sollte zwischen uns nicht wieder abreißen. In Münster sind wir offen für Ihre Wünsche, Ihre Bemerkungen zu unserer Arbeit und auch Ihre Kritik.

The Significance of the Papyri for Determining
The Nature of the New Testament Text in the Second Century:
A Dynamic View of Textual Transmission

Eldon Jay Epp

Case Western Reserve University (USA)

This study is largely an exercise in historical-critical imagination. It is an attempt to discover some things we do not know about the earliest stages of New Testament textual transmission by applying creative imagination to what we do know. The question, to be more specific, is whether we can take our limited knowledge of the earliest textual witnesses, combine it with the data we have about our later textual witnesses, and then think creatively about the process that must—or at least might—have produced it all. The approach proposed involves: first, exploring the dynamic relationships and movements (both secular and Christian) that must have occurred in the earliest centuries of textual transmission; second, utilizing textual complexions—commonly called text-types—to sort out the man-uscripts; and, third, bringing into view the early textual spectrum that results from, and is reflected in, the array of manuscript witnesses. In pursuing the first of these tasks, it will be instructive to offer two brief sketches, one of the general situation in the first few centuries of Christianity, and another of the specific environment of the earliest New Testament manuscripts and papyri.

The Dynamic Historical Situation of the Early Church

In looking at the earliest centuries of Christianity, that period when the New Testament text originated and began its odyssey of transmission, the word "dynamic" is constitutive. For too long the text of the New Testament has been conceived in static terms. It has often been assumed that one type of text existed only in one place and other types existed only somewhere else; or that one of these types on a rare occasion made its way solely to some other location; or that distinctive and persistent "local

71

texts" existed at a number of discrete localities; or that revisions and refinements of certain texts took place in isolated fashion in insulated locations. To be sure, all of these things probably happened, but much, much more was happening also—and simultaneously.

We focus, of course, on those first centuries when Christianity was expanding with rather phenomenal rapidity and in all directions within the vast Greco-Roman world until, already by the end of the second century, Christian centers existed from Edessa and Antioch and Caesarea in the East to Spain and Lyon and Rome in the West, and from Britannia and Sinope in the North to Carthage and Alexandria in the South.[1] This was not a static, but a dynamic world. And this was not an eastern world or a western world—it was both eastern and western; this was not a northern world or a southern—but both northern and southern. And things were happening: from its Judaean and Galilean origins, Jewish Christianity quickly spread to places like Antioch of Syria and Damascus, thence to Asia Minor and Macedonia, and to Greece and Rome.[2] As Mithraism spread to virtually every outpost of the Roman army, so—in the earliest generations—Christianity spread to innumerable Jewish settlements throughout that Greco-Roman world, and, of course, to non-Jewish centers as well.

The writings that were later to constitute the "New Testament" were in circulation, along with other Christian documents. For example, Jewish-Christian Gospels (later to be designated "non-canonical") were appearing around the middle of the second century in Syria-Palestine and Egypt, and during that same period and in the same areas Christian gnostic groups were flourishing and came into conflict with the main-stream church.[3] In Rome in 144 CE, Marcion—soon to be considered the arch-

---

[1]Compare the endpaper maps in W. H. C. Frend, *The Rise of Christianity* (Philadelphia: Fortress Press, 1984). For much of the summary of early Christianity that follows, I have used this volume as a general resource. In addition, I have relied upon the more cautious—and, for the earliest period, undoubtedly more accurate—work of Helmut Koester, *Introduction to the New Testament. Volume Two: History and Literature of Early Christianity* (Philadelphia: Fortress Press; Berlin/New York: Walter de Gruyter, 1982); and that of J. Neville Birdsall, "The New Testament Text," in *The Cambridge History of the Bible*, ed. P. R. Ackroyd and C. F. Evans (Cambridge: Cambridge University Press, 1970), vol. 1: *From the Beginnings to Jerome*, 308-377, whose discussion is always in full awareness of the church-historical context.

[2]See Koester, *Introduction*, 2:86-94.

[3]Ibid., 2:201-203; 219-233, esp. 232; and also 236.

heretic of the church—was excommunicated by the church of Rome. Even before this, early doctrinal definitions were underway, including— among a wide range of emerging issues—questions concerning the nature of Christ and his relation to God, the definition of church authority and organization, as well as liturgical practices and eschatological views, and the relation of church to empire. Differences in understanding these issues are reflected already in the New Testament writings and occur with increasing specification, for example, in *1 Clement, Didache, Epistle of Barnabas, Polycarp,* the *Letters* of Ignatius, the *Apocalypse of Peter,* the *Shepherd of Hermas,* as well as in Montanus, Tatian, Celsus, Hegesippus, and Irenaeus. The general heterodoxy of this initial period of Christianity is now well recognized, as is the early dominance in many areas of what the orthodox church would later call "heresies."[4] Certainly heterodoxy— "a syncretistic situation conducive to speculative thought without hier- archical control"[5]—was the mark of the earliest Egyptian period, which encompassed a variety of practices in Christianity, including gnostic forms of the young faith.

Meanwhile, forces outside Christianity were affecting it as well. Pliny the Younger, Governor of Bithynia in Asia Minor, wrote to the Emperor Trajan around 112 CE about "the contagious disease of this super- stition" (10.96), and Christian apologists, beginning with Quadratus and Aristides, soon issued their "invitations to a philosophical way of life."[6] Justin also sought to demonstrate the truth of the Christian faith, and died around 165 CE for confessing it, as did the aged Polycarp.

Then, by the end of the second century, the Greek New Testament was being translated into Latin, undoubtedly also into Syriac, and possibly

---

[4]For a convenient summary of these points, see Frederik W. Wisse, "The Use of Early Christian Literature as Evidence for Inner Diversity and Conflict," in *Nag Ham- madi, Gnosticism, & Early Christianity,* ed. C. W. Hedrick and R. Hodgson, Jr. (Peabody, MA: Hendrickson, 1986), 177-190.

[5]Frederik W. Wisse, "Prolegomena to the Study of the New Testament and Gnosis," in *The New Testament and Gnosis: Essays in Honour of Robert McL. Wilson,* ed. A. H. B. Logan and A. J. M. Wedderburn (Edinburgh: T. & T. Clark, 1983), 142. See also A. F. J. Klijn, "Jewish Christianity in Egypt," in *The Roots of Egyptian Christianity,* ed. B. A. Pearson and J. E. Goehring, Studies in Antiquity and Christianity (Philadelphia: Fortress Press, 1986), 161-175; note the following statement: "Egypt is a fine example of burning questions dealing with orthodoxy and heterodoxy, and with Jewish Christianity and gnosis," 175.

[6]Koester, *Introduction,* 2:338-340.

into Coptic.[7] It is both of interest and of considerable significance to observe that "in the first two centuries all the theologians who achieved fame in the West were themselves from the East (from Marcion and the Apologists through Irenaeus and Hippolytus)," and, therefore, that "all the significant theologians of any influence in the West in the early period came from Eastern church backgrounds, bringing their New Testament texts with them."[8]

With the coming of the third century, issues of Christian theology and philosophy were pursued in increasingly sophisticated fashion by Clement of Alexandria, Tertullian, Origen, Cyprian and others, involving, for example, controversies over rebaptism, penance, Easter, the trinity, and christology. Influential centers of Christian scholarship existed, for example, in Alexandria and Caesarea, and Origen was influential in both. Manichaeism was a threat, but the greater threat in the middle of the third century was the brief Decian persecution, affecting Christians in cities throughout the empire, followed by a similar period under Valerian several years later.

In the midst of these varied activities, both positive for the church's development as well as negative, and occurring variously in the East and the West and from North to South, the earliest Christian writings were continuing to circulate. This can be documented in a number of ways. Colossians (4:16) shows that letters were exchanged between churches and read, and 2 Peter (3:15-16) confirms a knowledge of "all" of Paul's letters, indicating that they were in movement. The Apostolic Fathers (ca. 90-130) quoted from the earlier Christian writings. Justin (ca. 150) knows two or more of our four Gospels. Marcion not only limited his canon to the Gospel of Luke and ten letters of Paul, but edited them critically. Tatian produced his *Diatessaron* in Syria around 175, beginning a competition between a single, harmonized Gospel and the four separate Gospels. Succeeding church fathers quoted from a wide range of writings, many of which were to become canonical. Final settlement of the New Testament canon was to come more than two centuries after the days of Justin and

---

[7]Birdsall, "The New Testament Text," 345-347; cf. Bruce M. Metzger, *The Early Versions of the New Testament: Their Origin, Transmission, and Limitations* (Oxford: Clarendon Press, 1977), 8, 287-290.

[8]Kurt Aland and Barbara Aland, *The Text of the New Testament: An Introduction to the Critical Editions and to the Theory and Practice of Modern Textual Criticism*, trans. E. F. Rhodes (Grand Rapids: Eerdmans; Leiden: Brill, 1987), 68.

Marcion, though the collection and authority of the four-fold Gospel and of the Pauline Corpus were clear enough by Irenaeus' time (ca. 180).

Though we can never know the actual extent of the circulation of Christian writings throughout the Roman world, the process was dealt a severe blow during the Diocletian persecution at the outset of the fourth century, when—beginning perhaps in 303—copies of Christian Scripture were confiscated and destroyed. Over the following two decades, events significant for the church—both positive and negative—continued, culminating in Constantine's opening of the Council of Nicaea in 325 and his establishment of the "new Rome" at Constantinople in 330, and, of course, in the achievement by Eusebius of an *Ecclesiastical History*.

The point of this hasty and quite inadequate survey of activities and movements in the first few centuries of Christianity is simply to recall the multifarious interactions in these tumultuous times and to suggest that copies of New Testament books—as well as those of other early Christian writings—were circulating within these complex situations and were interactive with the circumstances described and with innumerable others like them. Unfortunately, we cannot with certainty link any specific early manuscript with any specific event or person. Yet we can imagine—quite legitimately—the importance of biblical manuscripts again and again in this early Christian world. We can well envision their role in worship and homily, in teaching and polemic, in church consultations, and in times of persecution; and we can postulate their certain transfer from congregation to congregation, from church leader to church leader, and from scholar to scholar, within both orthodox and heterodox Christianity.

It is within this background of dynamic movement, development, and controversy that the earliest New Testament manuscripts must be examined, for—as has long been asserted but too little exercised—the text of the New Testament in its earliest stages was a vibrant, living text that functioned dynamically within the developing church. Textual criticism, therefore, can never be understood apart from the history of the church.[9]

---

[9]On the study of New Testament textual criticism in the context of church history, see especially Birdsall, "The New Testament Text," 311-316, 328-377; see also note 1, above. See also Aland and Aland, *The Text of the New Testament*, 49-54, 67-71. The latter work, however, exaggerates the lack of attention to church history by New Testament textual critics, for viewing textual variants as products of the church's tradition is a theme that has been pursued by a number of scholars over the past sixty years, though most notably by American and British textual critics; for a summary, see my *The Theological Tendency of Codex Bezae Cantabrigiensis in Acts*, SNTS.MS, no. 3 (Cambridge: Cambridge University Press, 1966), 15-21.

The Environment of the Earliest New Testament Manuscripts

In addition to this ecclesiastical background, we need also to sketch not only the situation with respect to the earliest manuscripts, including something of the environment they shared in the places where they were found, but also their general life setting in Christianity's dynamic first centuries. There are innumerable difficulties attending these tasks, as everyone recognizes, yet this is a crucial step if we are to make progress. One of the difficulties is that we know almost nothing about the specific provenance of our early manuscripts, except—of course—that the forty-five earliest ones all come from Egypt and that twenty of these (as well as seven others) were unearthed at Oxyrhynchus. Very little, however, is known about Christianity at Oxyrhynchus at the time these manuscripts were used and finally discarded—although this general area of Egypt is known to have been a center of Christian activity at a later time, that is, in the fourth and fifth centuries.[10]

Of the provenance of the other earliest papyri, such as the famous Chester Beatty ($\mathfrak{P}^{45}$, $\mathfrak{P}^{46}$, $\mathfrak{P}^{47}$) and the Bodmer papyri ($\mathfrak{P}^{66}$, $\mathfrak{P}^{72}$, $\mathfrak{P}^{75}$), still less is known, though it was reported at the time of their purchase that the Chester Beatty papyri were discovered in a pitcher in a ruined church or monastery near Atfih (Aphroditopolis) in the Fayyûm,[11] about one-third of the way down the Nile River from Oxyrhynchus toward Alexandria. A similar statement accompanied the purchase of $\mathfrak{P}^{52}$, the earliest New Testament fragment of all, which was assumed to have come either from the Fayyûm or from Oxyrhynchus.[12] It has also been surmised that the Beatty and Bodmer codices may have come from the same church library, though there is no proof.[13] Among the famous uncial manuscripts, it has been suggested on occasion that Codices Vaticanus (B) and Sinaiticus (ℵ)

---

[10]E. G. Turner, *Greek Papyri: An Introduction* (Oxford: Clarendon Press, 1968), 28.

[11]Colin H. Roberts, *Manuscript, Society and Belief in Early Christian Egypt,* Schweich Lectures, 1977 (London: Oxford University Press, 1979), 7.

[12]Colin H. Roberts, *An Unpublished Fragment of the Fourth Gospel in the John Rylands Library* (Manchester: Manchester University Press, 1935), 24-25; H. Idris Bell and T. C. Skeat, *Fragments of an Unknown Gospel and Other Early Christian Papyri* (London: Oxford University Press, 1935), 7.

[13]C. H. Roberts, "Books in the Graeco-Roman World and in the New Testament," in *The Cambridge History of the Bible,* ed. P. R. Ackroyd and C. F. Evans (Cambridge: Cambridge University Press, 1970), vol. 1: *From the Beginnings to Jerome,* 56.

represent two of the fifty parchment manuscripts that, according to Eusebius, were ordered by Constantine around 331 for his new churches in Constantinople, but this identification is based, most tenuously, on Eusebius' reference to "volumes of threefold and fourfold forms," which could, of course, fit the respective three-column and four-column formats of the two codices. However, Eusebius' words can be interpreted in other ways, and there are some reasons to think that Codex Vaticanus may have originated in Egypt.[14] Likewise, though Codex Alexandrinus (A) is usually assumed to have originated in Alexandria, it might have come from Constantinople or Caesarea.[15] All of this is to suggest that our knowledge of the provenance of early New Testament manuscripts is scant.

Accordingly, these sparse data would seem to offer precious little assistance in an effort to link our early manuscripts in some direct way with early church history. Difficult as the process is, the fact that all of the earliest manuscripts come from Egypt makes worthwhile any and every conceivable form of investigation of that Egyptian environment. Artifacts and manuscripts from Alexandria certainly would help, but papyri from Alexandria and the Delta region have not survived, and the ancient city of Alexandria is now below sea level,[16] raising several critical questions. For instance, were the cities in the Fayyûm or those farther removed from Alexandria, like Oxyrhynchus, Antinoe, or Hermopolis, in close touch with Alexandria or largely isolated from it? With what ease or difficulty did letters and literature circulate in these areas? What was the general level of cultural and literary activity in such places? Information on these matters will help us assess the role that the papyrus books originating in these localities might have played in society and the extent to which such books circulated within Egypt and in the Greco-Roman world generally.

We begin, then, by asking what we know of Christianity in Egypt in this period. Statements about our lack of knowledge are classic,[17] but the

---

[14]See Bruce M. Metzger, *The Text of the New Testament: Its Transmission, Corruption, and Restoration,* 2d ed. (New York/Oxford: Oxford University Press, 1968), 7-8; see also Birdsall, "New Testament Text," 359-360.

[15]Burnett Hillman Streeter, *The Four Gospels: A Study of Origins* (London: Macmillan, 1924; 5th impression, 1936), 120, note 1.

[16]H. Idris Bell, *Egypt from Alexander the Great to the Arab Conquest: A Study in the Diffusion and Decay of Hellenism* (Oxford: Clarendon Press, 1948), 10.

[17]For statements from Adolf Harnack and B. H. Streeter, see A. F. J. Klijn, "Jewish Christianity in Egypt," 161; from C. H. Roberts, see the opening sentence of his *Manuscript,*

beginnings of Christian faith in Alexandria and in other parts of Egypt must reach back to the first half of the second century, even though that cannot easily be documented. One might, however, argue for that conclusion from our earliest New Testament manuscript, $\mathfrak{P}^{52}$. This tiny fragment of the Fourth Gospel was written in the first quarter of the second century, but probably nearer 100 than 125;[18] the same may be said for the "Sayings of Jesus" fragment from Oxyrhynchus[19] and of Papyrus Egerton 2, usually referred to as "the Unknown Gospel."[20] The precise provenance of neither $\mathfrak{P}^{52}$ nor Egerton 2 is known, but doubtless they are from the Fayyûm or Oxyrhynchus,[21] and the "Sayings of Jesus" fragment is from Oxyrhynchus. In fact, certain affinities between the latter papyrus and $\mathfrak{P}^{52}$ suggest to some that they could have come from "the same early Christian community in Middle Egypt."[22]

Looking at the early date of these papyrus fragments and their likely provenance in the Fayyûm or Oxyrhynchus—that is, in Middle Egypt 150 to 200 miles up the Nile from Alexandria—suggests that Christianity was well established in those areas by around 100 CE. In addition, the very likelihood that a number of the very early Oxyrhynchus Christian papyri were private copies—copies belonging to individual Christians rather than to communities or churches[23]—reinforces the early presence of

---

Society and Belief, 1, also quoted by Birger Pearson, "Earliest Christianity in Egypt: Some Observations," in *The Roots of Egyptian Christianity*, ed. B. A. Pearson and J. E. Goehring, Studies in Antiquity and Christianity (Philadelphia: Fortress Press, 1986), 132.

[18]Colin H. Roberts, *An Unpublished Fragment of the Fourth Gospel in the John Rylands Library* (Manchester: Manchester University Press, 1935). Though earlier dated 125-150, recent opinion moves it back into the 100-125 period, perhaps very early in that quarter century. See Roberts, *An Unpublished Fragment*, 12-16; and Aland and Aland, *Text of the New Testament*, 85.

[19]Given the first position in Bernard P. Grenfell and Arthur S. Hunt, *The Oxyrhynchus Papyri: Part I* (London: Egypt Exploration Fund, 1898), 1-3, and plate.

[20]H. Idris Bell and T. C. Skeat, *Fragments of an Unknown Gospel and Other Early Christian Papyri* (London: Oxford University Press, 1935); Koester, *Introduction*, 2:222. Roberts, "Books in the Graeco-Roman world," 62, dates it "about the middle" of the second century.

[21]Roberts, *An Unpublished Fragment*, 24-25.

[22]Ibid., 25.

[23]Roberts, *Manuscripts, Society and Belief*, 9. He says "many, but not all" of our papyri may have belonged to individual Christians. For more on the non-professional quality of these papyri, see Roberts, "Books in the Graeco-Roman World," 62-63.

Christianity in Egypt, for the following reason: though possibly debatable, it is logical to assume that copies of authoritative books would first be in the possession of a church or community (for liturgical and instructional use) and only later be copied for private use. If so, the existence of private copies so far from Alexandria at so early a period suggests the early origin, rapid expansion, and significant saturation of Christianity in at least the lower third of Egypt at an early time.

Though this scenario is the most likely one, a *caveat* is in order. It is possible—following the line of argument to be presented below—that one or even all of these early Christian papyri could have been written elsewhere and brought into Egypt for use there, and such an event could have occurred immediately after the production of a papyrus manuscript or considerably thereafter. Should this have taken place many decades or as much as a century or more after their writing, these manuscripts could not so easily be used to document the presence of Christianity in Egypt in the early second century.

Yet it must be remembered that virtually all of the papyri are from Egyptian rubbish heaps and presumably, therefore, were in extended use— most likely in Egypt—prior to being discarded. Nevertheless, the possibility that manuscripts like $\mathfrak{P}^{52}$ could have been produced elsewhere and imported into Egypt is a further complicating factor and gives the whole matter an ironic twist: In determining the presence of Christianity in Egypt, the date that a papyrus manuscript was *discarded* may be more important than the date of its copying.[24] If, for example, it could be determined that $\mathfrak{P}^{52}$ was discarded in 175 or 200 or 250, and if we knew more about how long manuscripts were used in early Christian congregations before they were "retired" and replaced, we could work backward from the date of discard to the date of a probable presence of Christianity in Middle Egypt. Unfortunately, much less is known about when the manuscripts were cast on the rubbish heaps than about the date and provenance of writing—which is itself precious little—and the useful life of a papyrus manuscript in a liturgical setting is something I have not seen discussed.[25]

---

[24]I owe this point to Frederik Wisse, in discussion at the conference.

[25]Contrary to common opinion, papyrus is a durable substance: see my forthcoming article, "The New Testament Papyrus Manuscripts in Historical Perspective," in *To Touch the Text: Studies in Honor of Joseph A. Fitzmyer, S.J.* (New York: Crossroad, 1989).

Sites of Papyrus Finds in Egypt

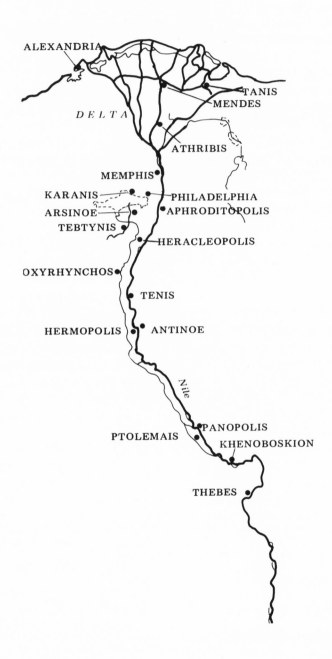

The non-Christian Egyptian papyri in general, however, provide information on two other factors highly relevant to our discussion and here there is greater clarity: first, the papyri attest extensive and lively interactions between Alexandria and the outlying areas, and also between the outlying areas and other parts of the Roman world, including Rome itself; and, second, they provide evidence of the wide circulation of documents in this early period. The following are a few examples. Papyri indicate that Jews were in touch with each other in the provinces.[26] One papyrus shows that of 325 Philadelphians registered as resident outside that village, sixty-four were resident in Alexandria.[27] Tax registers from Karanis suggest a population of five or six thousand there and "a small minority of Alexandrian citizens, who are probably absentee landlords," as well as Greeks from Alexandria and Roman veterans; and literary texts there include Homer's *Iliad* and Chariton's romance, *Chaereas and Callirhoe*.[28] Hermopolis (up the Nile from Oxyrhynchus) yielded an official letter of congratulation to a certain Plution upon his return from Rome, including quotations from Euripides and *Poimandres*.[29] A number of members of the Museum at Alexandria are connected by the papyri with estates in the outlying country. One prominent member of this scholarly group, around 200 CE in Philadelphia, can also be connected with Rome, leading E. G. Turner to remark that he was "a person therefore who might have carried books from Rome to Philadelphia."[30] Other members of this Museum elite can be documented in Antinoe (near Hermopolis) and in Oxyrhynchus. Documents from Oxyrhynchus, dating from around 173 CE, involve people who were obviously Alexandrian scholars (one of whom is known otherwise) and who discuss the procurement of books. Turner's conclusion on this is of interest:

---

[26]Roberts, *Manuscript, Society and Belief*, 4 (who refers, of course, to Victor A. Tcherikover and Alexander Fuks, eds., *Corpus Papyrorum Judaicarum*, 3 vols. [Cambridge, MA: Harvard University Press, 1957-1964], vols. 1 and 2).

[27]Ibid., 4.

[28]Turner, *Greek Papyri*, 80-81.

[29]Ibid., 85-86.

[30] Ibid., 86.

Here, for Oxyrhynchus at least, we tread firm ground:
a circle of persons exchanging notes on how to
procure and get copies made of works of scholarship,
who are themselves professional scholars.[31]

In addition, there is extensive papyrus evidence that documents
and letters were brought to Egypt from a wide range of localities and from
considerable distances, including Ravenna, Macedonia, Seleucia, Ostia,
Rome, and Constantinople, eliciting Turner's rhetorical question, "What
books or Christian texts might not have been carried in?" He adds that
these data serve to "alert the searcher to the possibility that other literary
(and religious) books, Latin or Greek, found in Egypt were the products of
scriptoria outside Egypt," though he admits that a desideratum in the field
is a criterion for identifying manuscripts copied outside Egypt.[32]

Oxyrhynchus also yielded an account of fees paid to a scribe for copying manuscripts. There were letters asking friends in Alexandria to buy
paper for them, or telling family members that inkwells and pens have
been left for their use, or revealing fine expression and writing style. An
interesting papyrus scrap lists subjects for student declamations which
would require the reading of Thucydides or Euripides.[33] In the villages in
the Fayyûm generally, Homer, Plato, Sophocles, and other Greek authors
are well represented.[34] Moreover, the papyrus texts of the "Acts of the
Alexandrian Martyrs," stemming from the first three centuries, represent
a "pamphletering literature, probably passed from hand to hand,"[35] and
there is evidence of wide circulation since specimens have been found as
far as 200 miles apart, beginning more than 150 miles from Alexandria at
Arsinoe, then at Oxyrhynchus, and perhaps also at Panopolis, 160 miles up
the Nile from Oxyrhynchus.[36] From these data, C. H. Roberts concludes:

---

[31]Ibid., 87.

[32]Ibid, 50-51, 96; see also Colin H. Roberts and T. C. Skeat, *The Birth of the Codex*
(London: Oxford University Press, 1983), 35.

[33]Ibid., 83-84, 87.

[34]E. G. Turner, *Greek Manuscripts of the Ancient World* (Oxford: Clarendon Press,
1971), 96.

[35]Roberts, *Manuscript, Society and Belief*, 3.

[36]Ibid.

> With this analogy in mind, we shall not be inclined to accept the view of some scholars that until the third century Christianity was confined to Alexandria when Christian manuscripts of second century date have been found in Middle and Upper Egypt .... . There is abundant evidence of a close and continuous relationship between the Greeks of Alexandria and the Greek middle class in the provincial towns and villages at all levels—economic, cultural, and personal.[37]

It is not easy, however, to determine precisely what economic, cultural, and personal life was actually like in a district capital such as Oxyrhynchus, where archaeological finds were minimal. It is, however, of interest—as we have already observed—how much can be discerned from "philological archaeology," that is, from the papyrus documents. We know something of the number of public buildings from records of a night watchman's rounds—including temples and two Christian churches; we have evidence, actually, of twenty temples, of gymnasia, of courts for playing ball and a racecourse, of a theater—seating 8,000 to 12,000 people—as well as a script on papyrus for a play of Euripides; and we have records of money allocated for a new street, of residents' addresses in named quarters of the city, and of soldiers stationed in Oxyrhynchus.[38] This is in addition to the correspondence and literary activity alluded to earlier, all of which adds up to a city full of cultural and intellectual pursuits, not to mention, of course, the everyday activities of life.

Similar data could be compiled for other cities in the Fayyûm or farther up the Nile, where papyri have been found, but what we have outlined will be sufficient to make the point that these were places not only of literacy but of literary activity and that they were in frequent and relatively easy communication—both through travel and letter writing—with Alexandria and other major areas in the Greco-Roman world. As further documentation, reference might be made, for example, to *P. Mich. Zenon* 10, a letter dated 257 BCE, which reports a two-month adventure by ship from Alexandria to southern Asia Minor; but the letter itself which told of the trip "took only nineteen days to get back to the village of Philadelphia

---

[37]Ibid., 4; see also Roberts and Skeat, *The Birth of the Codex*, 35.

[38]Ibid., 81-82; see also 78-88 for other localities and cultural information.

in the Arsinoite nome, some 250 kilometers up-river from Alexandria."[39] In addition, mundane commercial documents on papyrus show that the business dealings of the Philadelphian banker, Zenon, reached not only nearby Memphis, but all the way into the Nile Delta to places like Athribis, about seventy miles from Philadelphia, and Mendes, forty miles farther into the Delta near the Mediterranean Sea.[40]

Though one would not hastily equate the Christian production and use of books with the cultural literary activity of the Greco-Roman world, yet the Christian papyri—in our case the New Testament papyri—must be viewed within this active, vibrant world, and viewed with every degree of legitimate historical and creative imagination that can be brought to bear on the subject.

Textual Clusters and the Early Spectrum of New Testament Manuscripts

It is time, now, to look at the early New Testament text within this two-fold background of the church-historical context and the Egyptian cultural setting as revealed through the papyri. We must explore how our knowledge of the New Testament manuscripts might be combined with the information gained from their historical-cultural environment and then break through, if possible, to new insights into the earliest period of textual transmission. Should that elude us, we may hope at least for greater clarity on the issues that confront us in the early formative period.

Designations for the Textual Clusters

A first step (though by no means an indispensable one) is to take seriously the clarion call from the early post-World War II era that we abandon the anachronistic terminology used in the period prior to the discovery of the Chester Beatty and Bodmer papyri. Kenneth W. Clark issued that call already in 1948, before the Bodmer papyri were known, by saying that "the only studies made thus far [of the Chester Beatty Papyri] seem to approach these texts by reversing the centuries. We require a new mental attitude, wherein we . . . approach these earliest materials *de novo*,"

---

[39]Naphtali Lewis, *Greeks in Ptolemaic Egypt: Case Studies in the Social History of the Hellenistic World* (Oxford: Clarendon Press, 1986), 12.

[40]Ibid., 53-54. Note also from page 54, that the Zenon correspondence refers to the acquisition of papyrus rolls from the Delta region.

adding that "we should study the third-century witnesses in their own right."[41] More widely quoted—and rightly so—has been the statement of J. Neville Birdsall in 1958, who pointed out the fault "common to many contemporary scholars who attempt to discuss and define such early evidence as this by standards of later witnesses," adding specifically:

> Beyond the fourth century the divisions of "Neutral," "Western," "Caesarean," "Byzantine" (or corresponding terms) are apposite: but in the early period, which such a papyrus as p[66] reveals to us, these concepts are out of place. The task of present-day criticism is to inaugurate an era in which we begin from the earliest evidence and on the basis of its interpretation discuss the later.[42]

So, we shall abandon the long-standing but largely anachronistic and partially misleading designations of the past when discussing the earliest textual period, especially the terms "Neutral," "Western," and "Caesarean," and we shall try some new terms. Departure from the old categories is particularly important when dealing with the papyri, but we should go a step farther and abandon also, at least for the moment, the term "text-type," since the existence of such entities in the early centuries has been questioned in some quarters.[43] We shall substitute "textual group" or "textual cluster," assuming that these terms lack the offensive implications of a rigidly fixed form or a tightly integrated character and

---

[41]Kenneth W. Clark, "The Manuscripts of the Greek New Testament," in *New Testament Manuscript Studies: The Materials and the Making of a Critical Apparatus,* ed. M. M. Parvis and A. P. Wikgren (Chicago: University of Chicago Press, 1950), 20-21.

[42]J. Neville Birdsall, *The Bodmer Papyrus of the Gospel of John,* Tyndale New Testament Lecture, 1958 (London: Tyndale Press, 1969), 7.

[43]Most prominently Kurt Aland; see his "The Significance of the Papyri for Progress in New Testament Research," in *The Bible in Modern Scholarship,* ed. J. P. Hyatt (Nashville: Abingdon, 1965), 334-337; this article was updated in his "Die Konsequenzen der neueren Handschriftenfunde für die neutestamentliche Textkritik," in *Studien zur Überlieferung des Neuen Testaments und seines Textes,* ANTT, no. 2 (Berlin: Walter de Gruyter, 1967), 188-189; more recently, see Aland and Aland, *The Text of the New Testament,* 59, 64, 103, who distinguish between "different forms" of the text (which they say did exist prior to the third/fourth century) and "text types" (which they say existed only in the fourth century and after); cf. E. C. Colwell, "Method in Establishing the Nature of Text-Types of New Testament Manuscripts," in *Studies in Methodology in Textual Criticism of the New Testament,* NTTS, no. 9 (Leiden: Brill, 1969), 55: "Very few, if any, text-types were established by that time [A.D. 200]."

that they avoid the attribution to textual groups of an officially conveyed status. Then, if and as appropriate, we may bring back the term "text-type" in the course of the investigation.

It will be obvious to all that proposing new symbols in the field of New Testament textual criticism is an extremely hazardous venture, as witnessed by the fate accorded the schemes of Westcott-Hort, or von Soden, or F. G. Kenyon—all of which seemed appropriate enough in their respective periods of research, but, as scholarship passed them by, were soon out of date. Nor do I wish to suggest that proposing new terminology is either the burden of this paper or, for that matter, of any intrinsic importance. Yet, reluctance to start anew is, by default, to permit the perpetuation of anachronistic labels and to necessitate the repeated explanation of terms that already are used by all of us only with surrounding quotation marks.

In forming new designations, ideally we should begin with terms or symbols that are both simple and unbiased, or—alternatively—with terminology that has a genuine historical basis. On the latter approach, natural designations for New Testament textual clusters, for example, would be "the $\mathfrak{P}^{75}$ text," "the $\mathfrak{P}^{45}$ text," etc., but the obvious danger here is the same as that which brought about our present terminological crisis: who can say that even manuscripts like $\mathfrak{P}^{75}$ will remain either the earliest or the most distinctive representative of that particular textual cluster?[44] Rather, the use of arbitrary symbols is preferable, though it would be advantageous if we could employ some symbols that, at the same time, would also recognize and recall certain aspects of our past scholarship that are generally recognized as valid. That would make the symbols both more meaningful and easier to remember. So, rather than merely selecting in an arbitrary fashion the numbers 1, 2, 3, 4; or the Greek letters, alpha, beta, gamma, delta (as Westcott-Hort and Kenyon did, though with

---

[44] As to the likelihood of discovering additional New Testament papyri of importance, see the pessimistic statement in Aland and Aland, *The Text of the New Testament*, 75: "After the impressive growth in the number of manuscripts recorded in the nineteenth century by Gregory and in the twentieth century by the Institute for New Testament Textual Research, it is unlikely that the future will bring any comparable increases," though they go on to allow that recent finds at St. Catherine's Monastery on Mt. Sinai "could change the situation." Of course, the rising water table throughout Egypt, as a result of the high dam at Assuan, threatens the survival of any buried papyri; yet, the long-standing pessimism in the past about new finds in Egypt was repeatedly falsified by fresh discoveries (see Turner, *Greek Papyri*, 40).

different meanings[45]), I would suggest that we keep matters as simple as possible and use the letters A, B, C, and D when probing for the basic New Testament textual groups of the early period. These are symbols that will easily justify themselves, and yet will remain essentially unbiased regardless of future discoveries and developments. In this way we can make a fresh start—at least in appearances—with respect to our terminology, and yet retain connections that are sufficiently reminiscent of certain significant scholarly achievements in our evolving history of the text as to give the system immediate credibility. The four proposed groups are set forth in what follows.

Textual Group "A" — On this scheme, "A" would designate what is variously called the Majority text, or the Koine, or the later Byzantine; with the letter "A" suggesting such words as the "average" text (in the sense of ordinary or common), or the "accepted" text (with affinities to "textus receptus"), or the "ascendent" text (since it became the text that prevailed, though wrongly so), but also calling to mind Codex Alexandrinus (A), which is the oldest representative of this textual group—though only in the Gospels—and, of course, recalling Westcott-Hort's designation, "Antiochian."[46] (We could use "K" for Koine, or "M" for Majority, but there is a nice symmetry in using four consecutive letters of the alphabet.)

Textual Group "B" — The symbol "B" would be used to represent the character and quality of text found in $\mathfrak{P}^{75}$ and Codex Vaticanus (B), which are the major representatives of this textual cluster. Of the close relationship of the texts in these two specific manuscripts there can be no doubt. The symbol "B," while it may appear to perpetuate anachronistic procedures of the past—in that it appears to use a later manuscript name for an earlier textual phenomenon—is in reality quite neutral when it is seen simply as one of several consecutive letters of the alphabet. Yet, it has the advantage of easy recognition.

Textual Group "D" — The letter "D" (to skip over group "C" for the moment) would designate the kind of text found in $\mathfrak{P}^{29}$, $\mathfrak{P}^{48}$, and $\mathfrak{P}^{38}$, which in a later form is found in Codex Bezae (D). The use of "D" would rid us of the largely misleading term "Western," but would leave us with

---

[45]See Vincent Taylor, *The Text of the New Testament: A Short Introduction,* 2nd ed. (London: Macmillan, 1963), 6-7; Frederic G. Kenyon, *The Text of the Greek Bible: A Student's Handbook* (London: Duckworth, 1949), 197.

[46]B. F. Westcott and F. J. A. Hort, *The New Testament in the Original Greek* (Cambridge/London: Macmillan, 1881-1882), 2:142-146.

a well-established symbol for this textual cluster and—again—place it in a more unbiased setting.

   Textual Group "C" — Finally, the letter "C," which conveniently stands between "B" and "D," would represent the early "in-between" text that occurs, for example, in $\mathfrak{P}^{45}$ and in parts of Codex Washingtonianus (W). The letter "C," of course, recalls the term "Caesarean," though this is a name that should no longer be perpetuated; yet no harm will be done if, for some, it serves to recall the general kind of text found in this cluster.

   Before offering further explanations of this scheme, it should be observed that those who eschew the identification of text-types in the early period of New Testament textual transmission[47] will object to the entire enterprise; but such an approach appears to reflect more an obscurantism than a realistic attempt to come to terms with the early data, limited though it is. It seems to me that we should use as judiciously and as creatively as possible the data we have and venture boldly toward some scholarly progress—we should take risks, forge new paths—rather than close off the future by preemptive decisions or through judgments that by their very nature preclude advances in our knowledge of the past.

Definitions of the Textual Clusters

   The next steps are to define these textual clusters in greater detail (using the fresh symbols) and then to show how they are to be viewed dynamically within their general life setting in those earliest centuries of Christianity. Naturally, there is a fair measure of tentativeness in all of this, but that—as we say—"goes with the territory." Though textual criticism has shown itself to be—by its very nature—a highly conservative discipline, an overly cautious attitude when exploring theoretical issues will forestall the progress so urgently required in the field. We need to open some new windows, and—if possible—a few doors as well! A general survey of the situation of the text in the earliest known period will set the stage for these closer definitions of textual groups.

   The forty-five earliest New Testament manuscripts which are currently known, that is, those dating up to and including the turn of the third/fourth centuries, present us with a number of differing textual complexions. Everyone recognizes this, though not all agree on how they are

---

[47]See note 43, above.

to be differentiated or what to call them or what the range of difference means. These and other difficulties abound as we try to interrogate these aged witnesses and as we attempt to use them in theorizing procedures. Perhaps the most obvious difficulty is that most are highly fragmentary in nature. Yet, the first principle to be adopted in assessing the fragmentary papyri is clear enough: "If a fragment preserves a passage where there is any variation in the tradition, it is quite sufficient to signal the textual character of the whole manuscript," as Kurt Aland and Barbara Aland affirm in their recent book.[48]

A second difficulty is that all forty-five of these earliest manuscripts —as well as all the other NT papyri—are from Egypt, and Egypt only. Does this mean that the array of textual complexions they present all originated in Egypt? In answering that question, we should resist the temptation to look to later New Testament manuscripts that may represent other places and draw any conclusions; rather—at least at this stage of investigation— we should stay with the earliest manuscripts only and restrict our analysis to them alone. But does that not preclude the possibility of offering any sort of answer as to whether all the New Testament texts found on papyri originated in Egypt? No, for it seems to me that we do have a path toward an answer, though—by the nature of the case—it cannot be decisively demonstrated.

The answer as to whether the varying textual complexions of the earliest papyri all originated in Egypt—and, therefore, the answer to the more substantive question as to whether Egypt is representative of the *entire* early history of the New Testament text—that answer was implicit in our description of the movement of population and the circulation of letters and literature in Egypt in the first centuries of the Christian era. That is, if—as we have shown—there existed a lively and vigorous movement of people back and forth between Alexandria and the Greco-Roman world to the east and west and north, and also between Alexandria and the upper regions of Egypt, especially the Fayyûm and centers like Oxyrhynchus, and if—as we have shown—there was a brisk circulation of letters and of literature in these same areas, then we are compelled to give up, first, the notion that all of these textual complexions necessarily originated in Egypt, and, second, that they remained in or were confined to Egypt. In fact, the evidence from the non-New Testament papyri which reveals

---

[48] Aland and Aland, *The Text of the New Testament*, 58. They support the principle with the every-day analogy that "there is no need to consume a whole jar of jelly to identify the quality of its contents—a spoonful or two is quite enough!"

dynamic interchanges of people, letters, and books to and from Egypt, as well as within Egypt, actually would permit us to go to the logical extreme—if we wished—of asserting that *none* of the New Testament textual complexions necessarily originated in Egypt, though there is no reason to carry the matter that far. Suffice it to say that the breadth and intensity of the intellectual commerce between Egypt—even Middle and Upper Egypt—and the rest of the vast Mediterranean region between 30 and 300 CE supports the strong possibility—indeed the strong probability— that *the various textual groups presented by our Egyptian papyri represent texts from that entire Mediterranean region* (including, of course, those texts that might have originated in Egypt itself).

A dynamic view of New Testament textual transmission, then, envisions considerable movement of New Testament manuscripts to and from Egypt and within Egypt, at least in the period up to the Diocletian persecution beginning around 303. It also permits us, by inference, to put to rest the question as to whether Egypt adequately represents the textual spectrum of earliest Christianity—we may presume that it does.

Another line of argument can be employed to support the same conclusion in a more explicit fashion. Recently C. H. Roberts (with T. C. Skeat) has made a case that the *nomina sacra* (the uniform abbreviations of divine names and sacred terms in manuscripts) were a Christian creation established either by the church at Jerusalem before 70 CE, or by the church at Antioch slightly later—as a kind of "embryonic creed" of the first church—and that from there they "spread to Egypt and everywhere where Greek was written." This system, Roberts says, "was too complex for the ordinary scribe to operate without either rules or an authoritative exemplar"—because without one or the other it would have been difficult, even in a small Christian community, to determine which usages (of the secondary *nomina sacra*) were secular and which were sacred.[49] In addition, a case can be made that the *nomina sacra* and the codex form of book not only were both Christian inventions, but that both came into existence at the same place at about the same time. Moreover, both phenomena share the same characteristic: each serves effectively to differentiate Christian books from both Jewish and secular books.[50]

---

[49]The basic case is made in Roberts, *Manuscript, Society and Belief*, 44-46, where he argued for Jerusalem, but it is revised and supplemented in Roberts and Skeat, *The Birth of the Codex*, 57-61, where Antioch is favored.

[50]Roberts and Skeat, *The Birth of the Codex*, 57-58.

The presence in Egypt of "this remarkably uniform system of *nomina sacra*" in the earliest Christian manuscripts (all of which were codices) only slightly more than a century after their invention calls for explanation. Roberts' conclusion is that already "at an early date there were standard copies of the Christian scriptures."[51] On this theory, such standard copies would have to have been established in Jerusalem or Antioch and transmitted, either directly or through other centers, to Egypt. Others think that the *nomina sacra* (and also the codex form) might have originated at Alexandria or even Rome.[52] The point is that a highly technical, rigidly practiced *Christian* procedure was well established in Middle Egypt prior to the time of our earliest New Testament papyri, which in a rather striking fashion, regardless of its place of origin, attests to the active movement of New Testament manuscripts within the eastern Greco-Roman world—and at very least attests to early and active textual transmission within Egypt itself.

Though no one yet is asserting that the *nomina sacra* procedures and practices suggest that Christian scriptoria existed prior to 200, that is at least a possibility. What these practices do suggest with more certainty, however, is that the churches in this earliest period, at least in the East, were perhaps not as loosely organized as has been assumed,[53] and, therefore, they also were not as isolated from one another as has been affirmed. Indeed, at least one "program of standardization"[54]—the *nomina sacra*—was certainly functioning with obvious precision and care. Moreover, the exclusive use of the codex by Christians for biblical books in the earliest period[55] evidences a second standardization program—the very form that the books assumed appears to have been a matter of policy. We should not, then, "rule out of court" the likelihood that additional standard textual procedures were in operation at this very early time.

---

[51]Roberts, "Books in the Graeco-Roman World," 64.

[52]See Roberts, *Manuscript, Society and Belief*, 42-44; for arguments against Alexandria especially, see Roberts and Skeat, *The Birth of the Codex*, 54-57.

[53]These two points are made against views taken in Aland and Aland, *The Text of the New Testament*, 55-56, 59.

[54]The phrase is from Aland and Aland, *The Text of the New Testament*, 59; where, in their discussion of $\mathfrak{P}^{45}$, $\mathfrak{P}^{46}$, and $\mathfrak{P}^{66}$, they do at least allow for the possibility that the manuscripts could have been "imported from elsewhere."

[55]Roberts and Skeat, *The Birth of the Codex*, 42.

When—at long last—we now analyze the textual characteristics of our earliest New Testament witnesses, noting differences among readings that are sufficient to distinguish separate textual complexions, and when we subsequently trace lines of connection with later manuscripts of similar textual complexions, we must take these factors into account. Other significant observations will arise in the process of sketching the composition of the various textual clusters, to which we now turn.

Members of the "A" text group — The "A" text cluster, that is, the "accepted" text or the Koine or later Byzantine textual group, need not be further considered here, for the early papyri are not involved (although a few papyri of the sixth and seventh centuries do represent the "A" text). Furthermore, everyone recognizes that this textual group exists, though not until the fourth century—that is, after the period of the earliest papyri. Moreover, everyone also acknowledges that this can actually be called a "text-type."[56] The recognized constituent members can be found in the standard handbooks.[57]

Members of the "B" text group — The place to begin a description of the "B" textual cluster is with the striking and highly significant fact that the texts of $\mathfrak{P}^{75}$ and Codex Vaticanus (B) are almost identical, a fact which demonstrates that there is virtually a straight line from the text of a papyrus dated around 200 to that of a major, elegant manuscript of 150 years later.[58] Does this permit us to expect—or to require—that similarly direct connections will be found between other early papyri and certain later manuscripts? Not necessarily, for both the discovery of the New Testament papyri and the survival of later manuscripts are random phenomena, and no uniform or complete representation of the textual spectrum can be expected to have been preserved for us. So we take what we have, both of the early papyri and the later witnesses, and attempt a creative reconstruction of the transmission process, recognizing that it will always be partial and less than fully satisfying. Precisely because this is the

---

[56]See, e.g., Aland and Aland, *The Text of the New Testament*, 51, 64-69.

[57]E.g., Bruce M. Metzger, *A Textual Commentary on the Greek New Testament* (London/New York: United Bible Societies, 1971), xxx-xxxi; idem, *The Text of the New Testament: Its Transmission, Corruption, and Restoration*, 213.

[58]This hardly requires documentation, but both references and evidence may be found in Gordon D. Fee, "P75, P66, and Origen: The Myth of Early Textual Recension in Alexandria," *New Dimensions in New Testament Study*, ed. R. N. Longenecker and M. C. Tenney (Grand Rapids, MI: Zondervan, 1974), 24-28.

situation, the close affinity of $\mathfrak{P}^{75}$ and B is all the more striking, for it demonstrates that an early papyrus can stand very near the beginning point of a clearly identifiable and distinctive textual group that has been preserved with a high degree of accuracy over several generations and through a period that often has been assumed to have been a chaotic and free textual environment.

If we had several pieces of evidence like the $\mathfrak{P}^{75}$-B relationship, it would be plausible to argue that the situation was not chaotic, but quite orderly. Although that evidence eludes us due to the randomness of the survival of papyrus, the evidence we have does, to a certain extent, move in that direction. For it was more likely a semblance of standardization, rather than accident, that permitted the text of Vaticanus—over several generations—to maintain its close affinity to that represented in $\mathfrak{P}^{75}$. Vaticanus was not copied from $\mathfrak{P}^{75}$—they had a common ancestor[59]—so one must ask about the transmission process that would have produced this very similar resultant text. To answer that $\mathfrak{P}^{75}$ is a manuscript with a "strict" text[60] may be descriptive, but it does not answer the question *why*. Indeed, the very employment of the term "strict" in describing some early New Testament papyri implies—though it does not prove—that a form of standardization was operative in the transmission process already at an early time.

As a matter of fact, the discovery of $\mathfrak{P}^{75}$ nullified an older view of standardization, for the close affinity of $\mathfrak{P}^{75}$ with Codex Vaticanus swept away the cobwebs of a long-standing and commonly-held notion that Codex Vaticanus reflects only a third/fourth century recension. On the contrary, it can be demonstrated that the $\mathfrak{P}^{75}$-B textual tradition represents a relatively pure form of preservation of the text of a common ancestor,[61] and that $\mathfrak{P}^{75}$, therefore, is not itself an editorial adaptation or recension.[62] We are left, then, with the undoubted fact that a distinctive kind of text, *with both antecedents and descendants*, existed in the very early period of

---

[59]Fee, "P[75], P[66], and Origen," 33-40.

[60]Aland and Aland, *The Text of the New Testament*, 64, 93, 95.

[61]See the compelling series of arguments that lead to this conclusion in Fee, "P[75], P[66], and Origen;" on the recension view, see 20-24; on the view that there is a common ancestry of the manuscripts, see 33-40.

[62]Ibid., 32-33; cf. Aland and Aland, *The Text of the New Testament*, 64, 93, 95, where the term "strict" implies the same conclusion.

New Testament textual transmission. That text actually exists in an extant document from around 200 CE. It also had earlier antecedents, although it is difficult to specify their dates. However, a dynamic view of textual transmission—combined with the *nomina sacra* evidence—would suggest that not only the text of $\mathfrak{P}^{75}$ and its antecedents, but also other early New Testament papyri have a significantly earlier history in Judaea or Syria, as well as in Egypt. Moreover, there are enough hints that some early procedures of standardization were involved in the process to warrant calling the $\mathfrak{P}^{75}$-B cluster a "text-type." Therefore, I would not hesitate to affirm the existence of at least one text-type—which we can designate the "B text-type" *in the second century.*

The slightly earlier $\mathfrak{P}^{66}$ is usually associated with $\mathfrak{P}^{75}$ and the later Vaticanus in this textual group. It has been argued that $\mathfrak{P}^{66}$ is the product of a scriptorium.[63] Whether or not this is the case, the papyrus was produced by a "scribe-turned-recensor," who (though a careless workman) was himself correcting his text against a second exemplar and, in addition, appears intent on producing a more readable, common Greek style by abandoning Johannine style on numerous occasions (Johannine style, that is, as it is found in $\mathfrak{P}^{75}$ and B). Thus, his text moves away from that of $\mathfrak{P}^{75}$ (and toward the kind of readings later seen in the "A" type of text); but overall, the text of $\mathfrak{P}^{66}$ still is closer in character to that of $\mathfrak{P}^{75}$ (and B) than it is to other manuscripts,[64] although it falls short (by at least ten percentage points) of the seventy percent agreement required by current practice to demonstrate textual affinity (see below). Yet, to place a text like $\mathfrak{P}^{66}$ in a "text-type" like "B" does not diminish "B" as an actual text-type, for the motivations of the scribe of $\mathfrak{P}^{66}$—both his efforts to make the text readable and his quasi-scholarly activity in comparing and correcting his copy to a second exemplar—can be adequately recognized, providing thereby an explanation for his departures from his text-type norm. It may be a "wild" member of the group, but it is a group member nonetheless.[65]

---

[63]E.g., by Ernest C. Colwell and Gordon D. Fee; for documentation and arguments, see Fee, "p75, p66, and Origen," 30-31. On the "impossibility" of Christian scriptoria before 200 (except perhaps in Alexandria "about 200"), see Aland and Aland, *The Text of the New Testament*, 70.

[64]Fee, "p75, p66, and Origen," 30-31; cf. Gordon D. Fee, *Papyrus Bodmer II (P66): Its Textual Relationships and Scribal Characteristics.*, StD, no. 34 (Salt Lake City: University of Utah Press, 1968), esp. 9-14, 35, 76-83.

[65]A. F. J. Klijn's description of $\mathfrak{P}^{66}$ as "Neutral in a non-pure way" is accepted and confirmed by Fee, *Papyrus Bodmer II*, 35.

If this is an adequate analysis of $\mathfrak{P}^{66}$ and of its relationship to $\mathfrak{P}^{75}$ and Vaticanus, then we learn something significant about "text-types." A text-type is not a closely concentrated entity with rigid boundaries, but is more like a galaxy—with a compact nucleus and additional but less closely related members which range out from the nucleus toward the perimeter. An obvious problem is how to determine when the outer limits of those more remote, accompanying members have been reached for one text-type and where the next begins. We shall return to this issue in a moment.

To these witnesses for the "B-text"—$\mathfrak{P}^{75}$, Vaticanus (B), and $\mathfrak{P}^{66}$— can be added others, both among the papyri and among later manuscripts that share a similar textual complexion. These identifications necessarily must be quite tentative with respect to the fragmentary papyri. In addition, the classifications for all manuscripts should really be structured separately for various sections of the New Testament, particularly for the Gospels, for the Pauline letters, for Acts and the General Epistles, and for Revelation, because many manuscripts confine their contents to one of these groups. The matter is more complex, however, for "the textual history of the New Testament differs from corpus to corpus, and even from book to book; therefore the witnesses have to be re-grouped in each new section."[66] This is primarily the result of the way in which books were grouped in the transmission process, for the make-up of manuscripts varies vastly and many different combinations of books are to be found as one moves from manuscript to manuscript.[67] In addition, a number of manuscripts show "block mixture," that is, they contain sections reflecting one distinctive kind of text, and other sections reflecting another. Thus, any classification of manuscripts will lack the desired precision and neatness.

By definition, textual clusters, and especially text-types, can only become visible and be identified when lines of connection can be drawn between and among a number of manuscripts which share a similar textual complexion. Furthermore, standards must be established both to determine relationships between manuscripts and to differentiate distinctive textual groups from one another. These standards cannot be impressionistic or based on random samples, but must be grounded in a scientific and full comparison of agreement/disagreement in variation

---

[66]Ernest C. Colwell, "The Origin of Texttypes of New Testament Manuscripts," in *Early Christian Origins: Studies in Honor of Harold R. Willoughby,* ed. A. Wikgren (Chicago: Quadrangle, 1961), 138; reprinted under the title, "Method in Establishing the Nature of Text-Types of New Testament Manuscripts" in *Studies in Methodology,* 55.

[67]See Aland and Aland, *The Text of the New Testament,* 78-79, for statistics.

units (or in test readings, when large numbers of manuscripts are under consideration). The isolation of the variation units (or test readings) must then be followed by quantitative measures of textual similarities and differences. These methods have been extensively explored and utilized, as well as substantially refined, in the current generation of New Testament textual criticism.[68] As to the definition of "text-type," no one yet has surpassed that offered by Ernest C. Colwell:

> The quantitative definition of a text-type is a group of manuscripts that agree more than 70 percent of the time and is separated by a gap of about 10 percent from its neighbors.[69]

Although highly fragmentary manuscripts do not lend themselves readily to this process, the readings within their variation-units can be fully compared with those of any other manuscript. To such results the criterion earlier quoted must be applied:[70] the textual character of a whole manuscript can be signalled even by a fragment's agreement with a variation in the textual tradition; therefore significant agreement with other manuscripts should qualify even a fragmentary witness as a member of the textual cluster. The randomness of the fragmentary papyri raises additional questions, however. For example, in these situations is seventy percent agreement still the minimum to qualify as a "fellow member" of a textual group?

In spite of all these contingencies, the process of assessing textual complexions can go forward and relationships can be established. In the case of the B-text, the later "trajectory" of transmission would include — beyond 𝔓[75], Vaticanus (B), and 𝔓[66]—the fourth-century Codex Sinaiticus (א) (though not in John), Codex L (eighth century), and minuscules 33

---

[68]See the important theoretical work, and its application, by Gordon D. Fee, esp. his "Codex Sinaiticus in the Gospel of John: A Contribution to Methodology in Establishing Textual Relationships," *NTS* 15 (1968-1969): 23-44.

[69]Ernest C. Colwell and Ernest W. Tune, "The Quantitative Relationships between MS Text-Types," in *Biblical and Patristic Studies in Memory of Robert Pierce Casey*, ed. J. N. Birdsall and R. W. Thomson (Freiburg: Herder, 1963), 29; reprinted under the title, "Method in Establishing Quantitative Relationships between Text-Types of New Testament Manuscripts" in *Studies in Methodology*, 59.

[70]See *supra*, note 48.

(ninth century), 1739 (tenth century) (except in Acts), and 579 (thirteenth century), to mention only the most obvious.

Members of the "C" text group — In line with our stated principle of beginning at the beginning, we start with one of the early papyri that clearly differs in its textual complexion from that represented in the "B" text, namely, $\mathfrak{P}^{45}$. Since textual groupings can be defined only when lines of connection can be drawn to other similar manuscripts, we want to know if such connections exist for $\mathfrak{P}^{45}$. Since the time of its discovery and initial analysis, its most interesting connections have been found to be with Codex Washingtonianus (W) of the fifth century, but only in Mark 5:31-16:20 (since W is a classic example of block mixture). Elsewhere in the Gospels, its text has been described as "intermediate" between the Alexandrian (="Neutral") and "Western," to use the usual designations[71] and the usual methods,[72] or—to use our designation—its text stands between the "B" and "D" textual groups. Thus, $\mathfrak{P}^{45}$ was linked to a textual group called "Caesarean," a text-type considered, until recently, as a well-established one standing midway between "B" and "D." This is not the place to review the exigencies of the so-called "Caesarean" text,[73] but it is sufficient to say that the $\mathfrak{P}^{45}$-W kind of text cannot be described as either "Caesarean" or "pre-Caesarean" in Mark. Rather, it constitutes its own group, with further developments evident in f^{13}, but with no significant connections with its previously regarded "Caesarean" fellow members, chief among which were Codex Koridethi (Θ) and minuscule 565.[74] Yet the affinity of variation units between $\mathfrak{P}^{45}$ and W in Mark virtually reaches the seventy percent mark (68.9%), with $\mathfrak{P}^{45}$ and f^{13} registering 55.3% agreement, but no other manuscript agrees with $\mathfrak{P}^{45}$ any more than 44%.[75] Hence, the line or "trajectory" of the $\mathfrak{P}^{45}$ or "C" text, to the extent that it can be recognized at present, extends from $\mathfrak{P}^{45}$ to W (in Mark) and secondarily to f^{13}. Codex W, by the way, appears to have been written in

---

[71]Metzger, *The Text of the New Testament*, 37.

[72]See my forthcoming article, "The New Testament Papyrus Manuscripts in Historical Perspective," where the treatment of the papyri in the history of New Testament textual criticism is discussed in detail.

[73]See Larry W. Hurtado, *Text-Critical Methodology and the Pre-Caesarean Text: Codex W in the Gospel of Mark*, StD, no. 43 (Grand Rapids, MI: Eerdmans, 1981).

[74]Ibid., 88-89.

[75]Ibid., 63; cf. 86-87.

Egypt,[76] but—on the basis of principles earlier enunciated—it would. be premature and unwarranted to conclude that it might represent a text-type of Egyptian origin.

In the case of the "C" text, we cannot readily refer to the standard handbooks to find its constituent members. This is due to the fact that so much has changed in the discipline in the past decades.

Members of the "D" text group — Finally, four or five manuscripts (including one uncial) from the third or fourth century form another early cluster: $\mathfrak{P}^{29}$, $\mathfrak{P}^{48}$, $\mathfrak{P}^{38}$, **0171**, and perhaps $\mathfrak{P}^{69}$. These have a connection with Codex Bezae (D) of the fifth century. The reality of a D-text (long known as the "Western" text) is not doubted, although it has recently been asserted that its existence "as early as the second century" is "quite inconceivable."[77]

----

[76]Henry A. Sanders, *Facsimile of the Washington Manuscript of the Four Gospels in the Freer Collection* (Ann Arbor, MI: University of Michigan, 1912), v; though he gives no reason or explanation for the 4th century date.

[77]Aland and Aland, *The Text of the New Testament*, 55. However, their conception of the D-text is not clear, as appears from their several statements on the subject: (1) The claim that "it is quite inconceivable that the text of Codex Bezae Cantabrigiensis could have existed as early as the second century" (p. 55). (2) The assertion that Codex Bezae's "tendentious revision (or more probably that of its ancestor of the third/fourth century) is based on a papyrus with an 'early text' of this kind" (p. 51). (3) The reference to "the phantom 'Western' text" (p. 55). (4) The statement, while speaking of the "Early Text" (prior to the third/fourth century), that "we also find manuscripts, although only a few, which approach the neighborhood of the D text" (p. 64). (5) The affirmation that pre-third/fourth century manuscripts include "some which anticipated or were more closely akin to the D text, but not until the fourth century . . . did the formation of text types begin" (p. 64). (6) Finally, the claim that "the text found in Codex Bezae . . . represents (in its exemplar) the achievement of an outstanding early theologian of the third/fourth century" (p. 69). Apparently the Alands wish to differentiate between the "D text" and the "Western" text (as a geographical designation) (pp. 67-69), insisting that the latter is a "phantom" (yet for generations no one has seriously suggested that the "Western" text was western). A curiosity, therefore, is their repeated emphasis that there could be no early "Western" text because "no important personality can be identified at any time or place in the early Western church who could have been capable of the singular theological achievement represented by the text of the Gospels and Acts in the ancestor of Codex Bezae Cantabrigiensis (D)" (p. 69; cf. 54). Indeed, if one wanted to make the case (though no one does) that the "Western" text was western, it would not be essential to identify a specific, known individual capable of producing it; after all, the canonical Epistle to the Hebrews was produced by someone not only unknown to us now, but also unidentified in antiquity (witness Origen). In the final analysis, the Alands affirm that "only the Alexandrian text, the Koine text, and the D text are incontestably verified" (p. 67; cf. 243), but this apparently means the D text only after the second century (if we take seriously the strong statement on p. 55). Of these six statements, it seems that numbers 2, 4, and 6 are correct.

At the Notre Dame conference, Barbara Aland appeared to accept the term "proto" or "pre-D-Text" to describe the kind of text in manuscripts like $\mathfrak{P}^{29}$ and $\mathfrak{P}^{48}$, implying that the D-text (though in her view not in existence until the beginning of the third century)

Admittedly, the chronological gap between the earliest representatives and the major manuscript that connects with them is greater than the gap between $\mathfrak{P}^{75}$ and Vaticanus (B), yet it is no greater than that between $\mathfrak{P}^{45}$ and Washingtonianus (W). Of course, no one will claim that if we had extensive portions of $\mathfrak{P}^{29}$ or $\mathfrak{P}^{48}$, or of the other early manuscripts in this group, they would be virtually identical to Codex Bezae. This later manuscript, Codex Bezae, has a complex history of its own, and the text it contains has evolved over more time and perhaps through greater exigencies than did the text of Vaticanus, though it has been almost impossible to determine the nature and scope of those situations. Yet—and this is crucial—lines of connection *can be drawn* from the four or five early manuscripts to Codex Bezae, and a further "trajectory" can be traced into the tenth century in minuscule 1739 (Acts only) and to the thirteenth century with minuscules 614 and 383.

It is significant that all five of the early manuscripts placed in this category contain portions of Luke-Acts (**0171** also contains a portion of Matthew), and that three of them contain only portions of Acts ($\mathfrak{P}^{29}$, $\mathfrak{P}^{38}$, $\mathfrak{P}^{48}$). It is well known that the distinctive textual features of Codex Bezae are more prominent in Luke-Acts (and especially in Acts) than in Matthew, Mark, or John. Though accidental, it is nonetheless extraordinary that it is precisely the most noteworthy portions of the later representative, Codex Bezae, that—relatively speaking—are so numerously represented by very early manuscripts. Certainly that lends more credibility to the connection with Codex Bezae than would otherwise be the case and just as certainly it lends greater credibility to the identification of a "text-type" that includes Codex Bezae as a prominent member.

The preceding is simply a sketch of the constituent members of each textual group; many more could be added to the "A," "B," and "D" clusters (though not so easily to the "C" cluster [but see below]). However, our interest lies in the New Testament *papyri* and whether more of them can be fitted into the textual scheme outlined above. It would be premature—and presumptuous—for me to imply that independent judgments permit me to place the various remaining papyri into these groups, but many of them have been categorized by other individuals according to their textual complexions, and the following is at least suggestive of the result (though

---

represents a *process*, developing from a "proto D-Text" to a later, established "D-Text." In their book (p. 93), the Alands do refer to $\mathfrak{P}^{29}$, $\mathfrak{P}^{38}$, and $\mathfrak{P}^{48}$ as "precursors or branches of the D text." Yet, note their caution about using the prefix "pre-" for any textual group (p. 67).

new assessments and measurements undoubtedly are in order).[78] Most of the additional New Testament papyri, then, perhaps may be assigned to these textual groups as follows (the papyri are listed by century):

(1) *The "A" group:* $\mathfrak{P}^{84}$ (6th); $\mathfrak{P}^{68}$, $\mathfrak{P}^{74}$? (7th); $\mathfrak{P}^{42}$ (7th/8th).

(2) *The "B" group:* $\mathfrak{P}^{52}$ (2nd); $\mathfrak{P}^{46}$, $\mathfrak{P}^{64+67}$, $\mathfrak{P}^{66}$ (2nd/3rd); $\mathfrak{P}^{1}$, $\mathfrak{P}^{4}$, $\mathfrak{P}^{15}$, $\mathfrak{P}^{20}$, $\mathfrak{P}^{23}$, $\mathfrak{P}^{28}$, $\mathfrak{P}^{39}$, $\mathfrak{P}^{40}$, $\mathfrak{P}^{47}$, $\mathfrak{P}^{49}$, $\mathfrak{P}^{53}$, $\mathfrak{P}^{65}$, $\mathfrak{P}^{75}$, $\mathfrak{P}^{91}$, (3rd); $\mathfrak{P}^{13}$, $\mathfrak{P}^{16}$, $\mathfrak{P}^{72}$ [in Peter], $\mathfrak{P}^{92}$ (3rd/4th); $\mathfrak{P}^{10}$, $\mathfrak{P}^{62}$, $\mathfrak{P}^{71}$, $\mathfrak{P}^{86}$ (4th); $\mathfrak{P}^{50}$, $\mathfrak{P}^{57}$ (4th/5th); $\mathfrak{P}^{14}$ (5th); $\mathfrak{P}^{56}$ (5th/6th); $\mathfrak{P}^{33+58}$ (6th); $\mathfrak{P}^{3}$, $\mathfrak{P}^{43}$, $\mathfrak{P}^{44}$, $\mathfrak{P}^{55}$ (6th/7th); $\mathfrak{P}^{11}$, $\mathfrak{P}^{31}$, $\mathfrak{P}^{34}$ (7th); $\mathfrak{P}^{60}$, $\mathfrak{P}^{61}$? (7th/8th).

(3) *The "C" group:* $\mathfrak{P}^{45}$ (most of Mark). In addition, though fresh assessments must be made, the following papyri are identified as mixed, with elements of "B" and "D": $\mathfrak{P}^{27}$ (3rd); $\mathfrak{P}^{37}$? (3rd/4th); $\mathfrak{P}^{8}$, $\mathfrak{P}^{35}$ (4th); $\mathfrak{P}^{36}$ (6th).

(4) *The "D" group:* $\mathfrak{P}^{5}$, $\mathfrak{P}^{29}$, $\mathfrak{P}^{48}$, $\mathfrak{P}^{69}$? (3rd); $\mathfrak{P}^{37}$?, $\mathfrak{P}^{38}$, $\mathfrak{P}^{72}$ [Jude], **0171** (3rd/4th); $\mathfrak{P}^{25}$? (4th); $\mathfrak{P}^{19}$?, $\mathfrak{P}^{21}$? (4th/5th); $\mathfrak{P}^{41}$ (7th/8th).

Though the placement of each papyrus in these categories is subject to review and possible revision, this is a beginning. These lists take into account the papyri through number 76, with the addition of $\mathfrak{P}^{84}$, $\mathfrak{P}^{86}$, $\mathfrak{P}^{91}$, and $\mathfrak{P}^{92}$, for decisions on textual groupings are not readily available for the rest. Yet, sixty-one of these eighty papyri can be placed into the various textual groupings, or seventy-six percent of them. If their respective categorizations can be sustained, then seventy-six percent is a significant proportion. The textual complexion of the remaining ones will need to be clarified or initially determined (if possible). An obvious difficulty is that the procedure of classifying textual fragments really works only when there is a later comparative basis in larger bodies or surviving text that permits us to identify the kind or character of text that a particular papyrus represents. Small fragments that issue in no clear lines of connection to later materials are difficult to classify.

---

[78]I simply rely on Metzger, *Textual Commentary on the Greek New Testament*, xxix-xxx, and his earlier *Text of the New Testament*, 247-255, with modifications from other sources. I have consulted the original publications of the most recently available papyri and have adopted the editors' judgments when given.

Can this proposal on early textual groupings be buttressed in any other way? Certainly the quotations of church fathers from the same period are essential aspects of the data and should be utilized in the process of discriminating among early textual groups, and—though more complex and difficult—the early versions should be employed in the same way. The standard handbooks will indicate the textual groups that the various early fathers and versions support, but such a discussion would take us well beyond the reasonable scope of the present paper.

Conclusion

Did "text-types" exist in the first two centuries of Christianity? If so, how early and where? Though exact answers cannot be given to the latter questions, I have established reasonable grounds for concluding that three identifiable text-types were in existence around 200 CE or shortly thereafter: a "B" text-type, a "C" text-type, and a "D" text-type. I have also furnished reasons for justifying the existence of these text-types already in the second century. Though some may consider the "reasonable grounds" to be "speculative," I would rather call them "creative." Essentially, I have argued as follows:

(1) The dynamism of the early Christian environment in the first three centuries stimulated the movement of Christian writings (whether later to become "canonical" or "non-canonical") over wide areas of the Greco-Roman world and encouraged their use in various aspects of the liturgical and theological/intellectual life of the church.

(2) The dynamism of life in the Greco-Roman world—even in the outlying areas of Egypt (where most of the New Testament papyri were discovered)—permitted relatively easy travel and rather free transmission of letters and documents, so that the earliest New Testament papyri—though they have survived accidentally and randomly—are generally representative of the earliest New Testament texts used by the Christianity of the time in all parts of the Greco-Roman world. Incidentally, it is of more than passing interest that the New Testament papyri contribute virtually no new substantial variants, suggesting not only that virtually all of the New Testament variants are preserved somewhere in our extant manuscript tradition, but also that representatives of virtually all textual complexions have been preserved for us in the papyri.

(3) Several hints, found in the New Testament (and in other Christian) papyri themselves, suggest that standardization procedures were in

existence already in the late first or early second century for the transmission of Christian texts, such as the codex form, the *nomina sacra*
techniques, and the possible presence of scriptoria. These standardization
procedures permit us to claim that our very earliest New Testament
papyri had antecedents or ancestors as much as a century earlier than their
own time. This point is supported by the demonstration that the $\mathfrak{P}^{75}$-B
text had a common ancestor earlier than the third-century $\mathfrak{P}^{75}$ itself.

(4) By tracing lines of connection from the earliest papyri to later
manuscripts with similar textual complexions, the broad *spectrum* of the
early New Testament text can be viewed, revealing a range of differing
textual complexions, which—at their extremes—merge with or blend into
one another. To employ another model alluded to earlier, a number of
distinctive textual *trajectories* present themselves. This model has the
advantage of envisioning, in a chronological, developmental fashion,
extended series of related manuscripts in distinctive groups. Such trajectories not only begin with one or more papyri and extend forward for
several—and sometimes many—centuries, but they also extend backward
to the hypothetical antecedent manuscripts/texts that preceded the earliest
papyri. As we have observed, $\mathfrak{P}^{75}$ had an antecedent whose existence can
be established even though that manuscript itself is not extant, and the
same kind of text appears later in Codex Vaticanus. The result is that a
genuine trajectory can be drawn from a very early (though non-extant)
manuscript to $\mathfrak{P}^{75}$, and then to Codex Vaticanus, and on to later witnesses.
Moreover, since no canonical New Testament books were authored in
Egypt, the texts had to travel to Egypt; hence, manuscripts copied anew in
Egypt have trajectories reaching back to their antecedents in other parts of
the very early Christian world.

What is striking is that one or more of the earliest papyri can be
connected almost immediately to an early major uncial manuscript with a
similar textual complexion. The major, non-fragmentary uncials from the
fourth and fifth centuries are Sinaiticus (‫א‬), Vaticanus (B), Alexandrinus
(A), Ephraemi (C), Washingtonianus (W), and Bezae (D). Four of these
connect with papyri to form distinctive early textual groups: Vaticanus
and Sinaiticus for the "B" text-type; Washingtonianus for the "C" text-
type; and Bezae for the "D" text-type. Another uncial, Alexandrinus,
represents a later "A" text-type and, not surprisingly, connects with some
sixth and seventh century papyri; the remaining uncial, Ephraemi, is a
mixed, composite manuscript. If such lines of connection could not be
drawn, the claim for early "text-types" would be less credible, though by no
means discredited.

If all of the groups presented as neat a picture as the B-text trajectory described earlier, the trajectory model would be the most appropriate one, especially if the manuscripts representative of each text-type showed the requisite 70% agreement among themselves and also the required 10% difference in the percentage of agreements with the members of the adjacent text-types. Such a 10% gap can generally be shown when measuring manuscripts that have extensive portions of text (whether papyri, uncials, or minuscules), but such measurements are difficult and less significant when attempted with the fragmentary papyri. Therefore, unless measurements of the latter can be refined, it may be preferable to employ the "spectrum" model when describing the early text-types.

On the spectrum model, the primary colors (distinct text-types) can be seen immediately, namely, the B, C, and D text-types in the earliest period. As we look farther along in time, the A text-type presents itself as an identifiable hue on the textual spectrum. Many of the fragmentary papyri (as specified in the lists for the various textual groups above) will reveal the same strong colors that identify a text-type, but others will appear as shades of the brighter hues, and the early papyri will range broadly across the spectrum. Yet a spectrum is a spectrum: it has concentrations of primary and secondary colors, with gradations of merging and blending hues between them. This very well portrays the early textual situation, with three (or four) primary concentrations representing clearly identifiable early text-types and a spread of manuscripts between them.

(5) Therefore, (a) since clear concentrations of manuscripts with similar textual character existed in the earliest period of transmission accessible to us, and—to change the figure—since lines of connection can be drawn from the papyri to major manuscripts with recognizable textual complexions, and (b) since these concentrations or lines of trajectory identify clusters that in turn differentiate themselves sufficiently from other clusters, the claim that at least three distinct "text-types" existed in the dynamic Christianity of the second century can be made with considerable confidence.

Extra-Canonical Sayings of Jesus:
Marcion and Some "Non-received" Logia

Joël Delobel

Katholiek Universiteit van Leuven (Belgium)

At the 1981 session of the *Colloquium Biblicum Lovaniense*, I read a paper on "The Sayings of Jesus in the Textual Tradition."[1] That paper, which has been the starting point for further and more detailed research, and which also forms the background of this contribution, was introduced with the following comments:

> A whole series of the sayings of Jesus have not been taken into the critical text, either in the place where they are found in certain gospel manuscripts or elsewhere in the same gospel or in other gospels. A number of these readings have been called "extracanonical sayings" or "agrapha," but these names are perhaps not precise enough to be used in textual criticism. Indeed, "canonical" and "critical" do not always coïncide, and the canon has never been so fixed in detail as to determine for each verse which reading has to be considered as canonical. We therefore prefer the more neutral name "non-received logia" which exclusively refers to their text-critical situation in modern critical editions.

Before the discovery of the papyri, indirect evidence was the only access to the early text. But even since the publication of an impressive amount of papyrus material, our direct evidence from the earliest period is limited, fragmentary and accidental. Therefore, indirect information remains valuable. It is, however, delicate to evaluate, and there is always the temptation of wishful thinking, which turns vulnerable hypotheses into historical facts.

---

[1] "The Sayings of Jesus in the Textual Tradition. Variant Readings in the Greek Manuscripts of the Gospels," in *Logia. Les Paroles de Jésus. The Sayings of Jesus*, ed. Joël Delobel, BEThL, no. 49 (Leuven: University Press/Peeters, 1982), 431-457.

It is particularly attractive to identify Marcion as the earliest datable witness for certain readings, or even as their creator, but this identification is beset with thorny problems. Marcion's own Gospel text is not available as such, and its reconstruction from Tertullian, and to a lesser degree from Adamantius and Epiphanius, is fragmentary and hypothetical. Though Marcion's theological tendency is well-known, it is striking to see how a particular reading has been considered as "Marcionite" by one author, and "anti-Marcionite" by another. Both the addition and the omission of a particular passage have been attributed to Marcion. Therefore, unqualified reference to Marcion in a critical apparatus may be misleading if it leads the reader to the simple conclusion that Marcion is one of the witnesses, and thus that the reading is attested as early as the middle of the second century. Three examples may illustrate this problem.

Luke 6:5 (D), The Man who Worked on the Sabbath[2]

The most striking "non-received" saying is a passage particular to Codex D: "On the same day, seeing someone working on the Sabbath, he said to him: man, if you know what you are doing, you are blessed, but if you do not know, you are cursed and a transgressor of the law."

This remarkable short pericope with an intriguing saying of Jesus has led to different and even paradoxical explanations as to its origin and its situation at this point in Luke's gospel. The intervention of Marcion, especially, has been variously interpreted.

Harnack's View of Marcion's Role

According to Harnack,[3] Marcion knows the pericope at this place in Luke's gospel. The proof that in Marcion's Gospel, verse 5 ("The Son of

---

[2]The argument is part of a more comprehensive analysis in my essay: "Luke 6,5 in Codex Bezae: The Man Who Worked on Sabbath," in *À cause de l'Évangile: Études sur les Synoptiques et les Actes offertes an P. Jacques Dupont, O.S.B. à l'occasion de son 70e anniversaire*, LeDiv, no. 123 (Paris: Cerf, 1985).

[3]Cf. A. Harnack, *Marcion. Das Evangelium vom fremden Gott*, TU, no. 45 (Leipzig: Akademie-Verlag, 1921), 190* (in the critical apparatus). Harnack makes only a short remark: "Dieser vers (v.5) steht in D erst nach v.10; dort erst hatte ihn auch M.; denn Tert. zitiert ihn nach v.9: '*dominus sabbati*.' Epiphanius, *haer.*, Scholion 3, confirms that Luke 6:5: κύριός ἐστιν ὁ υἱὸς τοῦ ἀνθρώπου καὶ τοῦ σαββάτου, is certainly present in Marcion's text, but does not teach us anything about its place in Marcion's gospel. See also Harnack's *Neue Studien zu Marcion*, TU, no. 44.4 (Leipzig: J. C. Hinrichs, 1923), 36.

man is the Lord of the Sabbath") followed verse 9, is found, according to Harnack, in Tertullian's *adversus Marcionem*.[4]   Marcion would have omitted verse 5D because the pericope seems to stress the lasting—though reduced—validity of the Sabbath law, something which was unacceptable to Marcion. Because of this omission, the text has disappeared from the entire textual tradition except for D.

Vogels' View of Marcion's Role

According to H. Vogels too,[5] Marcion's Gospel placed Luke 6:5 after verse 9. In his opinion, this is made clear by Tertullian's reply. But, in contrast to Harnack, he thinks that Marcion himself is responsible for this transposition as well as for the introduction of verse 5D.

Tertullian's Witness

In our opinion, Tertullian's text does not permit any of these conclusions. The only evidence is that "Dominus Sabbati" is indeed mentioned in Tertullian, *adv. Marc.*, IV.12.11, after allusions to both Sabbath pericopes of Luke 6:1-11. But did not Tertullian himself make this "postponement"? The theme of v. 5, "The Son of man is Lord of the Sabbath," is clearly Tertullian's basic argument in the controversy with Marcion concerning Jesus' behaviour on the Sabbath. According to Tertullian, Jesus, as "Lord of the Sabbath," acts in line with the activity and the intention of the God-Creator and therefore he mentions "Dominus Sabbati" from the *beginning* of the discussion: "De sabbato quoque illud praetermitto, nec hanc quaestionem consistere potuisse, si non Dominum sabbati circumferret Christus" (IV.12.1). It is not surprising then to meet this

---

[4]Cf. *Tertulliani Opera. Pars I. Opera Catholica. Adversus Marcionem,* CChr.SL, no.1 (Turnhout: Brepols, 1954), 571 (IV.12.11). I have consulted the English translation in *Tertullian. Adversus Marcionem,* ed. E. Evans, OECT, 2 vol. (Oxford: Oxford University Press, 1972).

[5]H. Vogels, *Evangelium Palatinum,* NTA, no. 12.3 (Münster: Aschendorff, 1926), 97: "Ich möchte es als marcionitischen Einschub betrachten, wie wohl es sich anscheinend weder im Exemplar Tertullians, noch des Epiphanius gefunden hat, da die Gegner sonst schwerlich an dieser tendentiösen Erzählung stillschweigend vorübergegangen wären. Denn die gleiche Hand die dieses Sabbatarbeiterstück in Lk eingeschoben hat, hat offenbar auch den Vers 6,5 aus dem Gefüge herausgenommen und hinten 6,10 gestellt." This last remark, which we accept, does not necessarily imply that the "gleiche Hand" is Marcion's. Cf. the reaction by M.-J. Lagrange, *Critique textuelle,* 2 vols. (Paris: Gabalda, 1935), vol. 2: *La critique rationelle,* 66.

theme again *after* the reference to the sabbath pericopes in Luke 6. The two references to "Dominus Sabbati" form an *inclusio*. There is no need to suppose that Tertullian found this sequence in Marcion.

We may conclude that there is no sufficient ground to attribute the postponement of verse 5 after verse 9 to Marcion, and still less to make him responsible for the introduction of the "agraphon" at Luke 6:5.

Luke 11:2c, The Request for the Holy Spirit

In the Lukan text of the Lord's Prayer, a few witnesses include a request for the Holy Spirit. The origin of this passage has been discussed for over a century.[6] Once more, Marcion is at the heart of the discussion.

The evidence

The primary evidence for attributing the reading to Marcion comes from Tertullian, *adv. Marc.*, IV.26.3-4:

> 3) . . . Cui dicam "pater"? Ei, qui me omnino non fecit, a quo originem non traho, an ei, qui me faciendo et instruendo generavit? A quo spiritum sanctum postulem? 4) A quo nec mundialis spiritus praestatur an a quo fiunt etiam angeli spiritus, cuius et in primordio spiritus super aquas ferebatur? Eius regnum optabo venire, quem num-quam regem gloriae audivi, an in cuius manu etiam corda sunt regum? . . .[7]

For the Greek text of Luke 11:2c, instead of ἐλθέτω ἡ βασιλεία σου, a few witnesses have the following text:

MS 700 (11th cent.; British Museum MS Egerton 2610):
ἐλθέτω τὸ πνεῦμά σου τὸ ἅγιον καὶ καθαρίσατω ἡμᾶς

---

[6]See G. Schneider, "Die Bitte um das Kommen des Geistes im lukanischen Vaterunser (Lk 11,2 v.l.)," in *Studien zum Text und zur Ethik des Neuen Testaments. Festschrift zum 80. Geburtstag von Heinrich Greeven*, ed. W. Schrage, BZNW, no. 47 (Berlin/New York: Walter de Gruyter, 1986), 344-373.

[7]Cf. *adversus Marcionem* (see note 4, *supra*), 615. There is no evidence in Epiphanius concerning Marcion's text of Luke 11:2-4.

MS 162 (1153 AD; Rom. Barberini Gr. 449):
ἐλθέτω σου τὸ πνεῦμα τὸ ἅγιον καὶ καθαρίσατω ἡμᾶς

Gregory of Nyssa (d. 394), *De oratione dominica*, 3.737f. (PG 44, col. 1157C):
ἐλθέτω τὸ ἅγιον πνεῦμά σου ἐφ' ἡμᾶς καὶ καθαρίσατω ἡμᾶς

Maximus Confessor (d. 662), *Expositio orationis dominicae*, 1.350 (PG 90, col. 884B):[8]
ἐλθέτω σου τὸ πνεῦμα τὸ ἅγιον καὶ καθαρίσατω ἡμᾶς

The Holy Spirit in the Lord's Prayer according to Marcion

Harnack refers to Marcion as the earliest witness for our variant,[9] and on his authority several authors have taken over this hypothesis. However, this point of view is disputable.

As usual, Tertullian's reference to Marcion's text is not a literal quotation. Rather, he is discussing Marcion's heretical viewpoint, and in his argumentation alludes to various elements of Marcion's gospel.[10] According to Tertullian, the second petition ("Thy kingdom come") is not lacking in Marcion as in MS 700, but we find no trace of the first petition

---

[8]A facsimile of the page with this variant reading in the Lord's Prayer in MS 700 is in H. C. Hoskier, *A Full Account and Collation of the Greek Cursive Codex Evangelium 604* (London: Nutt, 1890). In the second of the three quotations of the text by Gregory of Nyssa, ἐφ' ἡμᾶς is left out. Maximus' possible dependence on Gregory is often supposed, cf. F. Hauck, *Das Evangelium des Lukas*, ThHK (Leipzig: Deichert, 1934), 149; B. M. Metzger, *A Textual Commentary on the Greek New Testament* (New York/London/Stuttgart: United Bible Societies, 1971), 155. Harnack and others also refer to *Acta Thomae*, c. 27: ἐλθὲ τὸ ἅγιον πνεῦμα καὶ καθάρισου τοὺς νεφροὺς αὐτῶν καὶ τὴν καρδίαν. However, it should be noted that, in its original context, this passage has no relation with the Lord's Prayer.

[9]Cf. A. Harnack, *Über einige Worte Jesu, die nicht in den kanonischen Evangelien stehen, nebst einem Anhang über die ursprüngliche Gestalt des Vaterunsers*, SPAW, no. 5 (Berlin: Reimer, 1904), 170-208; idem, "Der Ursprüngliche Text des Vater-Unsers und seine älteste Gestalt, in *Erforschtes und Erlebtes. Reden und Aufsätze*, ed. A. Harnack, SPAW, n.F., no. 4 (Gießen, 1923), 24-35; idem., *Marcion. Das Evangelium vom fremden Gott*, 2nd ed. (Leipzig: J. C. Hinrichs, 1924), 207*: "Da es nach Tert. sicher ist, daß bei M. die erst Bitte eine Bitte um den h. Geist war, wird sie so gelautet haben, wie wir sie durch Minusc. 700 al. 604, Cod. Vatic., olim Barb. IV, 31, Gregor v. Nyssa und aus Anspielungen kennen . . . ."

[10]It is not clear whether Tertullian is referring to his own text of the Lord's Prayer. Cf. A. Loisy, *L'évangile selon Luc* (Paris: Nourry, 1924), 315: "On dirait que le texte de Marcion est aussi bien celui de Tertullien"; also B. M. Metzger, *Textual Commentary*, 155. Contra: R. Freudenberger, "Zum Text der zweiten Vaterunserbitte," *NTS* 15 (1968-1969): 419-432.

"Hallowed be thy name." At the place where we would expect this petition, we read the question: "a quo spiritum sanctum postulem?" And Tertullian answers: "Him by whom not even mundane spirit is conveyed to me, or him who even makes his angels spirits and whose spirit at the beginning was borne upon the waters?" In other words, the God-Creator.

Before quoting Marcion among the witnesses for the logion in the form of MS 700, one should take into account the following data:

a. In Marcion, the first petition ("Hallowed be Thy name"), is absent, and apparently supplied by the reference to the spirit. In MS 700, it is the second petition ("Thy kingdom come") which is missing.

b. Though Tertullian is rendering each of the demands in a free formulation, adapted to his argumentation, the original verb is always maintained: "cuius regnum optabo *venire*; quis mihi *dabit* panem cottidianum; quis mihi delicta *dimittet*; quis non sinet nos *deduci* in temptationem." Is it probable then that the initial question: "a quo spiritum sanctum *postulem*?" is inspired by a petition with the verb *advenire* (ἐλθέτω)?

c. If we introduce the text of MS 700 into Marcion's gospel, both the first and second petitions in his text would start with the same verb ἐλθέτω. This is not impossible but it is surprising in view of the fact that all the other petitions have a different verb.[11]

d. One should not forget that Tertullian does not mention the second part of the logion καὶ καθαρίσατω ἡμᾶς at all. These words are too easily supplied by modern commentators without any trace in their source.[12]

---

[11]Cf. E. Lohmeyer, *Das Vater-unser*, 5th ed. (Göttingen: Vandenhoeck und Ruprecht, 1962), 186: "denn nun beginnen die beiden ersten Bitten auf fast unmögliche Weise mit einem 'es komme'." In Lohmeyers's opinion, this would have been the result of the insertion by Marcion of an existing text, which he cannot have created himself because of its Old Testament flavor (ibid., 186-187). Cf. A. Loisy, *Luc*, 316: "Les allusions de Tertullien suggéreraient plutôt: 'Soit ton esprit saint sur nous' etc." Cf. also W. Grundmann, *Das Evangelium nach Lukas*, ThHK, 3rd ed. (Berlin: Evangelische Verlagsanstalt, 1966), 232: "Die dem Vaterunser widersprechende Parallelität des zweimaligen 'es komme' bei Marcion verbietet diesen Text als ursprünglich anzusehen." According to F. Hauck, *Lukas*, 149, the double ἐλθέτω, which he accepts in Marcion, proves that the text is not original.

[12]Cf. I. H. Marshall, *The Gospel of Luke* (Grand Rapids: Eerdmans, 1978), 458; J. Jeremias, "The Lord's Prayer in Modern Research," *ET* 70 (1958-1959): 141-146, esp. 141.

If we may trust that Tertullian is really referring to Marcion's text (and not simply to his own copy of the gospel; see note 10, *supra*), we can safely conclude that a reference to the Holy Spirit was made in Marcion's text of the Lord's Prayer. But that does not prove a relationship between this reference and the form of the logion in Gregory of Nyssa and MS 700.[13] An interesting hypothesis to explain the variant with πνεῦμα ἅγιον in Marcion has been proposed recently. With ἁγιασθήτω τὸ ὄνομά σου, the theme of "holiness" was present,[14] and Marcion may have preferred the term πνεῦμα above the word ὄνομα which may have sounded too Jewish to Marcion.[15]

We conclude that an unqualified reference to Marcion in the critical apparatus at this point, suggesting that he had the same text as MS 700 and Gregory of Nyssa, is misleading.[16]

A recent defense of the presence of the full text (in the form of MS 700) has not convinced us; cf. J. Magne, "La réception de la variante 'Vienne ton Esprit Saint sur nous et qu'il nous purifie' (Lc 11,2) et l'origine des épiclèses, du baptême et du 'Notre Père'," in *EL* 102 (1988): 81-106. According to Magne, Tertullian makes his own choice within Marcion's text, in view of his polemic argumentation. So, he does not mention "hallowed be thy name," not because it was absent from Marcion's gospel, but because the reference to the "new" name of the Father could have been abused by the Marcionites to stress their distinction between the God of Jesus and the God-Creator. That the variant from MS 700 is only partially quoted by Tertullian, is because of the fact that the phrase "and cleanse us" is not useful for his argumentation. Though, in our opinion, such reasoning is not impossible, it seems to us that Magne's approach to the problem, based on a sort of *argumentum e silentio*, could lead to a very subjective reconstruction of Marcion's text.

[13]Cf. G. Schneider, "Die Bitte," 359.

[14]Cf. C. B. Amphoux, "La révision Marcionite du 'Notre Père' de Luc (11,2-4) et sa place dans l'histoire du texte," in *Recherches sur l'histoire de la Bible Latine*, ed. R. Gryson and P.-M. Bogaert, no. 19 (Louvain-la-Neuve, 1987), 110: "*Sanctum* est, en effet, un rappel possible de l'impératif de la première demande (lat. *sanctificetur*), surtout si l'on comprend *spiritum sanctum* comme une propositon infinitive dépendant du *postulem*: 'à qui demanderai-je (que ton) esprit (soit) saint?'"

[15]See e.g.: B. Weiss, *Die Evangelien des Markus und Lukas*, 9th ed. (Göttingen: Vandenhoeck und Ruprecht, 1901), 461, note: "von Markion an die Stelle der so stark alttestamentlich klingenden 1.Bitte gerückt . . . . " Cf. V. Rose, *Évangile selon saint Luc* (Paris, 1909), 113; J. M. S. Baljon, *Commentaar op het evangelie van Lukas* (Utrecht: Van Boekhoven, 1908), 270; M.-J. Lagrange, *Évangile selon Saint Luc*, 8th ed. (Paris: Gabalda, 1948), 323; H. von Baer, *Der Heilige Geist in den Lukasschriften*, BWANT, n.F., no. 3 (Stuttgart: Kohlhammer, 1926), 149-152. The reference to the "name" is indeed Jewish. On the other hand, it would not be correct to consider "spirit" as exclusively Christian and non-Jewish (cf. e.g. Joel 3:1ff!).

[16]Cf. Souter, Tasker, Vogels, Merk, Kilpatrick (*haec vel similia*). My argument in this section is part of a broader critical overview of the textual problems in the Lord's

Luke 9:54-56, The Reaction of the Disciples against the Samaritans

The longer text of Luke 9:54-56 provides three additions, two of which are sayings of Jesus. To clarify the subsequent discussion, we will indicate them as readings A, B, and C.

Reading A (at the end of 9:54 an impressive range of MSS add):
ὡς καὶ Ἠλίας ἐποίησεν

Reading B (at the end of 9:55, several MSS add, with variations):
καὶ εἶπεν· οὐκ οἴδατε (π)οίου πνεύματός ἐστε ὑμεῖς

Reading C (at the beginning of 9:56, we read the addition):
ὁ γὰρ υἱὸς τοῦ ἀνθρώπου οὐκ ἦλθεν ψυχὰς ἀνθπώπων ἀπολέσαι ἀλλὰ σῶσαι

Marcion: The Earliest Witness?

In several critical editions of the New Testament, Marcion is listed among the witnesses for the first two additions, or even for all three of them.[17] Several commentators present Marcion among the witnesses without mentioning any problem. It has become almost "classical" to refer to the opposite points of view of J. R. Harris and T. Zahn concerning Marcion's role at this point. According to Harris,[18] these passages are probably Marcionite. This is purely a suggestion, not a conclusion of long and detailed research. Yet Lagrange[19] and Loisy,[20] among others, agree

---

Prayer in Matthew and Luke in my essay, "The Lord's Prayer in the Textual Tradition. A Critique of Recent Theories and Their View on Marcion's Role," in the *The New Testament in Early Christianity*, ed. J.-M. Sevrin, BEThL, no. 86 (Leuven: Peeters, 1988), 243-309.

[17]For readings A/B, see N-A[26]; for readings A/B/C, see: Tasker ("perhaps"), Kilpatrick, UBS[3]. The correct reference to Epiphanius in N-A[26] (for reading B) has nothing to do with Marcion. The allusion to Luke 9:55 does not appear in the *haer.*, but in the *Ancor.* 26, 7; cf. *Epiphanius, Bd 1, Ancoratus und Panarion Haer. 1-33*, ed. K. Holl, GCS, no. 25 (Leipzig: J.C. Hinrichs, 1915), 35.

[18]J. R. Harris, *Codex Bezae. A Study of the So-Called Western Text of the New Testament*, TaS, no. 2.1, (Cambridge: Cambridge University Press, 1891), 233.

[19]M.-J. Lagrange, *Luc*, 286.

[20]A. Loisy, *Luc*, 287.

with this explanation, and Harnack defends the same opinion.[21] Indeed, when one takes all three readings together, they can be understood as a direct criticism of Elijah, and such a critical approach toward an Old Testament prophet certainly suited Marcion's ideas. In so far, one can suppose a purely Marcionite creation. Yet T. Zahn[22] does not agree. In his view, the longer text is the original one. It is obvious that Marcion had good theological motives to preserve it, but he did not create it himself, because such an extensive polemical addition is not usual in Marcion, and, moreover, it would have been explicitly rejected by his detractors. That the longer text, or part of it, has been conserved by many witnesses, also proves its originality for Zahn. One attempt to avoid possible abuse in an anti-Jewish polemical way may have been to retain only the first element (A), or only the last two elements (B/C) in the text. It is the combination of these three readings which gives to the longer text its sharpest polemical tendency.[23]

By referring to Marcion's influence, both Harris and Zahn greatly influenced the subsequent "established" opinion which considers Marcion as a witness to the longer text, as he is supposed to be responsible for its introduction or at least its preservation. However, Zahn has investigated the evidence in much detail in order to prove that Marcion did indeed know the longer text. It is worthwhile to look at the evidence and at Zahn's interpretation.

---

[21]Cf. A. Harnack, *Marcion*, 204*. He is doubtful about the presence of reading C because of lack of evidence, but is convinced of its Marcionite character: "...angesichts der überwältigenden Zahl von Zeugen gegen den Vers, kann er nicht ursprünglich sein. Wer aber sollte ihn hinzugefügt haben, wenn nicht Marcion?" Cf. 247*-248*.

[22]T. Zahn, *Das Evangelium des Lucas*, KNT, 4th ed. (Leipzig: Deichert, 1920), 399-403, 764-767. Cf. more recently: J. M. Ross, "The Rejected Words in Luke 9,54-56," *ET* 84 (1972-1973): 85-88. His reaction against the Marcionite hypothesis (for readings B and C): "The shorter form would have been clear enough for Marcion's purposes without embellishment. The other Marcionite alterations alter the substance of the text, whereas this merely brings out the existing point of the story."

[23]The suggestion has already been made by F. Blass, *Philology of the Gospels* (London: MacMillan, 1898), 94: "Then there is a difference of spirit between the Old and the New Testament, and Marcionite heresy, maintaining a different God for the former, might be justified from these verses. In order to prevent such dangers, it seemed to some orthodox man better to strike out that part of the narrative which might give offense."

The Evidence

The primary source for referring the longer text to Marcion is found in Tertullian, *adv. Marc.,* IV.23.8-9:

> 8) (Repraesentat creator ignium plagam Helia postulante in illo pseudopropheta). Agnosco iudicis severitatem, e contrario Christi lenitatem increpantis eandem animadversionem destinantes discipulos super illum viculum Samaritarum: agnoscat et haereticus ab eodem severissimo iudice promitti hanc Christi lenitatem: non contendet, inquit, nec clamabit nec vox eius in platea audietur: harundinem quassatam non comminuet et linum fumigans non extinguet. 9) Talis utique multo magis homines non erat crematurus. Nam et tunc ad Heliam: non in igni, inquit, dominus, sed in spiritu miti.[24]

The Interpretation of the Evidence by Zahn

Reading A: The presence of this element in Marcion's text is proved by Tertullian's reference to "Helia postulante" in a typically Marcionite antithesis between the severity of the Judge and the "lenitas" of Christ.

Reading B: Here Zahn refers to Tertullian's text in nr. 9: "in spiritu miti". This "translation" of 1 Kings 19:12 ($\phi\omega\nu\grave{\eta}$ $\alpha\check{\upsilon}\rho\alpha\varsigma$ $\lambda\epsilon\pi\tau\hat{\eta}\varsigma$) is so free that it can only be explained by the influence of reading B in Marcion.

---

[24]English translation by E. Evans:

> The Creator, at Elijah's demand, brings down a plague of fire upon that false prophet. I take note of a judge's sterness: and on the contrary of Christ's gentleness when reproving the disciples as they call for the same punishment upon that village of the Samaritans. Let the heretic also take note that this gentleness of Christ is promised by that same stern Judge: *He shall not strive,* it says, *nor shall his voice be heard in the street: a bruised reed shall not break, and smoking flax shall not quench.* Such a one was even less likely to burn men up. For even in reference to Elijah in his days, it says, *The Lord was not in the fire but in a gentle spirit* (Tertullian, *Adversus Marcionem,* 2:389).

T. Zahn proposes the following change in the first (restored) sentence of Tertullian's text: "(Repraesentat creator ignium plagam Helia postulante. In illo pseudopropheta) agnosco iudicis severitatem . . . ." He comments: "Die herkömmliche . . . durch Interpunktion ausgedruckte Verbindung der Worte *in illo pseudopropheta* bekennne ich schlechterdings nicht zu verstehen. Es müßte doch wenigstens das *in* vor *illo pseudopropheta* gestrichen werden, um letztere Worte als eine nachhinkende Apposition zu *Helia* verstehen zu können" (T. Zahn, *Lucas,* 765).

Reading C: From Tertullian, *De Carne Christi*, 12: "veni, inquit, animam salvam facere," Zahn concludes that Tertullian had reading C in his text (because other parallels are less convincing as a source of inspiration: Luke 19:10; Matt 18:[11]; John 3:17; 12:47). Zahn seems to conclude that there is no reason why Marcion would not have known the same text.

Critical Remarks

The whole construction is ingenious, but, after all, surprisingly weak. None of the readings is quoted as such in *adversus Marcionem*, not even in a partially recognizable way. One has to infer their presence in Marcion's text from mere allusions in Tertullian. And this evidence is extremely limited, especially for readings B and C.

Reading A: This reading clearly has the most chance of having belonged to Marcion's text. Yet, even this can be disputed! Indeed, as Zahn himself indicates, Marcion, in his comment on an earlier pericope in the same context (Luke 9:46-48), makes the antithesis between Christ (who takes a child as an example) and Elisha (who cursed the children in the name of the Lord, cf. 2 Kings 2:23-24), without any direct reference to Elisha in the NT text itself.[25] So, it cannot be excluded that the motive of fire coming down from heaven (cf. 2 Kings 1:10, 12) inspired him (as it may have inspired any scribe[26]) to mention Elijah, even if reading A was not in the text.

Reading B: Tertullian's expression "in spiritu miti" is not a very strong argument to prove that Marcion knew reading B. The only correspondence is "spiritus," indeed a rather unusual but not impossible word for "wind" (cf. "spiritus Boreae"). Its presence in the quotation from 1 Kings 19:12 in Tertullian does not prove that he found this in Marcion. Moreover, "mitis" is not only absent from reading B, but perhaps not even

---

[25]*Adv. Marc.*, IV.23.4: "sed (ecce Christus diligit parvulos, tales docens esse debere qui semper maiores velint esse, creator autem mursos pueris inmisit, ulciscens Heliseum propheten convicia ab eis passum)." Tertullian calls it "satis impudens antithesis."

[26]J. Mill supposed that Tertullian's text may itself be the origin of the reading in later MSS. Cf. J. Mill, *Novum Testamentum Graecum* (Rotterdam: Fritsch and Böhm, 1710), 44: "Caeterum a Tertulliano lecta fuisse haec, quod nos olim in Notis nostris affirmavimus, non ita liquidum. Illud magis verisimile est, exemplum Eliae, ab ipso (lib. *adversus Marcionem*, c. 23) aliisque notatum ad hunc locum occasionem dedisse huic interpolationi."

alluded to at all: indeed, the sentence is ambiguous,[27] because it may mean: "don't you realize of which (bad) spirit you are (by suggesting to ask for the fire)" or: "don't you know to which (good, holy) spirit you (actually) belong."

Reading C: In our opinion, there is really no way to prove that this reading belonged to Marcion's text. One should not overlook the fact that the quotation in Tertullian is not in *adversus Marcionem,* but in *De Carne Christi,* which does not teach us anything about Marcion's gospel.

As a result, we do not see sufficient evidence to claim Marcion as the earliest witness for the longer text of Luke 9:54-56. Again, a simple, unqualified reference to Marcion in the critical apparatus is disputable.

Conclusion

The attempt at reconstructing Marcion's text of the Gospel and at determining his influence on the textual tradition has been a major scientific performance. It is rather regrettable that most often very little of the intelligent remarks made by early twentieth-century scholars like Zahn and Harnack is found in recent commentaries. This is especially the case because some of their *hypothetical constructions* are briefly taken over without discussion or justification, and their summarizing statements are presented as *straight facts.*

Yet, as we have seen, their conclusions have often been based on limited evidence and ingenious but vulnerable constructions. As such their results deserve our attention and esteem, but not a new status as facts, which are not based on new evidence, but only on a lack of memory concerning the premises.

Our general conclusion would not be that, in the cases we have discussed, Marcion should disappear from the critical apparatus or from the commentaries, but that his name should not be mentioned without some qualifier recalling the problems related to his testimony.

---

[27]Cf. F. Godet, *Commentaire sur l'évangile de saint Luc,* 3rd ed., 2 vols. (Paris, 1888-1889), ad loc.

The Lost Old Syriac at Luke 1:35
and the Earliest Syriac Terms for the Incarnation

Sebastian P. Brock

Oriental Institute, University of Oxford (England)

This paper is concerned with the early Syriac renderings of the verb ἐπισκιάζειν in the phrase: πνεῦμα ἅγιον ἐπελεύσεται ἐπὶ σὲ καὶ δύναμις ὑψίστου ἐπισκιάσει σοι, found in Luke 1:35. This is a passage for which neither of the two Old Syriac manuscripts (Syr$^{sin.cur}$) is available. Evidence for the other Syriac versions is as follows:

> Diatessaron[1] = Peshitta: *rūḥā d-qudšā tītē w-ḥayleh d-ʿellāyā*
> *naggen layk(y)*
> Philoxenian[2] = Harklean: *rūḥā qaddišā nītē ʿlayk(y) w-ḥayleh*
> *da-mraymā naggen ʿlayk(y)*

---

[1]Attested in Syriac by a quotation in Ephrem's *Commentary on the Diatessaron*, 1.25 (*Saint Éphrem, Commentaire de l'Évangile concordant, texte syriaque*, ed. L. Leloir, CBM, no. 8 [Dublin, 1963]); Ephrem uses *aggen* a further time in this context at 2.5 (a section whose Syriac original has recently been recovered and published by L. Leloir, "Le Commentaire d'Éphrem sur le Diatessaron. Quarante et un folios retrouvés," *RB* 94 [1987]: 481-518). At *Comm. Diat.* 1.25, Ephrem paraphrases the biblical text with the words: *gmurtā...ʿemrat b-marbʿā*, "the Coal of Fire (Isaiah 6:6)...dwelt in the womb;" for which one might compare the early fifth-century Anonymous of Jerusalem who comments on Luke 1:35: τὸ δὲ "ἐπισκιάσει σοι" παρίστησιν, ὅτι εἰ καὶ ἐπὶ σὲ ἐπελεύσεται πνεῦμα ἅγιον καὶ ἐνοικήσει ἐν σοὶ ἡ τοῦ ὑψίστου δύναμις (see J. Reuss, *Lukas-Kommentare aus der griechischen Kirche*, TU, no. 130 [1984], 34).

The Arabic translation of the Diatessaron reads *taḥillu*; it appears that *ḥalla* is the standard rendering in Christian Arabic for *aggen* (thus, for example, it occurs in the early Arabic version of Acts, made from the Peshitta, at 10:44 and 11:15, rendering *aggnat* [ed. M. Gibson, *SS*, no. 7 (1899)]); accordingly, S. Pines' recent claim that *ḥalla* in the Arabic Diatessaron at Luke 1:35 represents a different Syriac verb (perhaps *nḥet*, "descend") is not justified: see his article "Gospel Quotations and Cognate Topics in ʿAbd al-Jabbār's *Tathbīt* in relation to Early Christian and Judaeo-Christian Readings and Traditions," *JSAI* 9 (1987): 195-278, esp. 206-208. The Persian Diatessaron (*ḥūlul kunad*) is clearly influenced by awareness of this Arabic usage. I have found no traces of any correspondent to the Syriac Diatessaron's *naggen* in the western Diatesaronic witnesses.

[2]For the Philoxenian text of this passage see G. Zuntz, *The Ancestry of the Harklean New Testament*, BASP, no. 7 [n.l., 1945]), 42, 71. The form of the Philoxenian as given

Before turning to the rendering of the Greek verb ἐπισκιάζειν it is worth drawing attention to a few other points in passing:

(1) The Holy Spirit is still treated grammatically as feminine in the Peshitta;[3] a shift to masculine, and a substitution of the adjective *qaddīšā*, known from the Harklean, can now be shown to go back to the Philoxenian.[4]

(2) The phrase (ἐπελεύσεται) ἐπὶ σέ, "upon you," in the first half is absent from both Diatessaron and Peshitta.

(3) The alteration of *ᶜellāyā* to *mraymā* in the Harklean can now also be shown to go back to the Philoxenian.

Returning to our main concern, we can see that the Syriac Diatessaron, Peshitta, Philoxenian and Harklean all represent ἐπισκιάσει σοι by *naggen ᶜalayk(y)*, using the verb *aggen* (afᶜel from the root *gnn*), which I shall leave untranslated, since no single English term is satisfactory.[5] The verb is of especial interest since (1) it has a background in Jewish Aramaic (Targumim), where it is employed in the context of salvific and protective

above can now be confirmed from quotations in works published subsequently, notably in *Philoxène de Mabbog. Commentaire du Prologue johannique* (MS Br. Mus. Add. 14 534), ed. A. de Halleux, CSCO, no. 381 (Louvain: Peeters, 1977), 41, line 2; 211, line 26; etc. For the relationship of the Philoxenian to the Harklean, see my essay "The Resolution of the Philoxenian/Harclean Problem," in *New Testament Textual Criticism: its Significance for Exegesis. Essays in Honour of Bruce M. Metzger*, ed. Eldon J. Epp and Gordon D. Fee (Oxford: Oxford University Press, 1981), 325-343. It should be noted that the Christian Palestinian Aramaic also uses *aggen* here.

[3]Even though in some other passages a reviser has altered the gender to masculine: see provisionally my essay "The Holy Spirit as Feminine in Early Syriac Literature," in *Women, Theology and the Christian Tradition*, ed. J. Soskice (forthcoming). The verb is sometimes tacitly altered to a masculine form (*nite*) in quotations by Babai (d. 628); see *Babai Magni. Liber de unione*, ed. A. Vaschalde, CSCO, no. 79 (Louvain: Peeters, 1915), 27, line 28; 39, line 19; 92, line 9. In the Arabic translation of the Diatessaron, the feminine form of the verb (preserved in MS A) is clearly original, despite its rejection by both Ciasca and Marmardji in their editions: see T. Baarda, "The Author of the Arabic Diatessaron," in *Miscellanea Neotestamentica*, ed. T. Baarda, A. F. J. Klijn, and W. C. van Unnik, NT.S, no. 47 (Leiden: Brill, 1978), 1:67-103, esp. 94.

[4]See note 2; the masculine is regular in the *Commentaire du Prologue johannique*.

[5]F. C. Burkitt translated the verb at John 1:14 as "sojourned among us": *Evangelion da-Mepharreshe* (Cambridge: Cambridge University Press, 1904), 1:423 (along with the alternative: "or 'cast its influence in us,'" cf. Acts v 15"); cf. 2:307. Baarda renders "dwelled among us" (for reference, see note 8, *infra*). The translation of the Peshitta New Testament by J. Murdoch (1896) uses "overshadow" in Luke and "tabernacle" in John, clearly reflecting the Greek, not the Syriac; G. M. Lamsa has "rest upon" and "dwelt among."

action by God;[6] and (2) it was evidently inherited from Jewish Aramaic by the translators of the Peshitta Old Testament and of the Syriac New Testament versions as a technical term denoting immanent divine action; thus in the Gospels *aggnat/aggen ban* translates ἐσκήνωσεν ἐν ἡμῖν at John 1:14 in all the Syriac versions[7] (Sinaiticus, however, is lost here):

Diatessaron[8] = Old Syriac (Syr^cur): *mellṭā pagrā hwāt w-aggnat ban*
Peshitta = Philoxenian = Harklean: *mellṭā besrā hwā w-aggen ban*

Elsewhere, too, in the Peshitta New Testament we encounter *aggen* for a variety of Greek verbs, with either the Spirit or the Word as subject.

What did the Old Syriac read at Luke 1:35? This is not just a matter for idle speculation, for the search for an answer will involve us in some important methodological problems concerning evaluation of quotations and allusions, and at the same time it will shed light on the interaction between the Biblical text and exegetical and liturgical traditions.

Early Quotations and Allusions

Of the four texts quoting Luke 1:35 which are adduced by Leloir in his *L'Évangile d'Éphrem*,[9] only #433 is from a work which is certainly by Ephrem (*Sermo de Domino*, 2), and the quotation conforms exactly to the Diatessaron (= Peshitta) form. There are two further passages from the

---

[6]See my "An Early Interpretation of *pāsaḥ*: *aggen* in the Palestinian Targum," in *Interpreting the Hebrew Bible: Essays in Honour of E. I. J. Rosenthal*, ed. J. A. Emerton and S. C. Reif (Cambridge: Cambridge University Press, 1982), 27-34.

[7]The Christian Palestinian Aramaic version, however, uses ʿmar, "dwell" (for this, see also note 21, *infra*).

[8]The Syriac Diatessaron is quoted explicitly by Ephrem in his *Commentary on the Diatessaron* 1.8. Aphrahat also supports *aggnat ban*; cf. T. Baarda, *The Gospel Quotations of Aphrahat the Persian Sage, I. Aphrahat's Text of the Fourth Gospel* (Meppel: Krips, 1975), 64-66.

[9]L. Leloir, *L'Évangile d'Éphrem d'après les œuvres éditées*, CSCO, no. 180 (Louvain: Peeters, 1958), 67-68, #422-#425. The same applies to I. Ortiz de Urbina, *Biblia Polyglotta Matritensia VI: Vetus Evangelium Syrorum et inde excerptum Diatessaron Tatiani* (Matriti, 1967), 10, #95-#99.

genuine hymns which appear to be allusions to Luke 1:35, since "the Power" is the subject of the verb and Mary the indirect object; in both cases, however, the verb used is not *aggen*, but *šrā*, "reside (temporarily)":

> *H. de Nativitate* 4:174:
> > *kad hū ger ḥaylā*   *šrā (h)wā b-karsā*
> > *hūyū sāʾer (h)wā*   *ʿūlē b-karsā*
> > When the Power resided in the womb
> > that same Power was fashioning babes in the womb.
>
> *H. de Nativitate* 21:6:
> > *šrā b-ʿubbā zʿūrā*   *ḥaylā dal-kull mdaddar*
> > In a small womb there resided the Power which guides all.

Ephrem, in common with much of later Syriac tradition (and with several earlier Greek writers) differentiates the Power from the Holy Spirit, identifying the Power as the Word.[10] Now *šrā b-* is Ephrem's standard term for the activity of the Word in the womb of Mary,[11] whereas his use of *aggen ʿal* is confined to explicit citations of Luke 1:35 in the *Commentary on the Diatessaron* and the *Memra on our Lord* (*Sermo de Domino*).

If one turns to later liturgical poetry (largely undatable, but much of it is likely to belong to the fifth/sixth centuries), we again find that *šrā b-* is the verb most commonly used in this context, whereas *aggen* is very much rarer. This can be seen very clearly, for example, in the case of the anonymous *Memra on the Nativity* in the sixth-century manuscript British Library Add. 17 181, for there *šrā b-* occurs twelve times, but *aggen* only once.[12] We encounter a similar phenomenon in the famous poets Narsai (d. ca. 500) and Jacob of Serugh (d. 521), for with them *šrā b-* appears

---

[10]See R. Cantalamessa, "La primitiva esegesi cristologica di Romani 1, 34 e Luca 1, 35," *RSLR* 2 (1966): 69-80; J. de Aldama, *Maria en la Patristica de los Siglos I y II* (Madrid, 1970), 140-166. For Ephrem see the *memra* on the Prologue of John, in *Sancti Ephraem Syri, Hymni et Sermones*, ed. T. Lamy, 4 vols. (Mechliniae, 1886), 2, col. 515 (this turns out to be *H. de Ecclesia* 35:18) and *Sermo de Domino Nostro* §2. In later Syriac exegesis most West Syrian writers identify the Power as the Word, while East Syrian writers often equate the Power with the Spirit.

[11]E.g. *Sermo de Domino nostro* 1; *H. de Nativitate* 3:20, 4:130, 12:9.

[12]For *šrā b-*, see fol. 37a2, 39a1, 46a2, 55a2, 65b1, 66b2, 72a1, 72b1, 74a1, 78a1, 81b1; for *aggen*, see fol. 55b2.

to be the standard terminology, while *aggen* occurs only rarely.[13] In the later liturgical collections, as represented by the West Syrian *Fenqitho* and the East Syrian *Ḥudra*, we can again readily observe that *šrā b-* is vastly more common than *aggen*.[14]

Nor is this phenomenon confined to poetry. Thus Philoxenus, for example, after quoting Luke 1:35, comments: "Thus the Word resided in the Virgin (*šrā ba-btultā*) and received his conception from her, and not in the human person who was taken from the Virgin."[15]

Furthermore, *šrā b-* is often found in combination with certain other verbs, notably *nḥet*, "come down" (so already in Ephrem, *Carmina Nisibena* 46:1, *H. de Resurrectione* 4:10, and very common in later liturgical poetry),[16] and *ʿal*, "enter" (so already Ephrem, *Hymni de Virginitate* 25:8).[17]

---

[13]E.g. (for *šrā b-*) Narsai, *Homily on the Nativity* (ed. McLeod, PO, no. 40, fasc. 1), lines 81, 92; Jacob of Serugh, *Homily on the Virgin* (ed. Bedjan, in his *Sancti Martyrii qui et Sahdona quae supersunt omnia*, [Paris/Leipzig, 1902]), 615, 616, 620, 621, 624, 629, 631, 636, 638. It is noticeable that in this homily Jacob only uses *aggen* (always with *b-*!) in explicit allusions to Luke 1:35; of particular interest is the following statement from page 631: "First the Spirit [came], and then the Power resided (*šrā*) in the pure woman, / just as was told her 'The Spirit shall come and the power *naggen*.' / The Power of the Most High is the Child from the Most High / who *aggen* in her in order to come to bodily birth."

[14]A glance at the pages covering *Subbārā* (Annunciation, corresponding to Western Advent) and the Nativity in *Fenqitho II* and *Ḥudra I* will quickly confirm this. I use the Mosul edition of the *Fenqitho*, 7 vols. (Mosul, 1886-96) and the Trichur edition of the *Ḥudra*, 3 vols. (Trichur, 1960-1962).

[15]*Philoxeni Mabbugensis tractatus tres de Trinitate et incarnatione*, ed. A. Vaschalde, CSCO, no. 9 (Louvain: Peeters, 1915), 58; cf. 100. Philoxenus is polemicizing against what he sees as the Nestorian understanding of Luke 1:35.

[16]E.g. *H. de Instauratione Ecclesiae* ([wrongly attributed to Ephrem] ed. Lamy), 3, col. 973; *H. de Epiphania* (in *Des Heligen Ephraem des Syrers Hymnen de Nativitate [Epiphania]*, ed. E. Beck, CSCO 186 (Louvain: Peeters, 1958]), 8:1; *Memra III on Nativity* (MS Br. Mus. Add. 17 181), fol. 55a2; *Memra VIII* (ibid.), fol. 72a1; Jacob of Serugh, *Homiliae II* (ed. Bedjan), 659; *Soghitha on Mary and the Angel* in *Sogyāthā mgabbyāthā*, (ed. Brock [Glane, 1982]), 27, stanza 49. In the *Ḥudra*, e.g. 1:129 = 159; the combination of verbs is extremely common in *Fenqitho II*: a *madrasha* on page 90b rephrases Luke 1:35 as follows: "The Holy Spirit is coming to you and sanctifying your womb, and the Power of the Most High is descending and residing in you (*w-nāḥet šāre bek(y) ḥayleh d-ʿellāyā*)."

[17]This is often found in conjunction with the idea of the Word entering Mary through her ear (a typological reversal of Eve's disobedience); thus always in the Syriac *Acts of John* (ed. W. Wright, *Apocryphal Acts of the Apostles* [London, 1871; reprint, Amsterdam: Philo, 1968]), 8, 16, 29; *Memra VI on the Nativity* (MS Br. Mus. Add. 17, 181), fol. 65b1; *Nachträge zu Ephrem* (ed. E. Beck, CSCO, no. 363 [Louvain: Peeters, 1975]), 37,

We can also observe that in the places where *aggen* does occur in the context of the incarnation, then very often the preposition *b-*, "in," has replaced *ᶜal*, "upon"; this feature is also common in prose writers (as well as poets) from the time of Philoxenus (d. 523) onwards.[18] Again, we sometimes find *šrā* used in conjunction with *aggen*,[19] while in the *Fenqitho*, or Syrian Orthodox festal hymnary, *šrā* can replace *aggen*[20] in clear adaptations of Luke 1:35; thus *Fenqitho* II, 173b: "The Holy Spirit shall come and the Power of the Most High shall reside within (*nešrē bgaw*) your womb."

If we turn to John 1:14, we will discover a similar situation, for there are two passages in genuine works by Ephrem where he is probably alluding to John 1:14, but used the verb *šrā*, not *aggen* (it will be recalled that all Syriac versions attest *aggen ban* here [only Sinaiticus is missing]):

> *H. de Resurrectione* 1:7:
> *brīk da-šrā ban*
> Blessed is he who resided in us.[21]

---

lines 23-24; *Soghitha I*, (ed. Beck, *supra*, note 16), stanzas 31, 49; Jacob of Serugh, (ed. Bedjan, *infra*, note 13), 616, 739; *Fenqitho II*, 124a, 160b.

[18]E.g. Narsai, *Homily on the Nativity* (ed. McLeod, *supra*, note 13), line 416; Jacob of Serugh, *Homilies* (ed. Bedjan, *supra*, note 13), 632-634; Isaac of Antioch (ed. Bedjan, *supra*, note 13), 796; *Philoxène de Mabbog. Commentaire du Prologue johannique* (ed. Halleux, *supra*, note 2), 196-197, 212, 236; *Philoxeni Mabbugensis tractatus tres de Trinitate et incarnatione* (ed. A. Vaschalde, CSCO, no. 9 [Louvain: Peeters, 1915]), 62, 90, 181, 195; *Dionysius bar Salibi, Commentarii in Evangelia* (ed. I. Sedláček and I.-B. Chabot, CSCO, no. 15 [Louvain: Peeters, 1906]), I.1:9, 77; (ibid, CSCO, no. 85 [Louvain: Peeters, 1922]), I.2:237, 246. It also occurs in the interpolated Syriac version of Proclus' *Tomus ad Armenios*, preserved in Ps. Zacharias Rhetor; see *Historia ecclesiastica Zachariae Rhetori vulgo adscripta* (ed. E. W. Brooks, CSCO, no. 83 [Louvain: Peeters, 1919]), I.1:138: *ḥayleh d-ᶜellāyā d-aggen ba-btultā* (there is no equivalent in the Greek, PG 65, col. 868C = *Acta Conciliorum Oecumenicorum* IV.2, p. 193); for this version of Proclus see L. van Rompay, "'Proclus' of Constantinople's 'Tomus ad Armenios' in the Post-Chalcedonian Tradition," in *After Chalcedon: Studies in Theology and Church History offered to A. van Roey*, ed. C. Laga, J. A. Munitiz, and L. van Rompay, OLoP, no. 18 (Louvain, 1985), 425-449, esp. 445-449.

[19]E.g. Jacob of Serugh, *Homilies* (ed. Bedjan, *supra*, note 13), 712; Babai, *liber de unione* (ed. Vaschalde, *supra*, note 3), 256; *Fenqitho II*, 91a, 95b, 126a.

[20]It can also replace, "shall come"; e.g. *Fenqitho II*, pp. 88b, 93a, 96b = 114a, 142a. In this context one might note that in the medieval Arabic revision of the Gospel text in Arabic *yaḥillu* (originally corresponding to *naggen*) replaces "shall come," since the Greek ἐπισκιάσει is translated literally "shall overshadow."

[21]This is the passage which Burkitt derived from Lamy's edition, commenting: "It is obvious that this (sc. verse) is a reference to John i 14 and 18;" see his *S. Ephraim's*

H. *de Ecclesia* 15:2:

    brīk (h)ū d-arken rawmeh wa-šrā ban

    Blessed is he who inclined his height and resided in us.

Implications and Problems

These phenomena raise some serious methodological problems. Before turning to these, however, it should be observed that at least we are readily provided with the explanation for the shift from *aggen ʿal-,* to *aggen b-,* in allusions to Luke 1:35; this is due to the influence of two separate factors: (1) the parallel with John 1:14, brought about in Syriac both by the use of the same verb in the two passages, and by the frequent identification of the Power of Luke 1:35 as the Word, thus giving the same subject to both passages; and (2) the extremely common use of *šrā b-* in identical contexts.

What are we to make of *šrā b-*? Is it a genuine reading of a Syriac biblical text at Luke 1:35? Does it represent the lost Old Syriac there? And if so, what about John 1:14, where at least the Curetonian, with *aggen,* is preserved?

In considering these questions it is important at the outset to recall that *šrā* is another Jewish Aramaic term used of salvific divine action;[22] it is in fact considerably more common in this context than the verb *aggen.* This fact suggests that the use of *šrā* in Syriac is more likely to go back directly to the Judaic roots of Syriac Christianity, rather than to have been

---

Quotations from the Gospel, TaS, 7.2 (Cambridge: Cambridge University Press, 1901, reprint, Nendeln: Kraus Reprint, 1967), 49. One might also compare *H. de Epiphania* 8:1, *bāʿē d-neṣrē ban,* and note that Babai sometimes uses *šrā* in paraphrases of this passage, e.g. *Liber de unione* (ed. Vaschalde), 94, *šārē w-ʿāmar w-maggen b-;* the latter is interesting in the light of the Christian Palestinian Aramaic rendering of John 1:14, using ʿmar, and the express statement of Jacob of Edessa (in a scholion to Severus' *Homily 15,* PO, no. 26:312) that the sense of *aggen* in John 1:14 was that of ʿmar, while in Luke 1:35 it was that of *aṭṭel,* "overshadow" (he explicitly bases himself on the Greek).

[22]*Šrā* is one of the standard verbs used in connection with the *Īqar Škīntā* ("Glory of the Presence") and *Rūḥā d-Qudšā* ("Spirit of the Sanctuary, Spirit of Holiness") in the Targumim. Normally the preposition is ʿal, "upon," or *bēn, bgaw,* "among, in the midst of," for people, whereas *b-,* "in," is used for place. This interestingly suits the later application to Mary of Old Testament types such as "Tabernacle, Second Heaven" (compare Palestinian Targum at Deut 3:24, 4:39). For the use of *šrā* with *škīntā* see D. Muñoz Leon, *Gloria de la Shekina en los Targumim del Pentateuco* (Madrid, 1977), 183-188, 204-207, 215, 220, 227, 229; and A. Goldberg, *Untersuchungen über die Vorstellung von der Schekhinah in der frühen rabbinischen Literatur,* SJ, no. 5 (1969), 239-248, 445-446.

a later import, seeing that by the fourth century at least (Ephrem, d. 373, being our *terminus ante quem*) hostility between the two religious communities would not have been conducive to such influences.[23]

Is one justified, on the basis of the quotations and allusions adduced above, to reconstruct the lost Old Syriac of Luke 1:35 as *...w-ḥayleh d-ᶜellāyā nešrē bek(y)*? In order to reach a decision it will perhaps be most helpful if we consider the implications of each of the two possible Suppositions.

Supposition 1: *šrā b-* does represent the lost Old Syriac at Luke 1:35. Here we have two possibilities which need to be considered:

(a) If the Old Syriac is later than the Diatessaron (the prevailing view today),[24] then we need to ask why the author of the Old Syriac decided to alter *naggen ᶜal-* to *nešrē b-*, and why the reviser(s) behind the Peshitta decided to alter back to *naggen ᶜal-*.

(b) If the Diatessaron is later than the Old Syriac, why did the Syriac Diatessaron alter *nešrē b-* to *naggen ᶜal-*?

---

[23]For Jews and Christians at Edessa see H. J. W. Drijvers's article under that title in *JJS* 36 (1985): 88-102 (mainly covering late-third to early-fifth century, a period later than that with which we are concerned).   The origins and early history of Syriac Christianity are notoriously obscure. The following points are relevant to the present argument:

(1) At least parts of the Peshitta Old Testament have their roots in an early form of the Targum tradition (see my remarks in *JThS* 29 [1978]: 550-551); if other parts are of Christian origin (as has recently been argued for the Psalms by M. Weitzmann, "The Origins of the Peshitta," in *Interpreting the Hebrew Bible* [*supra*, note 6], pp. 227-298), the translators must have had a Jewish background, in view of their good knowledge of Hebrew;

(2) These Judaic roots were still alive when the Old Syriac Gospels were produced (variously dated from the late-second to the early-fourth century CE) as shown by the choice of specifically Jewish vocabulary at times (e.g. *knuštā* for ἐκκλησία, Matt 18:17 ; further examples can be found in F.C. Burkitt, *Evangelion da-Mepharreshe*, 1:78-84);

(3) Many Jewish exegetical traditions were known to, and used by, early Syriac writers to an extent that goes well beyond what is found in early Christian writers using Greek or Latin; in general see my article "Jewish Traditions in Syriac Sources," *JJS* 30 (1979): 212-232.

[24]See for example Matthew Black, "The Syriac Versional Evidence," in *Die alten Übersetzungen des neuen Testaments, die Kirchenväterzitate und Lektionare*, ed. K. Aland, ANTT, no. 5 (Berlin/New York: Walter de Gruyter, 1972), 124-128; and B. Aland, in *TRE* (1980), 6.1:189-191.   For older views see B. M. Metzger, *The Early Versions of the New Testament* (Oxford: Oxford University Press, 1977), 45-46.

Since *nešrē b-* is a less close rendering of ἐπισκιάσει σοι than *naggen ʿal-* (compare, for example, Targum Noefiti with Ps.-Jonathan and Onkelos at Numbers 10:34),[25] this means that (a) would be less easily explainable than (b); on the other hand, the evidence available today seems to favour the priority of the Diatessaron, and so we are left with having to provide a reasonable explanation of (a) if we opt for Supposition 1.

Supposition 2: *šrā b-* does not represent the Old Syriac of Luke 1:35. Since the use of the phrase is clearly an early one in Syriac Christianity, with roots in Jewish Aramaic, we must accordingly find some other plausible explanation. If it does not originate in a written Syriac biblical text, could it then belong to the earliest oral kerygma in Syriac?

If that were so, then the passages where *šrā* occurs in what are apparently quotations of (or at least, allusions to) Luke 1:35 will simply be due to the interaction between the originally independent *šrā b-* of the oral kerygma with the written versions of Luke 1:35, among which we might then assume that the lost Old Syriac also had *naggen ʿal-*. The same would apply, *mutatis mutandis*, for John 1:14.

In any case we will need to ask why *aggen* was chosen by the author of the Syriac form of the Diatessaron (assuming now that this was prior to the Old Syriac); or, if the Diatessaron were originally composed in Syriac (as has recently been cogently argued),[26] then why did its author (whether or not one goes on to identify him as Tatian himself) select this particular Jewish Aramaic term which happens to have an intriguing background in the Exodus Passover narrative?[27]

Which of the two previous Suppositions are we to prefer? Several considerations incline me to opt for the second and to say that *šrā b-* does not represent the lost Old Syriac of Luke 1:35:

---

[25]Neofiti: *wʿnn ʾyqr škynth dY hwh mgn*; Onkelos (cp. Ps.-Jonathan): *wʿnn yqrʾ dY mṭl* (Ps.-Jonathan: *mṭll*).

[26]See W. L. Petersen, "New Evidence for the Question of the Original Language of the Diatessaron," in *Studien zum Text und zur Ethik des Neuen Testaments. Festschrift zum 80. Geburtstag vom Heinrich Greeven*, ed. W. Schrage, BZNW, no. 47 (Berlin/New York: Walter de Gruyter, 1986), 325-343, whose evidence led him to conclude it was Syriac. If Petersen is correct, and if (as would then seem likely) Tatian himself were the author, then the Syriac Diatessaron could be dated towards the end of the third quarter of the second century; if, however, the Syriac is a translation, then its date may be somewhat later.

[27]For a suggestion, see below.

(1)   Supposition 1(a) raises some problems, as we have
      already seen.

(2)   Supposition 1(b) would imply that šrā was also an Old
      Syriac reading at John 1:14, where the Curetonian
      already has *aggen* (it is, of course, conceivable that šrā
      represents the missing Sinaiticus, in which case the
      reading of the Curetonian would have to represent a
      later revision).

(3)   Supposition 2 makes good sense on purely general
      considerations: it is hardly conceivable that there would
      not have been, alongside (and probably prior to) any
      written Gospel traditions in Syriac, an oral kerygma in
      that language, and this kerygma cannot have failed to
      touch on the incarnation and how this took place; in so
      doing it would have been likely to use terminology that
      would already have been familiar in Jewish Aramaic in
      contexts of divine presence on earth.

We can in fact find good parallels for Supposition 2. First, we know
another term for the incarnation which must have a similar origin,
namely *lbeš pagrā*, "he put on the body," one of the most common early
Syriac terms for the incarnation.[28] Since, however, *lbeš pagrā* offers no
reference to Jesus' mother, there was ample place for the phrase šrā b- as
well. Second, we can observe an analogous phenomenon in the Peshitta
Old Testament where words or phrases with a background in the Jewish
Targumim survive in Syriac tradition independently of the actual biblical
text (Peshitta). A striking example is provided by Genesis 22:13, where all
Peshitta manuscripts speak of the ram which took the place of Isaac as the
sacrifice as being "caught in a branch" (*b-sawktā*); yet commentators and
homilists, from Ephrem onwards, regular speak, not of a "branch," but of a
"tree" (*īlānā*)—a tradition which has clear roots in the Targumim (Pales-

---

[28]For general background, see my "Clothing Metaphors as a Means of Theological
Expression in Syriac Tradition," in *Typus, Symbol, Allegorie bei den östlichen Vätern und
ihren Parallelen im Mittelalter*, ed. M. Schmidt, Eichstätter Beiträge, no. 4 (1982), 11-40.
The phraseology occurs in the Peshitta at Hebrews 5:7 and 10:5—renderings to which
Philoxenus was later to object (see my essay "The Resolution of the Philoxenian/Harclean
Problem," in *New Testament Textual Criticism* [supra, note 2], 329).

tinian and Babylonian traditions).[29] Thus I conclude that, despite some possible evidence that the Old Syriac read *nešrē b-* instead of *naggen ʿal-* at Luke 1:35, we should nonetheless reject this evidence and opt for our second Supposition.

The Lost Old Syriac Reading at Acts 2:3

I turn now to another textual problem involving *aggen*, where once more we have to evaluate the evidence of quotations. It has recently been claimed that the lost Old Syriac version of Acts 2:3 read *aggen* in the context of the tongues of fire coming upon the apostles at Pentecost (Greek ἐκάθισεν, ἐκάθισαν = Peshitta *īteb(w) ʿal*).[30] Various quotations, but above all an extended one from John of Dara (ninth century), are adduced in support of this reading. In order to evaluate such evidence properly, I believe we should look at the passage against the background of the development of the use of the term *aggen* in connection with the activity of the Spirit within Syriac literature as a whole.[31]

Besides its use in Luke 1:35 (where, however, as we have seen, the Word rather than the Spirit is most frequently understood as being the subject), *aggen* occurs with the Spirit as subject in the Peshitta in Acts 10:44 and 11:15, where the Greek in both cases has ἐπέπεσεν. More significant, however, is the fact that *aggen* takes on an important role in liturgical texts; in particular it occurs in the epiclesis of the most influential of all West Syrian anaphoras, that attributed to St. James (where it corresponds to the Greek ἐπιφοιτήσαν). In the East Syrian liturgical tradition it is also

---

[29]See my "Two Syriac Verse Homilies on the Binding of Isaac," *Muséon* 99 (1986): 77, 84. It is interesting that *ilana* is used as late as the eighteenth-century by Maphrian Shemʿun of Tur ʿAbdin; see *Tenḥōthō d-Ṭur ʿAbdīn*, ed. J. Y. Cicek (Monastery of St Ephrem, Holland, 1987), 68, line 3.

[30]A. Vööbus, "Die Entdeckung von Überresten der altsyrischen Apostelgeschichte," *OrChr* 64 (1980): 32-35; D. L. McConaughy, "Research on the History of the Syriac Text of Acts Chapters One and Two" (Ph.D. diss., University of Chicago, 1985). I am endebted to Dr. McConaughy for his kindness in sending me a copy of his dissertation.

[31]In general see my "Passover, Annunication and Epiclesis: Some Remarks on the Term *aggen* in the Syriac Versions of Luke 1:35," *NT* 24 (1982): 222-233.

found in the anaphora attributed to Theodore of Mopsuestia (where it is juxtaposed with *nešrē*).[32]

Under the influence of these biblical and liturgical passages *aggen* (and also, from the late-fifth century onwards, the derivative noun *maggnanuta*)[33] came to be seen as terminology especially to be associated with the activity of the Spirit; as a consequence, writers grew increasingly apt to introduce their use into contexts of other biblical passages, notably the Baptism of Christ,[34] the Transfiguration,[35] and the Pentecost narrative, where the Syriac biblical text employs quite different verbs.[36] As far as Pentecost is concerned, it is striking that there is absolutely no evidence for the use of *aggen* in this context in any fourth-century writer; indeed, the first definite evidence known to me for the use of *aggen* (or its derivative *maggnanuta*) in the context of the Pentecost narrative of Acts 2 comes from an early sixth-century East Syrian writer, Cyrus of Edessa.[37] It seems to me particularly significant that neither Narsai nor Jacob of Serugh ever uses the term in their homilies on Pentecost,[38] whereas in writers after Cyrus the use of *aggen* in this context is not uncommon.[39] It is also of

---

[32]See my "Annunciation...," 230-231; *aggen* is used in eucharistic contexts by Narsai (ed. Mingana, 1:353) and Jacob of Serugh (ed. Bedjan, 4:597); in Jacob the older term *šrā*, used by Ephrem (e.g. *H. c. Haereses* 42:9), is rather more frequent (e.g. ed. Bedjan, 2:217; 3:657).

[33]First attested in Narsai, *Hom.* 5 (ed. Mingana, 1:95) and Philoxenus, *Tractatus Decem* (dated ca. 482-484), PO 38:502; PO 39:726, 728.

[34]Thus *Fenqitho III*, 70a, 253b, 282a (with *šrā*), *Ḥudra I*, 484 = 497. Likewise often in the context of Christian baptism (already in *H. de Epiphania* 1:5, attributed, no doubt incorrectly, to Ephrem).

[35]Thus, *Fenqitho VII*, 323b; but not in the *Ḥudra*.

[36]Baptism of Christ: Matt 3:16 *nḥt* + *qwy* (Old Syriac), *nḥt* +ʾtʾ (Peshitta); Mark 1:10, Luke 3:22 *nḥt*; John 1:33 *nḥt* + *qwy*. Transfiguration: *aṭṭel*.

[37]*Six Explanations of the Liturgical Feasts by Cyrus of Edessa*, ed. W. F. Macomber, CSCO, no. 355 (Louvain: Peeters, 1974), 162, 164, 172, 178, 180, 182 (for the verb).

[38]Narsai, *Hom.* 27 and Jacob, *Hom.* 59. The word *aggen* is likewise missing from the anonymous prose homily wrongly attributed to Ephrem, *S. Ephraemi Syri...Opera Selecta*, ed. F. Overbeck (Oxford, 1865), 95-98; according to T. Jansma it may belong to the late-fourth or early-fifth century; see his "Une homélie anonyme sur l'effusion du Saint Esprit," *OrSyr* 6 (1961): 157-178.

[39]In addition to examples cited by McConaughy (*supra*, note 30), 180, e.g. *Fenqitho VI*, 197b, 198b, 199a, etc. (for the noun: 207b, 208a); *Ḥudra III*, 123, 130, 150-2, etc. It is sig-

interest here to observe the situation with the two Syriac translations, one sixth- and the other seventh-century, of Severus' *Homily 48 on Pentecost*, where he makes specific allusions to Acts 2:3 on two separate occasions. The earlier translation, perhaps the work of Paul of Kallinikos, preserved in British Library Add. 14 599, dating from 569 CE, is unpublished, whereas the revision of this by Jacob of Edessa (d. 708) has been edited in *Patrologia Orientalis* (PO) 35. The two texts in the two passages are as follows:

(1)   Add. 14 599, fol. 115a1:

     rūḥā d-qudšā ... b-leššānē d-nūrā šāken ᶜal šlīḥē
     The Spirit of holiness ...

         with tongues of fire rests upon the apostles;

   Jacob (PO 35:320, line 2):

     rūḥā qaddīšā ... b-leššānē nūrānē maggen ᶜal šlīḥē
     The Holy Spirit ...

         with fiery tongues *maggen* upon the apostles.

(2)   Add. 14 599, fol. 116a2:

     metiteh
     the coming (of the Holy Spirit)

   Jacob (PO 35:322, line 15):

     maggnanuta.

Unfortunately, the Greek original corresponding to the last term is lost; but even if one supposes that it was ἐπιφοιτάω/ἐπιφοίτησις[40] (the Greek term corresponding to *aggen/maggnanuta* in liturgical texts), it is striking that the sixth-century translation employs quite different Syriac roots, and it is only in the late seventh-century revision by Jacob that *aggen* appears. Interestingly enough, Jacob seems to have made exactly the same alteration to the earlier Syriac version of Severus' Hymns (by Paul of Edessa, early seventh century) in three passages which allude to Acts 2:3.[41]

---

nificant that the term is so common in these later liturgical texts; both the *Fenqitho* (VI, 201a, 202b, 207a, 210b, 212a) and the *Ḥudra* (III, 126, 132) also use *nḥet + šrā* in this context (or *aggen + šrā* in *Fenqitho* VI, 198b, 199a).

[40]The noun already occurs in Greek in the context of Pentecost in Isidore of Pelusium (early fifth century), PG, no. 78, col. 293B.

[41]See PO, no. 6:148, 151-152 (Paul had used the more archaic term *šrā*, the use of which had also been extended to the context of Acts 2:3; see at the end of note 39, *supra*).

This state of affairs suggests that we need to be very cautious before accepting the claim that John of Dara's quotation of Acts 2:1-10, containing *aggen* at 2:3, preserves the Old Syriac version of that verse. The case of a famous passage in the Peshitta Old Testament can illustrate how such an extraneous reading can actually get into biblical manuscripts at a late date. At Genesis 49:10 all early Peshitta manuscripts render the obscure Hebrew blessing of Jacob as follows:

> ᶜ*dammā d-nītē man d-dīleh (h)ī*
> until there comes he to whom it (fem.) belongs.

A large number of seemingly explicit quotations of the verse in Syriac writers from Ephrem onwards add *malkūtā*, "kingdom," at the end, thus identifying "it" as "the kingdom." As was the case with *īlānā*, "tree," at Genesis 22:13, this reading too has its origin in the Targum tradition, but Jansma seems to me to be correct in concluding that *malkūtā* does not belong to the original Peshita text.[42] Nonetheless, the word has entered into the margin of a ninth-century lectionary and into the text of two eleventh-century lectionaries and a number of biblical manuscripts of the twelfth century and later.[43]

Conclusion

By way of conclusion, I return to Luke 1:35. If I am correct in opting for the second of the two suppositions set out above, then this opens up two interesting avenues for further investigation, neither of which can be followed up here, although for the second I offer a speculative suggestion which might serve as the basis for further discussion:

> (1) the Jewish Aramaic background to the oral Syriac kerygma using *šrā b-* to denote the presence of the Word in Mary;

---

[42]T. Jansma, "Ephraem on Gen. XLIX,10," *ParOr* 4 (1973): 247-256. One might also compare the case of the pseudo-variant *rdaw*, "flowed," in place of *npaq(w)*, "came forth," found in many quotations of John 19:34, but due to deliberate contamination from John 7:38 (see my remarks in *OrChrA* 197 [1974]: 190-191, 211).

[43]MS 915 (mg), 1114.5, 12b2 in the notation of the Leiden Peshitta OT.

(2) the reasons why the Syriac translator (or compiler) of the Diatessaron selected *aggen ꜥal*, with its own Jewish Aramaic background, in order to render ἐπισκιάζειν.

On the second point it must be emphasized at the outset that *aggen* is by no means an obvious rendering for ἐπισκιάζειν: a literal translation was readily at hand in *aṭṭel*, "overshadow." Why, then, did the author of the Syriac Diatessaron choose instead to render the Greek verb by *aggen*, a term which had its background in the language of the Aramaic Old Testament? Could it be that he was aware of the connection, found in part of the Palestinian targum tradition, between *aggen* and the Hebrew *pāsaḥ* in the Passover narrative (Exodus 12),[44] and wished to link the early Syriac date for the conception of Jesus, 10th Nisan,[45] with the Passover narrative, thus providing a typological link between the passover lamb and Christ the paschal lamb: the former was confined on 10th Nisan (Exodus 12:3), and the latter was conceived on 10th Nisan; and both were sacrificed on 14th Nisan. The rationale for this dating of the annunciation/conception can in fact be taken back to the second century, for its basis lies in the assumption that Zechariah was High Priest, an identification already made in the *Protevangelium of James*. This identification gives a date, 10th Tishri = Day of Atonement, for his vision in the Temple, and by combining this with the six months of Luke 1:26 one can reach the date of 10th Nisan for the annunciation/conception. All these typological parallels and aspects were very familiar to Ephrem in the fourth century;[46] could they have also already been in the mind of the author of the Syriac Diatessaron?[47]

---

[44]See note 6, *supra*.

[45]E.g. Ephrem, *Comm. Diat.* 1:29; *H. de Nativitate* 4:34; 5:14; 17:2-3; *H. de Resurrectione* 4:13; and in several subsequent writers.

[46]See my "Annunciation" (*supra*, note 31).

[47]If this suggestion concerning the choice of *aggen* in Luke 1:35 is right, then one might compare the case of the Syriac Diatessaron's choice of "bars (*mokhloi*) of Sheol," instead of "gates of Hades," at Matt. 16:18, which may be a deliberate allusion to Psalm 106 (107):16, introduced in order to relate Matt. 16:18 to the Descent theme (Psalm 106 is linked with Christ's descent into the underworld in Greek tradition from the second century onwards); for this, see "Some Aspects of Greek Words in Syriac," in article IV of my *Syriac Perspectives on Late Antiquity* (London: Variorum, 1984), 95-98. It is interesting that in this case too there is again no trace of the reading in the the western Diatessaron witnesses.

ΔΙΑΦΩΝΙΑ—ΣΥΜΦΩΝΙΑ:
Factors in the Harmonization of the Gospels, Especially in the Diatessaron of Tatian

Tjitze Baarda

Rijksuniversiteit te Utrecht (the Netherlands)

An Enigmatic Complaint of Celsus

The pagan author Celsus is, according to his own remarks in the *Alethes Logos,* acquainted with the Gospels.[1] The Jew (whether a fictive person or not) whom Celsus puts on the stage suggests that the stories in the Gospels were not according to the true facts: "although I could say much about what happened to Jesus which is true and nothing like that which had been written by the disciples of Jesus—I leave that out intentionally" (II.13).[2] The Gospels were merely the outcome of their lies (ψευδόμενοι) and could be labelled as fictitious tales (πλάσματα) of these disciples (II.26).[3] In that connection Celsus (or his Jew) says (II.27):[4]

(1) μετὰ ταῦτα τινας τῶν πιστευόντων φησὶν

(2) ὡς ἐκ μέθης ἥκοντας εἰς τὸ ἐφεστάναι αὑτοῖς[5]

(3) μεταχαράττειν ἐκ τῆς πρώτης γραφῆς τὸ εὐαγγέλιον

(4) τριχῆ καὶ τετραχῆ καὶ πολλαχῆ

(5) καὶ μεταπλάττειν πρὸς τοὺς ἐλέγχους ἀρνεῖσθαι.

---

[1]For references to the Gospels, cf. E. Preuschen, *Antilegomena,* 2nd ed. (Giessen: Ricker, 1905), 63-68.

[2] Origen, *c. Cels.* 13.1-4 (M. Borret, ed., *Origène, Contre Celse, I,* SC, no. 132 [Paris: Cerf, 1967], 318).

[3]*c. Cels.* 26.2-3 (Borret, 354).

[4]*c. Cels.* 27:1-5 (Borret, 356).

[5]This is the reading of the manuscript (A), which implies the disciples of the original Gospels, but since the edition of Delarue one follows the suggestion of Bohereau (Notes, 374) to read αὑτοῖς (cf. Chadwick's rendering, provided in our text above).

Chadwick's rendering of this passage reads thus:

> After this he says that some believers, as though from
> a drinking bout, go so far as to oppose themselves and
> alter the original text of the gospels three or four or
> several times over, and they change its character to en-
> able them to deny difficulties in face of criticism.[6]

One may say that the observation of Celsus is rather enigmatic.[7]
Origen concluded that Celsus had made an unjust allegation against
Christianity, since such alterations of the Gospels were to be ascribed only
to sectarians such as the Marcionites, Valentinians and Lucanians, "who
indeed dared to falsify the Gospels by introducing their own philosophical
principles which were foreign to the meaning of the teaching of Jesus."[8]
Origen may have had in mind new Gospels which these movements
attempted to introduce, such as Marcion's Gospel or the *Gospel of Truth*.[9]
However, one cannot exclude the possibility that he was also thinking of
"corrections" within the text of the existing Gospels.[10]

Another explanation of the text is that Celsus was referring to the
plurality of the Gospels read in the churches. In that case, he may have
assumed that there originally was only *one* Gospel (see line 3 above: ἐκ
τῆς πρώτης γραφῆς), which became the source of those Gospels which were
current in the churches and held in esteem by the believers, either *three*
(τριχῆ, the Synoptic Gospels) or *four* (τετραχῆ, including the Gospel of John,
which was read in Alexandria and was gradually gaining ground in
Rome—Celsus may have lived in either of these cities), or even more

---

[6]H. Chadwïck, *Origen, Contra Celsum* (Cambridge: Cambridge University Press,
1953), 90.

[7]Cf. Chadwick, *Origen, Contra Celsum*, 90, n. 2; F. Mosetto, *I miracoli evangelichi
nel dibattito tra Celso e Origine* (Rome, 1986), 44.

[8]Cf. *c. Cels.* 27:5-14 (Borret, 356). Origen speaks of τῶν τολμησάντων ῥᾳδιουργῆσαι
τὰ εὐαγγέλια (lines 8-9.), people οἱ μεταχαράττοντες τὰ εὐαγγέλια (line 12).

[9]Cf. Chadwick, *Origen, Contra Celsum*, 90, n. 2, who considers this as a possible
interpretation ("Origen, however, may well be right...").

[10]Cf. E. Nestle, *Einführung in das Griechische Neue Testament* 3rd ed. (Göttingen:
Vandenhoeck & Ruprecht, 1909), 224-225 ("Zum Teil auf die Neuherstellung von Schriften,
zum Teil auf ihre Umänderung geht der bekannte Vorwurf des Celsus...und die Antwort des
Origenes"); cf. 219-227 ("Schriftfälschungen der Ketzer").

(πολλαχῇ) such as the Gospel of Marcion, the *Gospel of Truth,* the *Gospel according to Peter,* or whatever Gospel(s) Celsus may have come across.[11] From his work it is clear that he knew the "canonical" Gospels *and* other early Christian documents. If this explanation is adopted, one should render line 3: "to alter the character of the Gospel ever since it was written for the first time."[12]

However, one observation in his remarks suggests another explanation. Celsus writes that there are some believers who make changes and alterations "in order to be able to decline allegations." Now, the plurality of the Gospels enabled pagans and certain Christians to discover discrepancies between the various Gospels and, consequently, to deny the reliability of all or some of them. As a matter of fact, from early times onwards, scribes or commentators have often tried to prevent such criticisms by harmonizing Gospel texts with each other. The possibility cannot be excluded that Celsus was aware of this harmonizing process either by his own observation or by hearsay.[13]

The Plurality of the Gospels as a Problem

Whatever the meaning of the passage may have been, it is evident that in the middle of the second century the plurality of the Gospels became a major problem for Christian communities.[14] From the writings of Justin Martyr one may conclude that the Gospels of Matthew, Mark and

---

[11]Cf. R. Bader, *Der ΑΛΗΘΗΣ ΛΟΓΟΣ des Kelsos,* TBAW, no. 33 (Stuttgart/Berlin: Kohlhammer, 1940), 69, n. 2; Chadwick, *Origen, Contra Celsum,* 90, n. 2.

[12]Cf. H. U. Meyboom, *Verweerschrift tegen Celsus 1-11 (De Apologeten IV: Origenes I)* (Leiden: Sijthoff, 1924), 139.

[13]Cf. W. Bauer, *Das Leben Jesu im Zeitalter der neutestamentlichen Apokryphen* (Tübingen: J. C. B. Mohr/P. Siebeck, 1909), 493; A. Harnack, *Marcion. Das Evangelium vom fremden Gott,* 2nd rev. ed. (Leipzig: J. C. Hinrichs, 1924), 173, 254*; see also the rendering of R. J. Hoffmann, *Celsus, On the True Doctrine* (New York/Oxford: Oxford University Press, 1987), 64.

[14]Cf. O. Cullmann, "Die Pluralität der Evangelien als theologisches Problem im Altertum," in *Vorträge und Aufsätze 1925-1962,* ed. K. Fröhlich (Tübingen/Zürich: J. C. B. Mohr [Siebeck]/Zwingli Verlag, 1966), 548-565; T. Baarda, *Vier = Een. Enkele bladzijden uit de geschiedenis van de harmonistiek der Evangeliën* (Kampen: Kok, 1969); H. Merkel, *Widersprüche zwischen den Evangelien* (Tübingen: J. C. B. Mohr, 1971); H. Merkel, *Die Pluralität der Evangelien* (Bern/Frankfurt a.M./Las Vegas: P. Lang, 1978).

Luke were accepted as reliable records or *memoirs* of the apostles concerning the life and teaching of Jesus, and could be used as basic material for theological or ethical argumentation.[15]   It is, however, also evident that Justin had access to and used additional information either from current oral traditions or from other written sources.[16]   Moreover, as an antagonist of Marcion he must have been acquainted with Marcion's recension of Luke.

The fact that Justin did not (or hardly) pay any attention to the Fourth Gospel cannot be mere coincidence.[17]   It is a well-known fact that in part of the Roman church there was a tendency to reject this Gospel as Gnostic, most probably since it was held in high esteem in the circles of Valentinus.[18]   The severe attacks launched on the veracity of the Fourth Gospel by the orthodox Caius of Rome betray that the apostolicity and reliability of this document were still under discussion in Rome at that time.[19]   The ecstatic movement of the Montanists with its appeal to the *Paraclete* of John's Gospel and the argument of the Quartodecimans on the basis of the Johannine chronology may have contributed to reservations regarding this Gospel.[20]

The gradual acceptance of more than one Gospel made people aware also of their differences in contents. The Marcionites laid emphasis on the fact that the Gospels did not agree (διαφωνοῦσι τὰ εὐαγγέλια), but in fact differed greatly from each other (ἀντικεῖνται).[21]   This was especially

---

[15]H. von Campenhausen, *Die Entstehung der christlichen Bibel*, BHTh, no. 39 (Tübingen: J. C. B. Mohr, 1968), 196-197.

[16]Cf. J. Leipoldt, *Geschichte des neutestamentlichen Kanons I*, (Leipzig: J. C. Hinrichs, 1907), 130, n. 5; Von Campenhausen, *Die Entstehung der christlichen Bibel*, 198.

[17]Von Campenhausen, *Die Entstehung der christlichen Bibel*, 198, n. 99.

[18]Cf. Irenaeus, *haer.* III.11.7.

[19]Cf. Von Campenhausen, *Die Entstehung der christlichen Bibel*, 276-277.

[20]Cf. Leipoldt, *Geschichte des neutestamentlichen Kanons I*, 42-43; Merkel, *Widersprüche zwischen den Evangelien*, 37-41.

[21]Cf. *Dial. Adam.* 1.7 (W. H. van de Sande Bakhuyzen, ed., *Der Dialog des Adamantius* [Leipzig: J. C. Hinrichs, 1901], 14).

true for the Gospel of John in the view of some of its antagonists.[22] For Christians, the variety in contents and chronology became a problem that required a solution, since the disharmony caused doubts concerning the reliability of the Gospels. This is seen in the attacks of pagan philosophers, who emphasized the ἀσυμφωνία or διαφωνία of Gospel stories.[23] Using a different but equally-damaging logic, the Marcionites could conclude that, because of the differences of the other Gospels from their own Gospel, these other Gospels were unreliable (ὅθεν φαίνεται φάλσα).[24] Some Christians could go so far that they said that the author of the Fourth Gospel could bend the truth (ὁ δὲ ᾽Ιωάνης ψεύδεται).[25]

It is difficult to exaggerate the bewilderment that must have struck diligent students of the various Gospels, when they became aware of the insoluble differences among them. We may quote a later scholar, Origen, to illustrate this. In his *Commentary on John*, he treats the different chronologies and contents in the opening chapters of the four Gospels and concludes that "the truth of these matters must lie in their spiritual meaning":

> ... if the διαφωνία cannot be solved, one has to give up one's (historical) trust with respect to the Gospels, since (if one would take them literally) they would not be true and not written by a more divine spirit, or would be just casual memorabilia.[26]

> ... If someone carefully studies the Gospels with respect to the ἀσυμφωνία in historical matters, ... he gets dizzy and will *either* give up any attempt to establish the truth of (all four) Gospels, and—since he does not dare

---

[22]Cf. Epiphanius, *haer* 51.4.5 (K. Holl, ed., *Ancoratus und Panarion II*, GCS, no. 31 [Leipzig, 1922], 251-252), οὐ συμφωνεῖ τὰ αὐτοῦ βιβλία—the Gospel and the Apocalypse— τοῖς λοιποῖς ἀποστόλοις.

[23]Cf. especially the criticisms of the later Porphyry; Merkel, *Widersprüche zwischen den Evangelien*, 13ff.

[24]*Dial.Adam*.7.1 (Van de Sande Bakhuyzen, 14).

[25]Epiphanius, *haer*. 51.21.15 (Holl, 281).

[26]Origen, *Comm.in Joannem* X.3.2 (A. E. Brooke, ed., *The Commentary of Origen on S.John's Gospel* [Cambridge: Cambridge University Press, 1896], I:183.29-184.1.

to fully deny his belief with respect to (the story of) our
Lord—will at random choose one of them, *or* will
accept that the truth of these four (Gospels) does not lie
in the literal text.[27]

Since Origen adopts this attitude, he can maintain the thesis: τὸ
ἀληθῶς διὰ τεσσάρων ἕν ἐστιν εὐαγγέλιον.[28] The plurality called for unity,
and Origen transposed the essential unity from the letter to the Spirit.[29]
But those believers who were inclined to accept the historical truth of the
Gospels, and refused to apply the Alexandrian solution of allegorization to
overcome the difficulties, may have become "dizzy" when confronted
with the discrepancies between the various Gospels.

Textual Harmonization

Textual harmonization was most probably one of the attempts to
remove or neutralize the disagreements among the Gospels. Apart from
an amount of unconscious assimilation by scribes who inadvertently
reproduced the text of the Gospel with which they were most familiar, and
not the text of the exemplar being copied, there are certainly deliberate
alterations, omissions or additions.[30] Scribes consciously altered their
manuscript and made it conform it to that of the other Gospels, especially
when these latter texts stood in high esteem in their community because
of their archaic character or supposed apostolic origin. This process of
harmonization was not necessarily limited to the canonical Gospels, but
extended also to documents that were later labelled as apocryphal Gospels.

---

[27]*Comm. in Joannem* X.3.2 (Brooke, I:185.8-15).

[28]*Comm. in Joannem* fragmenta of V:7 (Brooke, II:232.17-18).

[29]Since the Spirit is the unifying factor, Origen could defend the verbal inspiration
of the Gospels; cf. R. M. Grant, *The Earliest Lives of Jesus* (London: SPCK, 1961), 53; R. P. C.
Hanson, *Allegory and Event*, (London, 1959); Von Campenhausen, *Die Entstehung der
christlichen Bibel*, 365; Merkel, *Widersprüche zwischen den Evangelien*, 96ff.

[30]For the process of harmonization in general, see E. Tov, "The Nature and Background of Harmonizations in Biblical Manuscripts," *JSOT* 31 (1985): 3-29; for the Gospels,
see G. D. Fee, "Modern Text Criticism and the Synoptic Problem," in B. Orchard et al., ed., *J.
J. Griesbach: Synoptic and Text-critical Studies 1776-1976* (Cambridge: Cambridge
University Press, 1978), 154-169, esp. 161-167.

Early oral material may also have influenced scribes, leading them to alter the text before them. It is most likely that this process started in the middle of the second century, when the awareness of the discrepancies gradually became a problem.

Such harmonization is very significant in Mark, as one can easily deduce from the phenomena found in the textual apparatus of this Gospel. Although Mark is most likely the source of other Gospels, it was particularly open to assimilation, especially in the form of additions, due to its succinctness and shortness. The so-called *Secret Gospel of Mark*, which was an expansion of the original text, and the Carpocratian recension of Mark make it clear that its text could easily be supplemented with material from other sources. The "Longer Ending" of Mark is another sign of the desire for completeness. The Freer Logion in Codex W demonstrates that this process went on for a long time. Even Mark's textual character changed due to the harmonization of its text with other Gospels, predominantly Matthew and Luke.

When the Western Text (D *d n*) omits διαγενομένου τοῦ σαββάτου and the names of the women from Mark 16:1, one may guess that this was done to conform Mark's communication to Luke 23:56, especially to avoid discrepancy between the two Gospels regarding the precise time when the women busied themselves with the spices. Thus the reading ἡτοίμασαν for ἠγόρασαν (Θ 565) is not the result of a misreading, but a deliberate attempt to remove a difference (cf. *attulerunt* for *emerunt* in *c* and *k*). In Mark 16:2, ἀνατέλλοντος (D *c d n q*) is apparently an attempt to smooth the difference between ἀνατείλαντος of the original text and the observation in John 20:1 that it was still dark. The message of the angel in Mark 16:6, assimilated to Matt 28:5 in Codex D (read ὁ ἄγγελος, φοβεῖσθε instead of ἐκθαμβεῖσθε | omission of οἶδα γὰρ ὅτι, τὸν Ναζαρηνόν | read εἴδετε ... τόπον for ἴδε ὁ τόπος), betrays the urge for assimilation in the Western Text.

Harmonization is not only found in the variant readings of scribes, who unconsciously or deliberately assimilated one text to another, but also in the comments of early fathers on real or apparent discrepancies in the text. Such harmonizations are often found in the writings of later authors, such as Eusebius, Augustine and Jerome.[31] Even in the works of Origen, who emphasizes such differences among the Gospels in order to prove that they must be read not on the basis of their literal or historical

---

[31]Cf. for references to these works, see my *Vier=Een*, 37, notes 79-82.

meaning, but understood in a spiritual way,[32] one finds instances of "harmonizing" where Origen attempts to show that discrepancies are only apparent and not real.[33] In his *Contra Celsum* (V.56) he writes in reaction to an observation of Celsus:[34]

> I do not think he (Celsus) noticed that Matthew and Mark have one, while Luke and John have two angels. But these statements are not contradictory (οὐκ ἦν ἐναντία). The writers that have one angel say that this one was he who rolled back the stone from the sepulchre, whereas those that have two say they stood before the women.... However, while it would be possible to substantiate now each of these statements, both as *historical* events (καὶ γεγενημένον) and as manifesting some *allegorical* meaning (καὶ δηλωτικόν τινος... τροπολογίας)... it is not relevant to the present undertaking but rather to commentaries on the Gospel.[35]

The Rise of Harmonies

One might say that the temptation to combine various sources and consequently create harmonies was "overwhelming" and that the urge was "in the air."[36] From the beginning of the Christian tradition, there was a tendency to combine the various oral and written sources of different types or genres into a narrative of the activities and sayings of Jesus. In itself, Mark is the result of such a procedure, but this Gospel in its turn served as one of the sources that enabled the creation of such Gospels as Matthew and Luke. And even the Gospel of John is the combination of

---

[32]Merkel, *Widersprüche zwischen den Evangelien,* 112-121.

[33]Merkel, *Widersprüche zwischen den Evangelien,* 98-108.

[34]See *infra,* 152-153.

[35]Chadwick, *Origen, Contra Celsum,* 307-308; Origen's explanation is not very convincing since he overlooks that Mark's one angel did not roll away the stone, and that in John the two angels do not appear to the women, but only to Mary.

[36]W. L. Petersen, *The Diatessaron and Ephrem Syrus as Sources of Romanos the Melodist,* CSCO, no. 475 (Louvain: Peeters, 1985), 21, n. 2.

different sources such as the *semeia* source and of some saying source. Each author combined current material in order to create a more complete narrative of the appearance of Jesus from a varying perspective.

From fragments of several so-called apocryphal Gospels of the second century, it is apparent that the process of combining different materials into one new Gospel began in earnest after the Synoptic Gospels and John had gained ground in several regional churches. It is very likely that such documents as the *Gospel of Peter*[37] and the *Gospel of the Ebionites*[38] were, to a certain extent, harmonies that combined materials from other sources including one or more of the "canonical" Gospels. The goal was probably not to create a "scholarly" work, the result of a careful analysis of the sources, but rather to produce a "popular" harmonization: a work which contained materials compiled from various sources so that readers would have more information about Jesus than could be found in any single underlying source.[39]

It has been assumed that the sayings of Jesus as quoted by Justin not only show a harmonistic pattern, but must also derive from some kind of a post-synoptic harmony,[40] or at least from some sort of church manuals or catechisms in which the sayings of Jesus were thematically collected in a harmonized form.[41] It has also been suggested that the procedure of harmonization may have been developed in the catechetical school of Rome, where Justin had been rector. Therefore, it should not surprise us that the name of Tatian, who was Justin's devoted pupil and successor in the school, has been connected with the the most successful harmonization of the Gospels, the *Diatessaron*.

---

[37]See R. E. Brown, "The *Gospel of Peter* and Canonical Gospel Priority," *NTS* 33 (1986/1987): 321-343.

[38]See D. A. Bertrand, "*L'Évangile des Ebionites*: Une harmonie Évangélique antérieure au Diatessaron," *NTS* 26 (1979/1980): 548-563.

[39]Cf. Brown, "The *Gospel of Peter* and Canonical Gospel Priority," 336.

[40]See E. Lippelt, *Quae fuerint Justini Martyris ΑΠΟΜΝΗΜΟΝΕΥΜΑΤΑ...* (Halle: M. Niemeyer, 1901), 2.

[41]Cf. A. J. Bellinzoni, *The Sayings of Jesus in the Writings of Justin Martyr*, NT.S, no. 17 (Leiden: Brill, 1967), 139-142.

Tatian's Harmony

The scholar who composed the most renowned harmony in the
second half of the second century was undoubtedly the man named in the
Ecclesiastical History of Eusebius:

> Tatian, the first chief of them (*sc.* the Encratite party),
> composed (συνθείς) sort of a combination (συνάφειάν
> τινα) and assemblage (συναγωγήν)—I do not know
> how—of the Gospels and called it *Diatessaron*, which
> is still in circulation among some people.[42]

It has been generally assumed that Tatian may have learned the
technique of harmonizing in Justin's school.[43]   If harmonizing Gospel
texts was really one of the goals of scholarship in this school, it would
indicate that there was an historical interest in the memoirs concerning
the life and teaching of Jesus which was different from the concern in the
Alexandrian school, where scholarship focused on the disagreements
among the various Gospels (it was in Alexandria that the synopsis of
Ammonius, also called a *Diatessaron*, was composed, enabling scholars to
easily note the differences[44]) in order to find the spiritual meaning of the
differing texts, if harmonization was not possible. Tatian disagreed with
Origen's hermeneutical procedure of allegorizing the Gospels. He wished
to take these sources as *memoirs,* historical material which had to be
approached with historical methods.[45] Thus Tatian sarcastically spoke to
the Greeks as follows:

> So take a look at your own records (ἀπομνημονεύματα)
> and accept us merely on the grounds that we too tell
> stories (μυθολογοῦντες, used with irony)... Mind now

---

[42]Eusebius, *h.e.,* IV.29.6 (E. Schwartz, ed., *Eusebius Kirchengeschichte* [Leipzig:
J.C. Hinrichs, 1903], I:392.1-2).

[43]Cf. Bellinzoni, *The Sayings of Jesus in the Writings of Justin Martyr,* 142.

[44]For the text see K. Aland, et al., ed., *N-A*[26], 73-74.

[45]*Or.* 21 (E.Schwartz, ed., *Tatiani Oratio ad Graecos,* TU, no. 4.1 [Leipzig: J. C.
Hinrichs, 1888], 23.7) speaks of διηγήματα "narratives."

what I say, men of Greece: do not *allegorize* either
your stories (μύθους) or your gods.[46]

So, in my view, Tatian composed his harmony in order to publish a
single, complete historical "Life of Jesus" based on the records and memoirs of the apostles, and the reason for this publication was his concept of
unity both in a philosophical and in an historical sense. His attack on the
Greeks is directed against their preferring the rule of many (πολυκοιρανίη)
to the rule of one (μοναρχία) both in philosophy and religion.[47] Christian
philosophy and religion are determined by the principle of unity.[48] This
principle led him also in his composition of the harmony. But before I
give my arguments, it has to be asked whether other factors might have
led him to this composition of a Life of Jesus.

The Argument of Economy and Practicality

One might be tempted to mention two other factors for the composition of the harmony: namely that of economy and practicality. The
harmony, as a more compact work than the Tetraevangelium, would
have been less expensive and easier to carry along on journeys.[49] There is
reason to consider these factors.

As to the economic factor, one should consider the fact that the
harmony is not much smaller than the Separate Gospels together. It com-
prised most material of Matthew and John, which would amount to 1,185
+ 879 = 2,064 verses, to which must be added the so-called *Sondergut* of
Luke (548) and Mark (61), so that the book would have contained roughly

---

[46]*Or.* 21 (Schwartz, 23:17-18, 22-23); M. Whittaker, *Tatian, Oratio ad Graecos,*
OECT (Oxford: Oxford University Press, 1982), 43.

[47]*Or.* 14 (Schwartz, 15:8-9).

[48]Cf. especially the observations by M. Elze, *Tatian und seine Theologie,* FKDG,
no. 9 (Göttingen: Vandenhoeck & Ruprecht, 1960), 58 126; cf. also my *Vier=Een,* 17ff.

[49]See W. L. Petersen, *The Diatessaron and Ephrem Syrus,* 21: "contrasted with its
sources, the harmony would be a compact work (advantageous in a day when the reproduction of books was expensive and their transportation difficult)..."; ibid., n. 2: "The cost of
reproducing a book, which is and was directly related to its bulk, should not be ignored
either." Petersen attributes a "minor role" to the idea of unity (contra Elze and Baarda),
and thinks that the temptation was simply overwhelming and the urge "in the air," apart
from the factors of economy and handiness.

2,673 verses, that is circa 75% of a Tetraevangelium. One should, however, not overlook the fact that Tatian's procedure of combining did not totally avoid doublets; moreover, he seems to have added other material from either an extra-canonical Gospel or oral tradition. In short, the saving is less than one might expect. An additional consideration should be given. We do not know anything about the prices of books in the second century. The first century epigrammatist Martial tells us that books of his were sold for one denarius in the bookshop of Tryphon, whereas the bookseller Atrectus sold one of his books for five.[50] Much of the cost of a book depended on the price of the papyrus scrolls used, as well as on the wages of copyists and correctors, and the design and decoration of the binding. If we realize that the harmony may have been destined for use at school or for liturgical use in the churches, then we may consider the fact that the first copies of the Diatessaron were possibly copied by the students and later on by monks, which would—just as in the case of the early Tetraevangelia—have kept the costs down.

The other factor is that of convenience: as a compendium, a harmony was easier to handle and carry along. Now we have seen that the size of the book would not necessarily have been much smaller than a Tetraevangelium. The papyrus manuscript $\mathfrak{P}^{45}$, including the Gospels and Acts, must originally have contained—according to the calculations of K. Aland—220 pages of 25 x 20 cm (text space 19 x 16 cm); without Acts its number would have been circa 170 pages, not much more.[51] If one wanted to save space, one could make use of small-sized editions,[52] between 12 or 15 cm high and 8 cm wide,[53] with a smaller uncial writing. This would have required less effort than creating a harmony. All this is apart from the question whether the book was intended for travellers.

It is true that Theodoret of Cyrrhus speaks of the harmony as a handy compendium when he writes, "However, not only those who belonged to Tatian's party made use of it, but also those who followed the

---

[50]Cf. W. Schubart, *Das Buch bei den Griechen und Römern*, ed. E. Paul, 3rd rev. ed. (Heidelberg: L. Schneider, 1962), 137, 140.

[51]K. Aland, *Repertorium der griechischen christlichen Papyri* (Berlin/New York: W. de Gruyter, 1976), I:269-270.

[52]Schubart, *Das Buch bei den Griechen und Römern*, 55, 118-119.

[53]For such pocket-bibles, see G. Milligan, *The New Testament Documents* (London: Macmillan, 1913), 196.

apostolic teachings." Concerning such use, he also gives the following explanation: first they did not perceive the wickedness of the composition (συνθήκη), that is, its heretical character; secondly, they used it "simply" or "silly enough" (ἁπλούστερον) as a compendium (ὡς συντόμῳ τῷ βιβλίῳ χρησάμενοι).[54] However, this is the private opinion of the bishop who thus tries to explain why they did not use the Separate Gospels. Was it also the opinion of those who used it and for whom was it the true Gospel text that was used in their churches for almost two centuries? Theodoret tells us that he found the book in more than two hundred of the churches of his diocese, that is, in about a quarter of his diocesan parishes. Apparently, these copies were used in the daily services, and were not private copies to be carried along, but official church books which may have had large sizes to enable the lector to read easily the text in the liturgy. They were not meant for the travel bag or for the sleeves of a mantle, but for the *capsa* of a local church. If people used the harmony as a handy "abridged" edition of the Gospels, they did so because it had been the standard book in the liturgy. But whatever the users of the harmony may have thought of it, it was hardly the motif of its author, Tatian, when he originally composed the Diatessaron.[55] The real motives are to be dealt with in the following paragraphs which deal with Tatian as a "herald of the Truth," Tatian as an historian, and Tatian as an apologist.

Tatian as a Herald of the Truth

Tatian the Assyrian had travelled through the world after having acquired a Greek education in which he may have studied philosophy and rhetoric. He had been initiated in Greek mysteries and had become acquainted with many arts and devices of the Greeks—in short, he had learned much about Greek religion and wisdom before he abandoned it.[56] What was the ultimate goal of all his travels, studies and initiations? It was a serious quest for the Truth, a pursuit of what is excellent with re-

---

[54]Theodoret of Cyrrhus, *haer.* I.20.3 (PG, no. 83 [Paris, 1864], col. 372:8-11.

[55]Cf. Elze, *Tatian und seine Theologie*, 126.

[56]See especially *Or.* 1.3 (Schwartz, 2:9-10); *Or.* 29.1 (Schwartz, 29:26-27); *Or.* 35.1 (Schwartz, 36:25ff.,37:1-2.); *Or.* 42 (Schwartz, 43:11). Cf. also Baarda, *Vier = Een*, 17 (notes pp. 94ff.); Elze, *Tatian und seine Theologie*, 16-17, 20-21.

spect to the Truth.[57]   It was in Rome that he found the Truth for which he
sought, when he happened to read some barbarian writings which contained doctrines that were older and more divine than those of the Greeks.
He became a reborn man by obtaining understanding of the Truth.[58]
Henceforth, he wanted to be a "herald of the Truth."[59]   What did Tatian
find attractive in the barbarian writings and the barbarian philosophy of
the Christians? It was the lack of arrogance, the artlessness of the authors,
the easy understanding of the narratives especially with regard to creation,
but above all the fact that the whole of their writings and doctrines was
governed by one principle: τῶν ὅλων τὸ μοναρχικόν.[60]

The lack of unity among the Greeks had struck him.[61]   They did
not agree (συνᾴδειν, ὁμοφωνεῖν), not even in their language.[62]   There was
such a discrepancy (στάσις) between them that it appears impossible to say,
who is a Greek.[63]   Moreover, there are differences—from town to town—
between the codes of law, whereas one should expect one and a common
constitution of state (μίαν ... καὶ κοινὴν πολιτείαν).[64]   With respect to religion their differences are likewise immense: how can one be respectful
towards those among whom there is such an amount of contradiction
(δογμάτων ἐναντιότης ... πολλή).[65]   The same goes for their philosophy: in
contrast to the Christians, who do not make use of differing subtleties of

---

[57]Cf. *Or.* 29.1 (Schwartz, 30:3-4); *Or.* 34 (Schwartz, 36:22); *Or.* 3 (Schwartz, 4:11-
12); Elze, *Tatian und seine Theologie,* 28ff.

[58]Cf. *Or.* 29.2-4 (Schwartz, 30:4-16); *Or.* 5.2 (Schwartz, 6:9-11); Elze, *Tatian und
seine Theologie,* 29, 33.

[59]*Or.* 17.1 (Schwartz, 18:20ff.); cf. *Or.* 42 (Schwartz, 43:11ff.), Elze, *Tatian und
seine Theologie,* 7, 32, 45.

[60]*Or.* 29.2 (Schwartz, 30:11); cf. *Or.* 14.1 (Schwartz, 15:9, τὴν μοναρχίαν); Elze,
Tatian und seine Theologie, 59f.

[61]*Or.* 26.2 (Schwartz, 28:4); Elze, *Tatian und seine Theologie,* 37.

[62]*Or.* 1 (Schwartz, 2:1ff.).

[63]*Or.* 1 (Schwartz, 2:5f.); for the languages, cf. also *Or.* 30.5 (Schwartz, 30:29-31:3).

[64]*Or.* 28.1 (Schwartz, 29:17ff.).

[65]*Or.* 8.5 (Schwartz, 8:21-27).

doctrine (δογμάτων ... ποικιλίαις),[66] their views are incoherent (δόγμασιν ἀσυναρτήτοις),[67] in their doctrines they contradict each other (ἐναντία ... ἑαυτοῖς δογματίζουσιν),[68] since they propose ideas that oppose each other (ἀντιδοξοῦσι δὲ ἑαυτοῖς).[69] Being themselves in all kinds of doctrinal conflicts (στασιώδεις ... τῶν δογμάτων), and not being in harmony with each other (ἀσύμφωνοι) in their traditions, they fight against those who are in harmony (συμφώνους), the Christians.[70] Disharmony belongs to the realm of the Evil one; harmony is from God.[71]

Unity and harmony are the hallmark of Christianity. However, the disharmony of the Gospels could not have escaped the attention of Tatian. Does not this disharmony of the sources reveal the unreliability of these early Christian documents or at least of some of them, as some of the Christians and certainly the pagan critics had charged? Since Tatian did not apply the allegorical method (for which he took the pagans to task), he had to deal with the various discrepancies in the early Christian sources in another way. If unity and harmony were characteristics of Christian faith, it should also be the distinguishing feature of the life of Christ. Therefore, it does not seem unlikely that this was the major factor that prompted Tatian to his attempt to write *one* harmonious life of Jesus, which means that behind his endeavor there was a clearly philosophical or theological interest: truth takes shape in unity and harmony.[72]

---

[66]*Or.* 32.1 (Schwartz, 33:2); Elze, *Tatian und seine Theologie,* 59.

[67]*Or.* 35.2 (Schwartz, 37:7).

[68]*Or.* 3.9 (Schwartz, 4:13-14.).

[69]*Or.* 3.10 (Schwartz, 4:16).

[70]*Or.* 25.5 (Schwartz, 26:28-27, 27:3-5).

[71]For this idea, see the quotation from another work of Tatian in Clement of Alexandria, *Stromata* III.12.81:1-3 (O. Stählin, ed., *Clemens Alexandrinus II, Stromata, Buch I-VI,* GCS [Leipzig, 1906], 232:22-29, 233:1-2); cf. Elze, *Tatian und seine Theologie,* 116ff.; F. Bolgiani, "La tradizione eresiologica sull' encratismo II, La confutazione di Clemente di Alexandria (Prima parte)," AAST.M 96 (1961-62) (Torino, 1962), 537-664.

[72]Cf. Baarda, *Vier = Een,* 19; Elze, *Tatian und seine Theologie,* 126; contra Merkel, *Widersprüche zwischen den Evangelien,* 69.

Tatian as an Historian

In my view, it is the quest for truth—which is implicitly the quest for unity and harmony—which underlies Tatian's composition of a harmony of the Gospels. But in composing such a book, he was obliged to act as an historian. Tatian faults Greek historians for their lack of historical accuracy,[73] and he speaks contemptuously about their dissent (στάσις) and discord (ἀσυμφωνία) regarding the date of Homer, which must catch the eye of everyone who will make an accurate investigation (ἐπ' ἀκριβὴς ἐξετάζειν).[74] He concludes that their historical views are false (ψευδεῖς).[75] In this respect Tatian's judgment agrees with that of Josephus, who also blames the Greeks for their disharmony (διαφωνία) in historical matters— something which is absent from the documents of the Jews who have not such a myriad of books that are discordant (ἀσύμφωνοι) and in contradiction with each other.[76] Symphony and harmony are hall-marks of truthfulness and reliability.[77] Likewise for Tatian, people whose chronological records (τῶν χρόνων ἀναγραφή) are inconsistent (ἀσυνάρτητος) cannot be reliable in their history. The cause of error in their descriptions is the fact that they composed stories which were not true (τὰ μὴ ἀληθῆ).[78] Accuracy (ἀκρίβεια) and truth (ἀλήθεια) are the devices of a good historian, and the proof of historical veracity is universal agreement in description.[79]

---

[73]*Or.* 31-41 (Schwartz, 32ff.).

[74]*Or.* 31.7 (Schwartz, 32:15-19). For ἀσυμφωνία as result of a wrong historical method among Greek historians, cf. Josephus, *Bell.* I.1 (H. St. J. Thackeray, ed., *Josephus II*, 5th reprint [Cambridge (Mass.): Harvard University Press/London: Hinemann, 1976], 2).

[75]*Or.* 31.7 (Schwartz, 32:19-20).

[76]Cf. Josephus, *Ap.* I.3.15-16 (H. St. J. Thackeray, ed., *Josephus I*, 5th reprint [Cambridge (Mass.): Harvard University Press/London: Hinemann, 1976], 168ff.), διαφωνεῖν, οὐ συμφωνεῖν, διαφωνία; cf. also I.23.

[77]*Ap.* I.8 emphasizes the fact that the books of the Jews are not only more archaic, but also have no διαφωνία: they do not have myriads of conflicting history books (βιβλίων ...ἀσυμφώνων καὶ μαχομένων); cf. W. C. van Unnik, *Flavius Josephus als historischer Schriftsteller* (Heidelberg: Schneider, 1978), 24-25.

[78]*Or.* 31.7 (Schwartz, 32:20-24).

[79]Cf. Josephus, *Ant.* 1, Prooemium (1), τὴν ἀλήθειαν; *Ap.* I.3, τἀληθές; I.27, ἀληθοῦς ἱστορίας; *Bell.* I.1, τὸ ἀκριβὲς τῆς ἱστορίας; cf. also *Ap.* I.26

This harsh judgment of Greek historiography and its inconsistencies could not have been pronounced without having repercussions for Tatian's own view of the inconsistencies which could be traced in the apostolic memoirs, especially with regard to their chronology. The possibility is not excluded that the book Προβλήματα, ascribed to Tatian and meant to clarify what was not clear (i.e., what was hidden) in the Scriptures, also dealt with problems arising from contradictions among the Gospels.[80]   However, a radical way to solve all the disharmony among the Gospels was to create a single new Gospel in the form of a harmony: "Le meilleur moyen, en effet, de prouver qu'il n'y avait de contradiction entre les évangiles était de fondre tous les quatre en un récit harmonique."[81]

Tatian's harmony is, in fact, an attempt at creating a *Life of Jesus Christ* out of all the material in the records or memoirs of the apostles (ἀπομνημονεύματα) which were in use in Justin's school.[82]   First, of course, he could not have missed Mark, which was held in high esteem in the Roman churches.   Secondly, he would have had to have used Matthew's Gospel, which was greatly respected, not only because it was connected with an apostle but also because there was a tradition that it was translated from the Hebrew.[83]   Third was the Gospel of Luke, which must have had an appeal to Tatian, since its author professed to have done historical research; there is reason to assume that Tatian was also acquainted with the Marcionite recension of this Gospel, which must have been part of Justin's library.[84]   Of course, Tatian would not have ignored earlier attempts to create harmonistic texts, especially if such attempts were under-

---

[80]For this book, see Eusebius' report on Rhodo, Tatian's pupil, in *h.e.* V.13.8 (Schwartz, 458:6-9); Von Campenhausen, *Die Entstehung der christlichen Bibel*, 190, n. 56; Baarda, *Vier = Een*, 19, 39-40, n. 107-108.

[81]J. P. P. Martin, *Introduction à la critique textuelle du Nouveau Testament*, Partie pratique, t. 1 (Paris, 1884), 494, cf. 495.

[82]Cf. Baarda, *Vier = Een*, 19, 40, n. 111; Grant, *The Earliest Lives of Jesus*, 19-20.

[83]This made it an "archaic" book and clearly fitted into Tatian's scheme: χρὴ τῷ πρεσβεύοντι κατὰ τὴν ἡλικίαν πιστεύειν, *Or.* 40.1 (Schwartz, 41:2-3.).

[84]Cf. T. Baarda, "'The Flying Jesus,' Luke 4:29-30 in the Syriac Diatessaron," *VigChr* 40 (1986): 313-341, esp. 336.

taken in Justin's school.[85]   Moreover, he seems to have used written and unwritten traditions that were known to him.[86]   However, his endeavor to create this harmony was justified only if it created a more accurate history of the life of Jesus in which the discrepancies of his sources were eliminated.

His greatest effort was undoubtedly his decision to introduce material from the Fourth Gospel into his history of Jesus. Those who opposed this Gospel emphasized the fact that in so many instances it was out of tune (οὐ συμφωνεῖ) with the writings of the apostles.[87]   If Irenaeus is justified in saying that the heretical period of Tatian revealed doctrinal influences of Valentinus,[88] one cannot exclude the possibility that Tatian had earlier contacts with the Valentinians in Rome who had a preference for this Gospel. From the remains of the Diatessaron it is clear that he followed this Gospel to a large extent in its chronology and made it, together with that of Matthew, the warp for the woof of the other Gospel materials. Perhaps one might conclude from this fact that Tatian accepted the Fourth Gospel as an authentic apostolic record.

Tatian's harmony was, as we can still deduce from the late witnesses to this work, a well-balanced piece of scholarly study, which presupposed a detailed comparison of the sources.[89]   His purpose must have been (to borrow Papias' words in his judgment of Mark) to write a history in an accurate way (ἀκριβῶς), not leaving out anything (μηδὲν παραλιπεῖν) nor giving false information (ψεύσασθαι τι ἐν αὐτοῖς). But Tatian also sought to avoid Papias' criticism of Mark's arrangement of the material (οὐ μέντοι τάξει); it is here that his great emphasis on historical "accuracy" (ἀκριβεία, the lack of which he had reproached in Greek historians) must have urged him to reconstruct accurately the chronology of the life of

---

[85]On this matter, see the forthcoming article by W. L. Petersen, "Textual Evidence of Tatian's Dependence Upon Justin's ΑΠΟΜΝΗΜΟΝΕΥΜΑΤΑ," *NTS* 36 (1990).

[86]Cf. J. H. Charlesworth, "Tatian's Dependence upon Apocryphal Traditions," *HeyJ* 15 (1974): 5-12 (see his references to G. Messina and G. Quispel); H. J. W.Drijvers and G. J. Reinink, "Taufe und Licht, Tatian, Ebionäerevangelium und Thomasakten," in *Text and Testimony. Essays on New Testament and Apocryphal Literature in Honour of A. F. J. Klijn*, ed. T. Baarda, A. Hilhorst, et al. (Kampen: Kok, 1988), 91-110.

[87]For the Alogi, cf. Epiphanius, *haer.* 51.4.5 (Holl, 251:24-252:1).

[88]Cf. Eusebius, *h.e.* IV.29.2 (Schwartz, 165).

[89]Cf. Grant, *The Earliest Lives of Jesus,* 29.

Jesus.[90]   One might apply to his harmony what Tatian himself wrote about the human body: despite all its different elements, "there is in the overall plan a harmonious agreement" (κατ' οἰκονομίαν συμφωνίας ἐστιν ἁρμονία).[91]

In order to create this harmonious composition Tatian had to weigh his sources, to evaluate the reliability of every detail in them, to reject what did not fit the overall plan, to transpose narrative material to more suitable positions, to add what was necessary to create a chronologically smooth course for the narrative, and to omit what did not seem reliable in the sources, all this in order to achieve the ultimate goal of one reliable story of the life of Jesus. Such a task could only be performed on the basis of scholarly preparations and with a well-considered plan and premeditated historical criteria. One of the required preparatory tasks was to create a kind of a synopsis of the sources, because such an enormous task as he had set himself could not be fulfilled just with "scissors and paste." One may perhaps say that the Diatessaron had a practical purpose; it still rested on very scholarly preparatory studies.

Tatian as an Apologist

This study is an attempt to show that the idea of unity and harmony in Tatian's concept of truth led him to the creation of *one* complete history in which the discrepancies of the sources were resolved. This served an apologetic purpose. After all, one could not blame others, pagans or Christian dissidents, for inconsistencies, if the historical sources of the Christian philosophy remained contradictory. One has to show that it is possible to read these sources in such a way that together they could present us with one harmonious history, even where these sources demonstrated a large amount of discrepancies. One of the most difficult problems is undoubtedly the diversity with which these sources related the narratives of the Resurrection.[92]   How can an historian like Tatian

---

[90]Cf. his emphasis on ἀκρίβεια: *Or.* 37 (Schwartz, 38:19); *Or.* 38 (Schwartz, 39:6); *Or.* 39 (Schwartz, 39:25); *Or.* 41 (Schwartz, 41:15-42:16), especially with respect to the chronological order.

[91]*Or.* 12.5 (Schwartz, 13:7-8).

[92]A gloss in MS Vat. Syr.154 preserves the following observation: "Titianos the heretic is as some say the one who made this (sc.the Diatessaron). And when he arrived at

create a harmonious narrative on the basis of the diverse sources, when he had not yet been able to consult the reconstruction of H. Frhr. von Campenhausen?[93]   He did it his own way.   In order to demonstrate Tatian's procedure some examples of his reconstruction will be given here, all of which may have an implicit apologetic tendency.

When Theodore bar Koni speaks concerning Tatian and his Diatessaron, he relates how Tatian in composing this work arrived at the pericope of the Resurrection and saw that the testimonies of the four Gospels were different, because—as Bar Koni guessed—each of them had described that Jesus arose from the dead when He had appeared to them. Now, in order not to choose one of these testimonies and leave out the three others, Tatian (in order to do justice to all four) spoke thus: "In the night when the first day of the week dawned, our Lord arose from the dead."[94] This was apparently the first verse of the Resurrection story in Tatian's Diatessaron, for which one may find support in the *Demonstrations* of Aphrahat and partly in the Syro-Sinaitic Gospels.[95]   The implication of such an opening of the Resurrection narrative is that Jesus had already arisen *before* the angel descended from heaven to roll away the stone. The thrust of this addition to the narrative is most probably apologetical, for it prevents the criticism of people like Celsus, who ironically wrote: ὁ γὰρ τοῦ θεοῦ παῖς, ὡς ἔοικεν, οὐκ ἐδύνατο ἀνοῖξαι τὸν τάφον, ἀλλ' ἐδεήθη ἄλλου ἀποκινήσαντος τὴν πέτραν: "The son of God, it seems, was not able to open the tomb, but needed someone else to move away the stone."[96]

---

the story of the Resurrection and saw that it was so different, he gave up his work" (cf. my *Vier=Een*, 51-53; reprinted in an English translation as "The Resurrection Narrative in Tatian's Diatessaron according to Three Syrian Patristic Witnesses," in T. Baarda, *Early Transmission of Words of Jesus* [Amsterdam: Vrije Universiteit Uitgeverij, 1983], 103-115, esp.105-106); the gloss is a misunderstanding of an observation made by Theodore bar Koni; cf. *infra*, n. 95.

[93]H. Frhr. Von Campenhausen, *Der Ablauf der Osterereignisse und das leere Grab*, (Heidelberg: C. Winter, 1966), who did not even mention his early predecessor (even where he could have done so; cf. n. 97, *infra*).

[94]For the text, a translation, and discussion of it, see my *Vier=Een*, 53-55; or *Early Transmission*, 106-109.

[95]Baarda, *Vier=Een*, pp. 59-60; idem, *Early Transmission*, 110-112.

[96]*c. Cels.* V.52.11-13 (Borret, III:146). Von Campenhausen, *Ablauf*, 20, thinks that one could interpret Matthew's text as follows: "Auf diese Weise ergibt sich, wahrscheinlich wieder ganz ungewollt, die seltsame Folgerung, dass Jesus vorher aus dem noch geschlossenen Grabe durch den Felsblock hindurch gefahren sein muss," but he notes that

In the same passage, Celsus wrote about the appearance of the angels: καὶ μὴν καὶ πρὸς τὸν αὐτοῦ τοῦδε τάφον ἐλθεῖν ἄγγελον, οἱ μὲν ἕνα, οἱ δὲ δύο, τοὺς ἀποκρινομένους ταῖς γυναιξὶν ὅτι ἀνέστη: "furthermore, they say that an angel came to the tomb of this very man—some say one (angel), but some two—who replied to the women that he was arisen."[97] His criticism—although made *en parenthèse*—is that the Gospels vary in the number of the angels. Tatian prevents such criticism by harmonizing the sources in this way. First—after Jesus had risen—the angel descends from heaven, rolls away the stone, and sits upon it; by his appearance, he scares the guards (Matt 28:2-3); but, in contrast to Matt 28, he does not speak to the women. Next, Tatian adds a textual element, namely, "after this angel had departed"; only then do the women proceed and enter the tomb. There they find the youth (Mark 16:5) who addresses them; then stupified by his words, two other men appear and give them the "Lucan" message (Luke 24:4ff.). With this sequence[98] Tatian tries to disarm such historical criticisms as those found in Celsus' refutation of Christianity.

There is a third criticism of Celsus regarding the resurrection story: namely, the appearance of Jesus to a mentally unbalanced woman. His criticism is expressed in the following passages:

> ὅτε μὲν ἠπιστεῖτο ὢν ἐν σώματι, πᾶσιν ἀνέδην ἐκήρυττεν·
> ὅτε δὲ πίστιν ἂν ἰσχυρὰν παρεῖχεν ἐκ νεκρῶν ἀναστάς,
> ἐνὶ μόνῳ γυναίῳ καὶ τοῖς ἑαυτοῦ θιασώταις κρύβδην
> παρεφαίνετο.[99]

> ἀνέστη ποτὲ αὐτῷ σώματι ... νεκρὸς δ'ἀνέστη καὶ τὰ
> σημεῖα τῆς κολάσεως ἔδειξε καὶ τὰς χεῖρας ὡς ἦσαν
> πεπερονημέναι, τίς τοῦτο εἶδε; Γυνὴ πάροιστρος, ὥς
> φατε, καὶ εἴ τις ἄλλος τῶν ἐκ τῆς αὐτῆς γοητείας.[100]

---

even Origen did not dare to draw this conclusion (ibid., n. 111). If he had taken notice of Tatian, he could have seen that even before the late Middle Ages (see again, n. 111) Tatian had interpreted the text this way.

[97] *c. Cels.* V.52.10-11 (Borret, III:146).

[98] I follow here the data of the Arabic Diatessaron, lii.48-55; A.-S. Marmardji, ed., *Diatessaron de Tatien* (Beyrouth: Imprimere catholique, 1935), 506, 508.

[99] *c. Cels.* II.70.9-12 (Borret, I:452).

[100] *c. Cels.* II.55.12, 17-20 (Borret, I:414).

Celsus blames Jesus for having appeared only to his followers after his resurrection, and not in public; and again he speaks of the appearance to a woman, but now he describes her as an hysterical female. Since he speaks both times of the woman first, he may refer the tradition preserved in Mark 16:9-10 and John 20:11ff.; the most likely is the first passage, Mark 16:9-10, since there it is said that from Mary of Magdala, to whom Jesus appeared first, seven demons were driven out. But from the evidence of the oriental Diatessaronic witnesses, Tatian seems to have changed the episode by making the woman to whom Jesus appeared first to be Mary, the mother of Jesus, not Mary of Magdala.[101] This change in the narrative would avoid the criticism that Jesus' appearance was only the hysterical hallucination by one woman, who had once been possessed by demons.

Conclusion

The Diatessaron was a careful attempt to create *one* historical account of the words and deeds of Jesus, as far as they could be reconstructed on the basis of the memoirs of the apostles contained in the various Gospels, predominantly those which later on received canonical status. The basic idea of the harmony was that the truth becomes visible in unity and harmony. The sources contained discrepancies and contradictions, but by using historical methods the historian could demonstrate that one universal biography of Jesus could be created which solved the διαφωνία of the sources in the συμφωνία of a harmony. The realization of the philosophical idea of unity as a hallmark of truth in a real, harmonious composition of the history of Jesus served an apologetic purpose. Once composed it turned out to be a practical compendium, which by the way may have been sold in some bookshops for three-quarters the price of a Tetraevangelium. But this was not Tatian's purpose. In some way Tatian wanted to replace the sources and their contradictions with a new document that surpassed all these sources and would avoid the criticisms that pagans and Christian dissidents made on the basis of the existing Gospels; it was not intended to be a fifth Gospel, but rather, what it actually became in the early Syriac-speaking churches, *the* Gospel.

---

[101]See T. Baarda, "'Jesus and Mary' (John 20,16f.) in the Second Epistle on Virginity ascribed to Clement," in *Studien zum Text und zur Ethik des Neuen Testaments. Festschrift zum 80. Geburtstag von Heinrich Greeven*, ed. W. Schrage, BZNW, no. 47 (Berlin/New York: W. de Gruyter, 1986), 11-34; and T. Baarda, *The Gospel Quotations of Aphrahat the Persian Sage* (Meppel: Krips, 1975), I:254-257 (par.122); cf. II:484-487.

Epilogue

In a few paragraphs, your editor wishes to summarize four major themes which emerged from the conference proceedings. They are glossed with comments made by participants during both the formal and informal discussions.

(1) It was striking how the Western Text—or, as Prof. Epp proposed, conglomeration "D"—still dominates discussions of the Gospels in the second century. The antipodes may be represented by quotations from Profs. Aland and Koester. Their remarks, made during the discussion, but not in this sequence, have been harmonized: Aland: "There is no evidence of the Western Text in the second century." Koester: "Read Justin Martyr." When Prof. Birdsall observed that it has been twenty years since the second volume of A. F. J. Klijn's *A Survey of the Researches into the Western Text of the Gospel and Acts* appeared, and that a new conspectus was, perhaps, desirable, it seems he was right. Prof. Birdsall's lecture has remedied that lacuna to some degree; but, perhaps, if we prevail on Prof. Klijn, we may yet wring another volume from him, now that he has the leisure of a professor emeritus. It was felt that periodic comprehensive summaries of research in a field such as the Western Text are valuable for disseminating specialized research and creating a consensus.

(2) The theme of harmonization is larger and more important than ever. There were probably pre-Tatianic Gospel harmonies, as Prof. Baarda points out. Our best evidence suggests that Justin used a harmony. But perhaps the most stimulating remarks on Gospel harmonies were those by Prof. Koester, who would extended their line back to the very earliest stages of Gospel development. This is a new and important perspective, ripe for future investigation. However, opposition was already forming during the conference, and not without just cause. Profs. Aland and Wisse both pointed out that there is a difference between a writer using sources, rather as an undergraduate cribs a term paper from several encyclopedia articles, and a real harmonization, such as we find in the *Diatessaron* where, to use Vööbus' word, the work is a fine "filigree" of texts. This is a vital distinction, and cannot be ignored. Nevertheless, Prof. Koester's thesis has intrinsic merit, for we often seem to encounter subtle harmonizations in second-century works.

(3) The necessity of a clean method was emphasized in all of the papers, especially in that of Prof. Wisse. Both he and Prof. Aland would lay the *onus probandi* on those who challenge the early "Alexandrian"

text, as represented in $\mathfrak{P}^{75}$ and B. Against this, however, the chant was heard: "Read Justin Martyr."   In the view of some, there is indeed a burden of proof, and it rests squarely upon the defenders of the Alexandrian text, who are called upon to explain the presence of the numerous "Western" readings in the second century: in Justin, Tatian, Clement, the *Gospel of Thomas*. This area cries out for further study of the most subtle, nuanced and dispassionate sort.

(4) Prof. Aland spoke at some length about the necessity of bringing research on the Gospels in the second century—often conceived of as a purely text-critical task—into contact with early church history, linguistics and higher criticism. She pointed out that the great Hans Lietzmann was an early church historian—an appointment which both she and her husband, Kurt Aland, share.   The intimate connection with historical studies—indeed, the entire antique world—was underscored in Prof. Epp's review of the migration of texts in antiquity. It was further emphasized in Prof. Baarda's argument that the Diatessaron was created in response to pagan criticisms of disunity among the gospels. The theme occupied a central place in the papers of Prof. Delobel and Prof. Brock. As their careful work demonstrated, one cannot blithely accept citations from the Fathers and Versions as evidence for the second-century text. Rather, each individual citation or variant must be minutely examined. This requires knowledge of the period, the culture, and the language, as well as historical vision. Compartmentalization is the bane of such research.

We thank our guides for having led us on this trek back to the second century; now that the way is familiar, it is hoped that more will undertake the journey.

Index of Passages

Hebrew Bible

New Testament

Other Early Christian Writings

Index of Names and Subjects

Index of Manuscripts and Versions